DOCUMENTS OF MODERN POLITICAL THOUGHT

DOCUMENTS OF MODERN POLITICAL THOUGHT

EDITED BY

T. E. UTLEY

AND

J. STUART MACLURE

CAMBRIDGE

AT THE UNIVERSITY PRESS

1957

CAMBRIDGE UNIVERSITY PRESS
Cambridge, New York, Melbourne, Madrid, Cape Town,
Singapore, São Paulo, Delhi, Mexico City

Cambridge University Press
The Edinburgh Building, Cambridge CB2 8RU, UK

Published in the United States of America by Cambridge University Press, New York

www.cambridge.org
Information on this title: www.cambridge.org/9781107621794

First published 1957
First paperback edition 2013

A catalogue record for this publication is available from the British Library

ISBN 978-1-107-62179-4 Paperback

PREFACE

Our debts are too numerous to be acknowledged exhaustively, but we must mention the extremely valuable advice given to us by Mr Michael Derrick of *The Tablet*, Mr E. H. Carr of Trinity College, Cambridge, and Mr T. H. Willetts, formerly of Manchester University. None of them is, of course, in any way responsible for the contents of this book.

At the stage of planning the book, we continually consulted Professor Cecil Driver, Chairman of the Department of Political Science at Yale University. It is impossible to exaggerate what this book owes in its final form to the influence of his wide knowledge and long teaching experience.

LONDON
August 1957

T.E.U.
J.S.M.

ACKNOWLEDGEMENTS

The authors' thanks are due to the following for permission to quote copyright matter:

Messrs Bowes & Bowes (M. Oakeshott: *Political Education*); The Clarendon Press (Sir Ernest Barker: *Reflections on Government*); Messrs Hamish Hamilton and Messrs Little, Brown & Co. (Walter Lippmann: *The Public Philosophy*); 'The Times' (article on *Majority Rule*); Oxford University Press (Lord Hugh Cecil: *Conservatism*); Messrs Allen & Unwin and Messrs Simon & Schuster (Bertrand Russell: *Authority and the Individual*); Messrs Stevens & Sons (Sir Alfred Denning: *The Road to Justice*); Messrs Routledge & Kegan Paul and The University of Chicago Press (F. A. Hayek: *The Road to Serfdom*); Messrs Allen & Unwin and The Macmillan Company, New York (R. H. Tawney: *Equality*); Messrs Allen & Unwin (Barbara Wootton: *Freedom under Planning*); the Central Office of the Labour Party (*Labour Party Manifesto 1945*); Messrs Penguin Books (Lord Hailsham: *The Case for Conservatism*); the Conservative Research Department (*Conservative Party Manifesto 1955*); Messrs Victor Gollancz and Messrs Simon & Schuster (François Lafitte, *The New Outline of Modern Knowledge, Section IV*); The University of Chicago Press (Bertrand de Jouvenel: *Sovereignty*); Messrs Secker & Warburg and The University of Chicago Press (George Kennan: *American Diplomacy 1900-1950*); Messrs Hollis & Carter and The University of Chicago Press (Jacques Maritain: *Man and the State*); The Catholic Truth Society, London (*The Rights of Man, Quadragesimo Anno, Divini Redemptoris*); National Catholic Welfare Conference (*La Solennita della Pentecoste, Divini Illius Magistri*); the Editor of 'The Round Table' and the Ford Foundation (*Apartheid and the Scriptures*); Messrs Charles Scribner's Sons (Reinhold Niebuhr: *Moral Man and Immoral Society*); Messrs G. Bell & Sons and the author (H. Butterfield: *Christianity and History*); S.C.M. Press and Messrs Harper & Brothers (Report of the Second Assembly of the World Council of Churches: *Social Questions* and *Inter-Group Relations*); Messrs Longmans Green (Report of the Church of Scotland Commission on Communism: *The Church Faces the Challenge*); Messrs Lawrence & Wishart (for the extracts from Lenin and Stalin).

The Editor of 'The Round Table' wishes to point out that the views expressed in the quotation from *Apartheid and the Scriptures* are unrelated to the opinions of himself or of the 'Round Table' Group in the Union of South Africa.

CONTENTS

GENERAL INTRODUCTION

This book is divided into five parts, not because we are under the impression that the whole field of political thought can be neatly divided by rigid lines of demarcation but because for the sake of orderly presentation some such division has to be made.

Part I, entitled *Representative Democracy*, brings together writings by authors as far afield as India, France and the United States, linked by a common acceptance of the institutions of parliamentary democracy. To call this a school of political thought might be to create an impression of greater coherence than in fact exists: on the other hand the area of practical agreement is sufficiently large to justify an arrangement of this kind.

Communism, which forms Part II, can reasonably be described as a coherent orthodoxy and the documents for this section have been drawn from the writings of Marx, Engels, Lenin, Stalin and Khrushchev. Part III, *Papal Political Theory*, falls into a different category in that in one sense it represents an official policy, but not one binding upon all members of the Roman Catholic Church. It is therefore something which can be presented as a coherent doctrine but cannot be elevated to the level of articles of faith.

The last two parts are on an altogether slighter scale. Part IV, on *Romantic Authoritarianism*, of which Nazism and Fascism were examples, has been included because it was felt that to regard these doctrines as extinct so soon after the Second World War would be a mistake even if their present influence did not justify treating them at exhaustive length. Part V, on *Protestant Political Thought*, is an attempt to illustrate a trend in current political thinking which, though not expressed in any organised political movement, has a considerable influence in shaping political opinion on certain major issues.

The anthology is the unworthy successor of Professor Michael Oakeshott's *Social and Political Doctrines of Contemporary Europe* which was published in 1938. The principles of selection adopted here, however, have necessarily been somewhat different. Professor Oakeshott's aim was to describe 'official political thought', that is to say, the doctrines laid down by authority as the basis of the various political regimes in Europe. In pre-war Russia, Germany and Italy the doctrinal foundations of the state were defined in authoritative, official pronouncements which it was obligatory upon all to accept; the prevailing spirit in the democratic countries of Western Europe and in the U.S.A. was one of extreme indifference to political philosophy, the only remarkable exception to this rule being the Roman Catholic Church whose beliefs on politics and society as defined in Papal encyclicals were accepted by its members with very few noticeable variations.

Today, the only clearly defined and compulsory orthodoxy which is in fact the basis of political regimes is Marxist Communism. Germany and Italy have at least been partially reclaimed for the western tradition of representative democracy. At the same time, there has been a notable increase of interest in political philosophy in the countries which have this tradition. There has emerged in Europe a series of Christian Democratic parties, predominantly Catholic in composition, which profess to represent the Catholic tradition in social and political thinking in a form adapted to the conditions of the age; the policies of these parties, however, differ widely, and, in practice, their approach to politics is extremely empirical; while there has, therefore, been an apparent accession of influence to Catholic political thinking this influence is much more diffuse than it used to be, and it is no longer possible, for example, to treat an authoritarian regime like that of Portugal as an example of the form which Catholic political thought is most likely to take in practice.

In short, when Professor Oakeshott wrote his book, there were at least three orthodoxies, Marxism, Nazism and Fascism, which professed to be embodied in detail in political and social institutions; today, there is a much more complicated interaction of political traditions and the connection between political theory and political practice over much of the world is much more difficult to trace. This, of course, has always been so in those countries which live under representative democracy; in Britain, for example, it is possible to distinguish something which may be called Conservative theory from something which may be called Socialist theory, but it is equally clear that Conservatism has played an important part in influencing the practical character of British Socialism and that conceptions which are socialist in origin have an important place in shaping the policy of the Conservative Party.

The motives which induce men to associate themselves for the purposes of political action are infinitely various, and belief in common doctrines is only one of them. Sometimes a common body of beliefs about the nature and ends of politics does express itself to some extent in a common policy, and, wherever possible, connections of this sort have been indicated, but they are not always to be found and at times can only be fraudulently established. If the chapter headings of this book were to be taken as indicating the prevailing division of opinion in the world on the great practical questions of policy, the result would be dangerously misleading. There are different ways of arriving at the same conclusions and different conclusions can be derived from the same doctrinal source. To say that a man accepts the political and social teaching of the papacy is not to say that he will necessarily follow some particular course of political and social action to be inferred directly from that teaching; in fact, the acceptance of this teaching has been shown to be compatible with wide differences of view on constitutional, social and economic subjects, and conversely to say that a man belongs to the British Labour Party is not necessarily to say that he accepts in the abstract all or most of the social and economic doctrines on which that Party is ostensibly based. In this connection, another complicating phenomenon must be noted: a political theory can acquire the character of a myth which is significant not so much for its intellectual content as for its symbolic influence as an instrument for maintaining party unity; by this means, people of widely different political aims can be kept in the same political party, at the cost of some measure of strain, for an almost indefinite time; in this case, profession of a common political doctrine is of very little value as evidence of a common political purpose.

The proper way of studying politics is to consider the various groups into which men divide themselves for the purposes of political action, and to ask what makes them so divide themselves; to do this for the whole of mankind, to catalogue all possible combinations of motive, to set everything in exactly the right context, is a task which it is certainly impossible to perform. What can be done and what has been attempted here is to distinguish certain broad trends of reflection on the great questions with which political thought is perennially concerned, to indicate the connection between these trends and the actual policies of governments and parties when that connection is visible, and, where it is not, to point out the varieties of practical interpretation of which the same body of political doctrine is capable. Even in the case of Marxism, it would be a bold man who would profess to be able to predict policies on the strength of a knowledge of the pure word of doctrine. It is possible to argue that all schools of political thought are but rationalisations of experience; indeed, this view is strongly represented in several extracts appearing in this book. If this is so, the inadequacy of any classification of political ideas which does not describe the circumstances from which they arose and in which they are professed is too obvious to need emphasising.

It might reasonably be asked, therefore, whether there is in fact any justification for political thought. To this the answer must be that every practical policy towards the problems of government and society implies, however obliquely, some assumption about the ends of government and society and the means by which they should be pursued. These assumptions may well be, in origin, rationalisations of the interests or wishes of some particular body of people: for example, the arguments by which representative democracy is justified were very largely invented after representative democracy had been achieved. Nevertheless, once formulated, they both influenced the development of representative democracy in the countries of its origin and led other countries to adopt it. The character of these arguments, therefore, became an important force in the world; representative democracy might have been different or might have ceased to exist altogether had a different sort of argument been employed for its *ex post facto* defence.

Similarly, historic divisions of principle which arose in the course of particular practical controversies may seem at times to have become irrelevant to practical affairs. Is it not, it may be asked, a matter of indifference that some men defend universal suffrage on the ground that all men have a natural right to participate in government, and that others defend it on the ground that it has been shown to be universally that form of government which ministers most effectively to the happiness of mankind? Emphatically, it is not. In so far as the utilitarian defence of democracy is sincerely held, and in so far as the utilitarian habit of mind persists, faith in democratic institutions is not protected from the test of experience; in so far as it rests on *a priori* grounds which may be maintained in the teeth of calamity, it is so protected. The differences between Edmund Burke and Tom Paine may seem to be a purely historical interest in this country today when the institutions which Paine advocated have come to be defended indifferently on his and Edmund Burke's grounds; but if a new constitutional issue, like the reform of the Second Chamber, were to emerge into practical politics, this ancient conflict of principle would acquire a new relevance. The doctrinal assumptions implicit in practical policies, however unconsciously they may be taken for granted, are therefore of extreme practical importance. What has to be remembered is that in stating these assumptions in the abstract an act of abstraction has been committed. Such acts are legitimate and useful so long as they are recognised for what they are.

The object of this book, then, is to isolate the doctrinal assumptions implicit in contemporary political thought. A doctrine is a statement claiming the authority and objectivity of truth and claiming acceptance as a matter of moral duty. Even the empiricist's assertion that nothing can and ought to be affirmed to be universally true about politics has, therefore, the character of a doctrine. We are fixing our minds on what claims to be permanent and universal, therefore, even when our illustrations are taken from statements which bear the colour of some temporary and local setting. Politics is the art of directing the common life of communities each of which is subject, in temporal affairs, to the dominion of one sovereign authority. It is concerned, therefore, with the ends which this sovereign authority should pursue, the limits within which it should operate and the means which it should adopt. From time to time comprehensive statements purporting to cover all these topics and claiming to be internally consistent are made, and these are commonly called philosophies of politics. These philosophies, however, are not the only source of doctrinal assumptions about politics, and it is comparatively rare to find any one of them consciously professed. Modern political philosophy is at least equally influenced by ideas about some particular aspect of politics which do not arise from a fully developed philosophy of politics. It has, for instance, been thought worth while to include a brief section on Protestant political thought, although there is certainly nothing which can properly be described as a Protestant philosophy of politics. The justification is that certain trends in Protestant theological and ethical thinking have a marked bearing on some present-day political questions, notably on relations with the Soviet Union.

The aim of this book is, therefore, strictly limited; it is concerned with one factor in the shaping of policies, namely the doctrinal factor. Where the doctrinal assumptions embedded in contemporary political opinions can be illustrated from contemporary sources, with reasonable clarity, they have been so illustrated; where they can be more clearly or economically expressed by quotations from more distant sources, these have been employed, the criterion always being the extent to which the ideas illustrated may fairly be said to influence opinion today. Whenever possible, sources easily accessible in English have been preferred.

Two further points require explanation: in politics the word 'contemporary' has the habit of being rapidly outdated. A great part of Professor Oakeshott's pre-war compilation appears to have been rendered irrelevant by the war. It would show more courage than prudence, however, to leave out of account those doctrines of romantic authoritarianism which lay at the root of Nazism and Fascism, and which still have a lingering influence in the defeated countries. A short section on these doctrines has therefore been included. In particular the theory of democratic socialism is at present in a stage of transition: it has been thought best, therefore, to describe it at the peak of its power in Britain in the years immediately following the war.

Finally, Professor Oakeshott's book was geographically limited to Europe. No such specific limitation is imposed upon this book. The world, we are accustomed to being told, is more interdependent than ever before. In a book of this size, it has only been possible to illustrate the broadest trends; it may be safely said, however, that none of the ideas here illustrated is in its present influence confined to Europe. It is equally true that all the great contemporary movements in political thought are European in origin, a fact which persists in spite of the decline in the material strength of Europe, and for this reason almost all the quotations reproduced here are from European or American sources.

The most that is claimed for these extracts is that they may help the student of contemporary politics to distinguish in them some extremely broad principles which influence contemporary opinion, while not always or even generally determining its divisions.

T. E. UTLEY

J. STUART MACLURE

3 *January* 1956

PART I

REPRESENTATIVE DEMOCRACY

INTRODUCTION

The extracts which appear in Part I are intended to illustrate the various types of political thought which prevail in those countries where what has come to be described as the 'Western system' of representative democracy exists. In their very nature, the institutions of these countries do not rest on a systematic and authoritatively defined philosophy of politics. Furthermore, the various political theories which peacefully co-exist within them cannot be easily differentiated. Part of the condition of this peaceful co-existence is a high degree of interaction; the lines of demarcation are wavering and indistinct; it is impossible to say, for example, at precisely what point an economic doctrine becomes Socialist or when exactly a theory of liberty ceases to be Liberal.

Accordingly, it has been thought desirable to present some central topics in the form of a debate and to allow the different strands of political thought to be revealed in this context.

Section A deals with the premises from which political thought begins. The extracts from Locke set out the foundations of a philosophy of politics which may be conveniently described as *a priori* Liberalism. This philosophy begins by postulating that all men everywhere have certain indefeasible human rights—life, liberty and property—which it is the business of society and the state to preserve, the defence of which constitutes the justification of all political authority and the criterion by which political institutions should always be judged. The extract from Bentham puts forward an alternative basis for Liberalism; rejecting the theory of *a priori* rights, it sets up human happiness as the single goal of society and government. While it is important to make this distinction between two types of Liberalism, it is even more important to notice the qualities which are common to them both: both are concerned to discover a universal pattern for political organisation and a universal standard for the judgment of institutions. Both are individualist in the sense that they seek the proper ends of government in the life of the individual and hold it possible to think of the rights of the individual in the abstract without any necessary reference to the conditions of the political community in which he lives. This does not mean that Liberalism in either of these forms takes no account of social and historical circumstances in recommending policy, but merely that in both these forms it pursues an abstract and universally valid theory of politics.

The third extract expresses what may conveniently be described as the 'Empirical Conservative' approach to politics. In it, Professor Oakeshott restates Burke's belief that political theory should begin not with abstract principles and the search for universally valid patterns but with the study of particular communities. Only from knowing what a community is and what the laws of its being as revealed in history are, is it possible to discover what it ought to be. There are absolute truths about politics but they are expressed in ever-changing institutional forms, and it is never possible wholly to separate what is permanent from what is contingent. The politician has to discover what trends are at work in the particular society with which he is concerned and to choose which of them to foster.

Here, then, a fundamental rift in Western political thought appears: the rift between political theories which begin by enunciating principles which profess to be universally valid, and political theories which, holding that there are very few things which can be rationally affirmed to be universally true, tentatively infer principles from the study of particular circumstances.

This initial distinction made, it is possible to see these two traditions at work in the discussion of contemporary problems. Section B deals with majority rule. The extract from Sir Ernest Barker expresses a conventional Liberal defence of majority rule, in which it is possible to see at work the influence of both *a priori* assumptions about human rights and the utilitarian theory that political science is concerned with discovering ways of making human beings happy. The extracts from Mr Walter Lipmann and from *The Times* show the empirical tradition at work, criticising democracy by reference to the results which it is held to produce—passion and uncertainty in the handling of foreign affairs and a tendency for the mass to dominate the exceptional minority.

Section C on the proper limits of authority illustrates by an extract from its classical exponent, John Stuart Mill, the Liberal principle that society should not control the individual except in so far as the individual's behaviour affects society; an empirical criticism of this proposition is provided by the extract from Fitzjames Stephen; the extract from Lord Russell sets out the Liberal claim for freedom in matters of opinion, basing it on the utilitarian argument that truth tends to result from the competition of ideas. Lord Hugh Cecil defends the Conservative-empirical position—that it is impossible to consider the individual and the state as opposing abstractions and looks for the foundation of liberty in the spirituality of human beings. Finally the extract from Sir Alfred Denning expresses a principle for the limitation of state power which is accepted by all the theorists in the tradition under discussion—the principle of the rule of law.

Section D is concerned with the relationship between liberty and economic justice. At this point, an important rift appears in the Liberal tradition: at its outset, Liberal individualist economics tried to reconcile the conflict between liberty and justice by putting forward the theory that, in economic affairs, free competition automatically produces social harmony and well-being. This theory, in its modern version, is illustrated by the extract from Dr Hayek. Socialism, however, is itself an offshoot of the Liberal tradition: the extract from Professor Tawney illustrates how the principle of personal liberty can be used to justify the conscious direction of the community's economic life in the common interest; Miss Barbara Wootton contends that planning for determinate economic ends is compatible with, and, by implication, necessary to, cultural freedom; the practical consequences of this line of thought are revealed in the extracts from the British Labour Party's Manifesto of 1945.

The Conservative-empirical reaction is hostile to both the economic individualism represented by Dr Hayek and the collectivism represented by Professor Tawney, Miss Wootton and the Labour Party Manifesto. It is expressed in the extract from Lord Hailsham, which sets out the view that statesmanship should aim at holding a balance between extremes, and that the balance at this moment needs redressing on the side of individualism rather than of collectivism. The extract from Sir Winston Churchill defines the current Conservative doctrine of the basic minimum, the theory that the state should establish a level of economic well-being beneath which no one should be allowed to fall but should otherwise leave the field open for private enterprise; the extract from the Conservative Party

Manifesto of 1955 gives expression to another economic doctrine which empirical Conservatism embraces today—the doctrine that the state's function is not to conduct economic life but to hold the ring between contending economic interests.

Contemporary thinking about the function of the state in relation to economic affairs has produced a large measure of agreement. That agreement is expressed in the concept of the Welfare State as illustrated by the extract from M. Lafitte.

The two short extracts included under Section E, Decentralisation, are intended to illustrate a recurring theme in contemporary political thought in the West, a desire to reconcile liberty and authority by the fostering of group life on the assumption that the two can be more easily reconciled in small communities. A comment on the origin of this desire by M. de Jouvenel is also included.

The various views of the nature of international relations which have been advanced in recent years cannot be adequately treated in an anthology of this size, but the argument would not be complete without some illustration of two broad theories on the subject: extracts from the Atlantic Charter are included as typifying that Liberal view of international relations which postulates an international society analogous to the national state in the sense that it can be subject to a rule of law designed to preserve national and human rights. The objections of a 'Conservative-empiricist' to this approach are stated in the extract from Mr George Kennan.

In conclusion, an extract is reproduced from the Constitution of the Republic of India. It gives expression to the practical constitutional results which follow from an attempt to apply to the building of a new state the ideas presented in the collected documents.

SECTION A

FOUNDATIONS

JOHN LOCKE, '*A Priori*' *Liberalism*

To understand political power right, and derive it from its original, we must consider what state all men are naturally in, and that is, a state of perfect freedom to order their actions and dispose of their possessions and persons, as they think fit, within the bounds of the law of nature; without asking leave, or depending upon the will of any other man.

A state also of equality, wherein all the power and jurisdiction is reciprocal, no one having more than another; there being nothing more evident, than that creatures of the same species and rank, promiscuously born to all the same advantages of nature, and the use of the same faculties, should also be equal one amongst another without subordination or subjection; unless the lord and master of them all should, by any manifest declaration of his will, set one above another, and confer on him, by an evident and clear appointment, an undoubted right to dominion and sovereignty . . . .

But though this be a state of liberty, yet it is not a state of licence: though man in that state has an uncontrollable liberty to dispose of his person or possessions, yet he has not liberty to destroy himself, or so much as any creature in his possession, but where some nobler use than its bare preservation calls for it. The state of nature has a law of nature to govern it, which obliges every one: and reason, which is that law, teaches all mankind, who will but consult it, that being all equal and independent, no one ought to harm another in his life, health, liberty, or possessions: for men being all the workmanship of one omnipotent and infinitely wise Maker; all the servants of one sovereign Master, sent into the world by His order, and about His business; they are His property, Whose workmanship they are, made to last during His, not another's pleasure: and being furnished with like faculties, sharing all in one community of nature, there cannot be supposed any such subordination among us, that may authorise us to destroy another, as if we were made for one another's uses, as the inferior ranks of creatures are for ours. Every one, as he is bound to preserve himself, and not to quit his station wilfully, so by the like reason, when his own preservation comes not in competition, ought he, as much as he can, to preserve the rest of mankind, and may not, unless it be to do justice to an offender, take away or impair the life, or what tends to the preservation of life, the liberty, health, limb, or goods of another.

And that all men may be restrained from invading others' rights, and from doing hurt to one another, and the law of nature be observed, which willeth the peace and preservation of all mankind, the execution of the law of nature is, in that state, put into every man's hands, whereby every one has a right to punish the transgressors of that law to such a degree as may hinder its violation: for the law of nature would, as all other laws that concern men in this world, be in vain, if there were nobody that in the state of nature had a power to execute that law, and thereby preserve the innocent and restrain offenders. And if any one in the state of nature may punish another for any evil he has done, every one may do so: for in that state of perfect equality, where naturally there is no superiority or jurisdiction of one over another, what any may do in prosecution of that law, every one must needs have a right to do.

And thus, in the state of nature, 'one man comes by a power over another'; but yet no absolute or arbitrary power, to use a criminal, when he has got him in his hands, according to the passionate heats, or boundless extravagancy of his own will; but only to retribute to him, so far as calm reason and conscience dictate, what is proportionate to his transgression; which is so much as may serve for reparation and restraint: for these two are the only reasons, why one man may lawfully do harm to another, which is that we call punishment.

Men being, as has been said, by nature, all free, equal, and independent, no one can be put out of this estate, and subjected to the political power of another, without his own consent. The only way, whereby any one divests himself of his natural liberty, and puts on the bonds of civil society, is by agreeing with other men to join and unite into a community, for their comfortable, safe, and peaceable living one amongst another, in a secure enjoyment of their properties, and a greater security against any, that are not of it. This any number of men may do, because it injures not the freedom of the rest; they are left as they were in the liberty of the state of nature. When any number of men have so consented to make one community or government, they are thereby presently incorporated, and make one body politic, wherein the majority have a right to act and conclude the rest.

For when any number of men have, by the consent of every individual, made a community, they have thereby made that community one body, with a power to act as one body, which is only by the will and determination of the majority: for that which acts any community, being only the consent of the individuals of it, and it being necessary to that which is one body to move one way; it is necessary the body should move that way whither the greater force carries it, which is the consent of the majority: or else it is impossible it should act or continue one body, one community, which the consent of every individual that united into it, agreed that it should; and so every one is bound by that consent to be concluded by the majority. And therefore we see, that in assemblies, empowered to act by positive laws, where no number is set by that positive law which empowers them, the act of the majority passes for the act of the whole, and of course determines; as having, by the law of nature and reason, the power of the whole.

And thus every man, by consenting with others to make one body politic under one government, puts himself under an obligation, to every one of that society, to submit to the determination of the majority, and to be concluded by it.

The great end of men's entering into society being the enjoyment of their properties in peace and safety, and the great instrument and means of that being the laws established in that society; the first and fundamental positive law of all commonwealths is the establishing of the legislative power; as the first and fundamental natural law, which is to govern even the legislative itself, is the preservation of the society, and (as far as will consist with the public good) of every person in it. This legislative is not only the supreme power of the commonwealth, but sacred and unalterable in the hands where the community have once placed it; nor can any edict of any body else, in what form soever conceived, or by what power soever backed, have the force and obligation of a law, which has not its sanction from that legislative which the public has chosen and appointed; for without this the law could not have that, which is absolutely necessary to its being a law, the consent of the society; over whom nobody can have a power to make laws, but by their own consent, and by authority received from them. And therefore all the obedience, which by the most solemn ties any one can be obliged to pay, ultimately terminates in this supreme power, and is directed by those laws which it enacts; nor can any oaths to any foreign power whatsoever, or any domestic subordinate power, discharge any member of the society from his obedience to the legislative, acting pursuant to their trust; nor oblige him to any obedience contrary to the laws so enacted, or farther than they do allow; it being ridiculous to imagine one can be tied ultimately to obey any power in the society, which is not supreme.

Though the legislative, whether placed in one or more, whether it be always in being, or only by intervals, though it be the supreme power in every commonwealth; yet first, it is not, nor can possibly be absolutely arbitrary over the lives and fortunes of the people: for it being but the joint power of every member of the society given up to that person, or assembly, which is legislator; it can be no more than those persons had in a state of nature before they entered into society, and gave up to the community: for nobody can transfer to another more power than he has in himself; and nobody has an absolute arbitrary power over himself, or over any other, to destroy his own life, or take away the life or property of another. A man, as has been proved, cannot subject himself to the arbitrary power of another; and having in the state of nature no arbitrary power over the life, liberty, or possession of another, but only so much as the law of nature gave him for the preservation of himself and the rest of mankind; this is all he doth, or can give up to the commonwealth, and by it to the legislative power, so that the legislative can have no more than this. Their power, in the utmost bounds of it, is limited to the public good of the society. It is a power, that hath no other end but preservation, and therefore can never have a right to destroy, enslave, or designedly to impoverish the subjects. The obligations of the law of nature cease not in society, but only in many cases are drawn closer, and have by human laws known penalties annexed to them, to enforce their observation. Thus the law of nature stands as an eternal rule to all men, legislators as well as others. The rules that they make for other men's actions, must, as well as their own and other men's actions, be conformable to the laws of nature, *i.e.* to the will of God, of which that is a declaration; and the 'fundamental law of nature being the preservation of mankind', no human sanction can be good, or valid against it.

Though in a constituted commonwealth, standing upon its own basis, and acting according to its own nature, that is, acting for the preservation of the community, there can be but one supreme power, which is the legislative, to which all the rest are and must be subordinate; yet the legislative being only a fiduciary power to act for certain ends, there remains still 'in the people a supreme power to remove or alter the legislative', when they find the legislative act contrary to the trust reposed in them: for all power given with trust for the attaining an end, being limited by that end; whenever that end is manifestly neglected or opposed, the trust must necessarily be forfeited, and the power devolve into the hands of those that gave it, who may place it anew where they shall think best for their safety and security. And thus the community perpetually retains a supreme power of saving themselves from the attempts and designs of any body, even of their legislators, whenever they shall be so foolish, or so wicked, as to lay and carry on designs against the liberties and properties of the subject.

From *Second Treatise on Civil Government.* (1690)

JEREMY BENTHAM, *Utilitarian Liberalism*

The sole object of the legislator is to increase and to prevent pains; and for this purpose he ought to be well acquainted with their respective values. As pleasures and pains are the only instruments which he employs, he ought carefully to study their power.

If we examine the value of a pleasure, considered in itself, and in relation to a single individual, we shall find that it depends upon four circumstances:

1st Its intensity
2nd Its duration
3rd Its certainty
4th Its proximity

The value of pain depends upon the same circumstances.

But it is not enough to examine the value of pleasures and pains as if they were isolated and independent. Pains and pleasures may have other pains and pleasures as their consequences. Therefore, if we wish to calculate the tendency of an act from which there results an immediate pain or pleasure, we must take two additional circumstances into the account, *viz:*

5th Its productiveness
6th Its purity

A productive pleasure is one which is likely to be followed by pleasures of the same kind.

A productive pain is one which is likely to be followed by pains of the same kind.

A pure pleasure is one which is not likely to produce pains.

A pure pain is one which is not likely to produce pleasures.

When the calculation is to be made in relation to a collection of individuals, yet another element is necessary:

7th Its extent

That is, the number of persons who are likely to find themselves affected by this pain or pleasure.

When we wish to value an action, we must follow in detail all the operations above indicated. These are the elements of moral calculation; and legislation thus becomes a matter of arithmetic.

From *Theory of Legislation,* (1789), ch. viii,
'The Measure of Pleasures and Pains'.

Michael Oakeshott, *Conservative Empiricism*

The understanding of politics as the activity of attending to the arrangements of a society under the guidance of an independently premeditated ideology is, then, no less a misunderstanding than the understanding of it as a purely empirical activity. Wherever else politics may begin, they cannot begin in ideological activity. And in an attempt to improve upon this understanding of politics, we have already observed in principle what needs to be recognised in order to have an intelligible concept. Just as scientific hypothesis cannot appear, and is impossible to operate, except within an already existing tradition of scientific investigation, so a scheme of ends for political activity appears within, and is valuable only when it is related to, an already existing tradition of how to attend to our arrangements. In politics, the only self-moved manner of activity detectable is one in which empiricism and the ends to be pursued are recognised as dependent, alike for their existence and their operation, upon a traditional manner of behaviour.

Politics is the activity of attending to the general arrangements of a collection of people who, in respect of their common recognition of a manner of attending to its arrangements, compose a single community. To suppose a collection of people without recognised traditions of behaviour, or one which enjoyed arrangements which intimated no direction for change and needed no attention, is to suppose a people incapable of politics. This activity, then, springs neither from instant desires, nor from general principles, but from the existing traditions of behaviour themselves. And the form it takes, because it can take no other, is the amendment of existing arrangements by exploring and pursuing what is intimated in them. The arrangements which constitute a society capable of political activity, whether they are customs or institutions or laws or diplomatic decisions, are at once coherent and incoherent; they compose a pattern and at the same time they intimate a sympathy for what does not fully appear. Political activity is the exploration of that sympathy; and consequently, relevant political reasoning will be the convincing exposure of a sympathy not yet followed up and the convincing demonstration that now is the opportune moment for recognising. For example, the legal status of women in our society was for a long time (and perhaps still is) in comparative confusion, because the rights and duties which composed it intimated rights and duties which were nevertheless not recognised. And, on the view of things I am suggesting, the only relevant reason to be advanced for the technical 'enfranchisement' of women was that in all or most other important respects they had already been enfranchised. Arguments drawn from abstract natural right, from 'justice' or from some general concept of feminine personality, must be regarded as either irrelevant, or as unfortunately disguised forms of the one valid argument; namely, that there was an incoherence in the arrangements of the society which pressed convincingly for remedy. In politics, then, every enterprise is a consequential enterprise, the pursuit, not of a dream, or of a general principle, but of an intimation. What we have to do with is something less imposing than logical implications or necessary consequences: but if the intimations of a tradition of behaviour are less dignified or more elusive than these, they are not on that account less important. Of course, there is no piece of mistake-proof apparatus by means of which we can elicit the intimation most worth while pursuing; and not only do we often make gross errors of judgment in this matter, but also the total effect of a desire satisfied is so little to be forecast, that our activity of amendment is often found to lead us where we would not go. Moreover, the whole enterprise is liable at any moment to be perverted by the incursion of an approximation to empiricism in the pursuit of power. These are imperfections which can never be eliminated. But it is to be believed that our mistakes will be less frequent and less disastrous, and our achievements more manageable, if we escape the illusion that politics can ever be anything more than the pursuit of intimations; a conversation, not an argument.

Now, every society which is intellectually alive is liable, from time to time, to abridge its tradition of behaviour into a scheme of abstract ideas; and on occasion political discussion will be concerned, not (like the debates in the *Iliad*) with isolated transactions, nor (like the speeches in Thucydides) with policies and traditions of activity, but with general principles. And in this there is no harm; perhaps even some positive benefit. It is possible that the distorting mirror of an ideology will reveal important hidden passages in the tradition, as a caricature reveals the potentialities of a face; and if this is so the intellectual enterprise of seeing what a tradition looks like when it is reduced to an ideology will be a useful part of political education. But to make use of abridgement as a technique for exploring the intimations of a political tradition, to use it, that is, as a scientist uses hypothesis, is one thing; it is something different, and something inappropriate, to allow political activity itself to appear as the activity of amending the arrangements of a society so as to make them agree with the provisions of an ideology. For when this happens a character has been attributed to an ideology which it is unable to sustain, and we find ourselves directed by a false and a misconceived guide: false, because in the abridgement, however skilfully it has been performed, a single intimation is exaggerated and proposed for unconditional pursuit and the benefit to be had from observing what the distortion reveals is lost when the distortion itself is given the office of a criterion; misconceived, because the abridgement itself never, in fact, provides the whole of the knowledge used in political activity.

There will be some people who, though in general agreement with this understanding of political activity, will suspect that it confuses what is, perhaps, normal with what is necessary, and that important exceptions (of great contemporary relevance) have been lost in a hazy generality. It is all very well, it may be said, to observe in politics the activity of exploring and pursuing the intimations of a tradition of behaviour, but what light does this throw upon a political crisis such as the Norman Conquest of England, or the establishment of the Soviet regime in Russia? It would be foolish, of course, to deny the possibility of serious political crisis. But if we exclude (as we must) a cataclysm which for the time being made an end of politics by altogether obliterating a current tradition of behaviour, there is little to support the view that even the most serious political upheaval carries us outside this understanding of politics. A tradition of behaviour is not a fixed and inflexible manner of doing things; it is a flow of sympathy. It may be temporarily disrupted by the incursion of a foreign influence, it may be diverted, restricted, arrested, or become dried-up, and it may reveal so deep-seated an incoherence that (even without foreign assistance) a crisis appears. And if, in order to meet these crises, there were some steady, unchanging, independent guide to which a society might resort, it would no doubt be well advised to do so. But no such guide exists; we have no resources outside the fragments, the vestiges, the relics of its own tradition of behaviour which the crisis has left untouched. For even the help we may get from the traditions of another society (or from a tradition of a vaguer sort which is shared by a number of societies) is conditional upon our being able to assimilate them to our own arrangements and our own manner of attending to our arrangements. The hungry and helpless man is mistaken if he supposes that he overcomes the crisis by means of a tin-opener: what saves him is somebody else's knowledge of how to cook, which he can make use of only because he is not himself entirely ignorant. In short, political crisis (even when it seems to be imposed upon a society by changes beyond its control) always appears within a tradition of political activity; and salvation comes from the unimpaired resources of the tradition itself. Those societies which retain, in changing circumstances, a lively sense of their own identity and continuity (which are without that hatred of their own experience which makes them desire to efface it) are to be counted fortunate, not because they possess what others lack, but because they have ready mobilised what none is without and all, in fact, rely upon.

In political activity, then, men sail a boundless and bottomless sea; there is neither harbour for shelter nor floor for anchorage, neither starting-place nor appointed destination. The enterprise is to keep afloat on an even keel; the sea is both friend and enemy; and the seamanship consists in using the resources of a traditional manner of behaviour in order to make a friend of every inimical occasion.

A depressing doctrine, it will be said—even by those who do not make the mistake of adding in an element of crude determinism which, in fact, it has no place for. A tradition of behaviour is not a groove within which we are destined to grind out our helpless and unsatisfying lives: *Spartam nactus es; hanc exorna.* But in the main the depression springs from the exclusion of hopes that were false and the discovery that guides, reputed to be of superhuman wisdom and skill, are, in fact, of a somewhat different character. If the doctrine deprives us of a model laid up in heaven to which we should approximate our behaviour, at least it does not lead us into a morass where every choice is equally good or equally to be deplored. And if it suggests that politics are *nur für die Schwindelfreie*, that should depress only those who have lost their nerve.

From *Political Education*, Inaugural Lecture, (1951).

SECTION B

MAJORITY RULE

Sir Ernest Barker, *The Liberal Case for Democracy*

There is an obvious, and a profound, sense in which the process of democracy is itself scientific, and indeed may justly be called the most scientific process possible, in view of the nature of the material which has to be handled and the character of the problem which has to be solved; nor is the process any the less scientific because it is conducted by ordinary men and women, acting not in a laboratory or in a temper of quiet abstraction, but in the hurly-burly of their contacts and among the frictions which contacts produce.

The material to be handled is man: the problem to be solved is the government of man. It is the never-ending problem—always being solved, and never finally solved—of making, repairing, and maintaining an adjustment of human relations which satisfies (or is generally calculated to satisfy) the moral claims of right made upon one another by human individuals and by groups of such individuals. Now such an adjustment, which satisfies claims of right, can only be attained if there is present, in addition to claims of right and in answer to claims of right, a corresponding and responsive body of acknowledgements of duty. If we have a sense of right and make claims of right for ourselves, we have also a sense of duty and make acknowledgements of duty to others; and without this sense and these acknowledgements no claims of right (our own included) would ever be more than claims. It is acknowledgements of duty which turn claims of right into actual rights, actively recognised and therefore really enjoyed. We may therefore say that the government of man, or the adjustment of human relations within a political society, is ultimately based upon, and cannot exist without, the moral foundation of an acknowledgement of duty to others. This is the same as to say that it is based upon, and cannot exist without, a sense of moral obligation—the sense that I have, and must admit, and must fulfil, certain duties to my neighbour. It is true that the sense of our rights, and our claims of right, spring first to our mind. It is true again that, for this reason, political philosophy has often based itself on claims of right, and has often been couched in terms of 'natural rights' or 'the rights of man'. But it also is true that reflection must always carry us back to the sense of duty and the acknowledgement of obligation. Rights without duties are like men without shadows: they only exist in fairy tales. Any claim of right is ultimately an appeal to the sense of duty and the acknowledgement of obligation. 'I must give' is something which must underlie 'I ought to have'. That is why Kant proclaimed that true politics must first do homage to morals, and why political philosophy must always turn from the theory of Tom Paine to the theory of Kant.

The problem handled by government is therefore that of making an adjustment of human relations which satisfies moral claims of right because, and to the extent that, it is supported by moral acknowledgements of duty. What is the scientific method of attaining this adjustment?

There is one method which is not in itself scientific, though it may be the beginning and the first stage of a scientific method. This is the method of simple quantitative measurement. In itself, and in isolation, it is the method of a thin or mathematical democracy, which is something different from a rounded or scientific democracy. If we pursue only this method, we are guilty of a double abstraction. In the first place we confine our attention to abstract claims of right, forgetting the necessary foundation of acknowledgements of duty. In the second place we confine ourselves to measuring abstractly the number of persons who advance one claim of right, or one set of claims of right (grouped, for example, in the programme of a party), over against the number of those who advance another and opposing claim or set of claims. On the basis of this mathematical datum we proceed to make an adjustment, which may obviously range (if we still confine ourselves to mathematical considerations) over the whole indeterminate area which lies between the alternative of conceding the whole of its claim to the majority and the alternative of conceding a part of their claims to both sides in proportion to their numbers. This procedure has one merit. It supplies one definite datum: it registers exactly the number of claimants of right. On the other it has some obvious defects.

In the first place, though the datum, so far as it goes, is certain, the adjustment is uncertain. There is nothing scientific in an adjustment which is left with so large a latitude of undetermined discretion. In the second place, the datum supplied, although it is definite, is far from adequate. We want to know the quantity of claimants of rights, but we also want to know something more. We want to know the quality, or the value, of the claim which they make. In order to know that, we want to know how far, and with what degree of intensity, the claim appeals to, and is backed by, an acknowledgement of duty. For unless there is that acknowledgement of duty, the claim is only an abstract claim to which there is no foundation.

We are thus driven to demand a method of adjustment which starts from an adequate knowledge of the whole of the relevant data, and then proceeds, by an adequate assessment of the significance of the different data, to action based on that knowledge. The only scientific method of government—the only scientific way of adjusting human relations—will be a method which can satisfy that double demand. Democracy—provided that it is something more than the thin and mathematical democracy of mere measurement of majorities and minorities; provided that it attains the dimensions of a rounded or scientific democracy, engaged in the rational process of discussion, and constructing by means of discussion a reasonable adjustment or compromise—can meet and satisfy the demand. In the first place, it collects, in a full and unparalleled way, a complete survey not only of claims of right, but also of acknowledgements of duty. It sets the community itself to speak and to produce its own register and record of the data. No survey made from outside can produce the record: no external observation can register the data: the claims of right and the acknowledgements of duty, being things of the mind, must come forth and speak for themselves, through every organ by which they can find their speech and utterance. If they do this, then, in the very act of its being done, democracy already begins to achieve a second result. The process of collecting the data of the problem proves itself to be also a beginning of solution. The differences do not merely register themselves as what they separately are: they do not merely state themselves independently and in isolation: they begin, in the act and moment of statement, to enter into relations with one another—relations of attack and defence, of action and reaction—by which they are modified and adjusted even while they are being formulated and expressed. An adjustment is thus already immanent in the very statement of the problem. It is also 'immanent' in another sense. Adjustment does not proceed from any authority outside the parties themselves, or follow any process except the process in which they are themselves engaged. It is no act of external imposition, which might be this, or that; it has no quality of arbitrary selection: it comes, as a scientific solution should always come, from the very data of the problem.

So far as democracy proceeds by way of genuine discussion; so far as it succeeds in bringing one claim of right into argument with another, and in eliciting acknowledgements of duty to meet and face claims of right; so far, again, as it succeeds in inducing men to make for themselves compromises between different claims, and to achieve for themselves a union and correspondence between rights claimed and duties acknowledged; so far as it does these things, it is already true, in itself and as it stands, to the ideal of scientific government. If it then adds to its general method the particular machinery of expert scientific commissions, it is not tempering or qualifying its methods by that addition. Still retaining its own complete and final responsibility—still setting different claims to speak for themselves and present their own cases, and still seeking to promote a voluntary adjustment between the different cases presented—it has simply erected a special court to give a preliminary hearing to the cases, and it has simply empowered that court to make recommendations for the guidance of the community in achieving a voluntary adjustment between the cases. The method of the expert scientific commission is ancillary to, and in accordance with, the general method of parliamentary democracy—a method, in its nature and intention, no less scientific, but working on a grander scale, and with an unbroken continuity, in the ultimate court of final and absolute decision.

From *Reflections on Government* (1942), ch. viii, 'The Reform of Parliamentary Democracy: Planning'.

WALTER LIPPMANN, *An Empirical Critic of Liberal Democracy*

Experience since 1917 indicates that in matters of war and peace the popular answer in the democracies is likely to be No. For everything connected with war has become dangerous, painful, disagreeable and exhausting to very nearly everyone. The rule to which there are few exceptions—the acceptance of the Marshall Plan is one of them—is that at the critical junctures, when the stakes are high, the prevailing mass opinion will impose what amounts to a veto upon changing the course on which the government is at the time proceeding. Prepare for war in time of peace? No. It is bad to raise taxes, to unbalance the budget, to take men away from their schools or their jobs, to provoke the enemy. Intervene in a developing conflict? No. Avoid the risk of war. Withdraw from the area of the conflict? No. The adversary must not be appeased. Reduce your claims on the area? No. Righteousness cannot be compromised. Negotiate a compromise peace as soon as the opportunity presents itself? No. The aggressor must be punished. Remain armed to enforce the dictated settlement? No. The war is over.

The unhappy truth is that the prevailing public opinion has been destructively wrong at the critical junctures. The people have imposed a veto upon the judgments of informed and responsible officials. They have compelled the governments, which usually knew what would have been wiser, or was necessary, or was more expedient, to be too late with too little, or too long with too much, too pacifist in peace and too bellicose in war, too neutralist or appeasing in negotiation or too intransigent. Mass opinion has acquired mounting power in this century. It has shown itself to be a dangerous master of decisions when the stakes are life and death.

The compulsion to make mistakes

The errors of public opinion in these matters have a common characteristic. The movement of opinion is slower than the movement of events. Because of that, the cycle of subjective sentiments on war and peace is usually out of gear with the cycle of objective developments. Just because they are mass opinions there is an inertia in them. It takes much longer to change many minds than to change a few. It takes time to inform and to persuade and to arouse large scattered varied multitudes of persons. So before the multitude have caught up with the old events there are likely to be new ones coming up over the horizon with which the government should be preparing to deal. But the majority will be more aware of what they have just caught up with near at hand than with what is still distant and in the future. For these reasons the propensity to say 'No' to a change of course sets up a compulsion to make mistakes. The opinion deals with a situation which no longer exists.

When the world wars came, the people of the liberal democracies could not be aroused to the exertions and the sacrifices of the struggle until they had been frightened by the opening disasters, had been incited to passionate hatred, and had become intoxicated with unlimited hope. To overcome this inertia the enemy had to be portrayed as evil incarnate, as absolute and congenital wickedness. The people wanted to be told that when this particular enemy had been forced to unconditional surrender, they would re-enter the golden age. This unique war would end all wars. This last war would make the world safe for democracy. This crusade would make the whole world a democracy.

As a result of this impassioned nonsense public opinion became so envenomed that the people would not countenance a workable peace; they were against any public man who showed 'any tenderness for the Hun', or was inclined to listen to the 'Hun food snivel'.

From *The Public Philosophy* (1955), ch. II,
'The Malady of Democratic States'.

THE GOVERNORS AND THE GOVERNED

When I describe the malady of democratic states as a derangement in the relation between the mass of the people and the government, I am, of course, implying that there is a sound relationship and that we should be able to know what it is. We must now examine this assumption. We are looking into the relationship between, on the one hand, the governing or executive power, and, on the other hand, the elected assembly and the voters in the constituencies. The best place to begin is in the simple beginnings of our constitutional development—in the medieval English Parliament—before the essential functions and their relation had become complicated by their later development.

No relationship, sound or unsound, could exist until the functions of execution and representation had become differentiated. In primitive societies they are not differentiated. Under the Norman and Angevin rulers the differentiation had not yet occurred. These rulers 'judged and legislated as well as administered'. But by the thirteenth century the differentiation is already visible, and the essential relation in which we are interested can be recognised. There is a writ issued under Henry III in 1254, summoning Parliament. The sheriff of each county is ordered to 'cause to come before the King's Council two good and discreet Knights of the Shire, whom the men of the county shall have chosen for this purpose in the stead of all and of each of them, to consider along with knights of other shires what aid they will grant the King'.

Let us note the dualism. There is the government, which means the King and his Council of prelates and peers. Then there are the Knights of the Shires, representing the men of the counties. They are to meet, and the King will ask the Knights what aid they will grant to him. This is the basic relationship. The government can act. Because it can act, it decides what action should be taken, and it proposes the measures; it then asks the representatives of those who must supply the money and the men for the means to carry out its decisions. The governed, through their representatives, the two Knights of the Shire from each county, give or withhold their consent.

From the tension and the balance of the two powers—that of the ruler and that of the ruled—there evolved the written and the unwritten contracts of the constitution. The grant of aid by the ruled must be preceded by the ruler's redress of their grievances. The government will be refused the means of governing if it does not listen to the petitions, if it does not inform, if it does not consult, if it cannot win the consent of, those who have been elected as the representatives of the governed.

The executive is the active power in the state, the asking and the proposing power. The representative assembly is the consenting power, the petitioning, the approving and the criticising, the accepting and the refusing power. The two powers are necessary if there is to be order and freedom. But each must be true to its own nature, each limiting and complementing the other. The government must be able to govern and the citizens must be represented in order that they shall not be oppressed. The health of the system depends upon the relationship of the two powers. If either absorbs or destroys the functions of the other power, the constitution is deranged.

There is here a relationship between governors and governed which is, I would contend, rooted in the nature of things. At the risk of reasoning by analogy, I would suggest that this duality of function within a political society has a certain resemblance to that of the two sexes. In the act of reproduction each sex has an unalterable physiological function. If this function is devitalised or is confused with the function of the other sex, the result is sterility and disorder.

In the final acts of the state the issues are war and peace, security and solvency, order and insurrection. In these final acts the executive power cannot be exercised by the representative assembly. Nor can it be exercised after the suppression of the assembly. For in the derangement of the two primary functions lie the seeds of disaster.

THE PEOPLE AND THE VOTERS

A recent historian of the Tudor Revolution, Mr G. R. Elton, says that 'our history is still much written by whigs, the champions of political freedom', and that 'while the safeguards against despotism have long been understood and often described—strong rule, preventing anarchy and preserving order, requires still much exploration'. There have been periods, he goes on to say, of which the Tudor Age was one—and our own, we may add, is another—when men were so ready to be governed, being so oppressed by disorder, that they have preferred strong government to free government.

The Western liberal democracies are a declining power in human affairs. I argue that this is due to a derangement of the functions of their governments which disables them in coping with the mounting disorder. I do not say, indeed it is impossible to know surely, whether the malady can be cured or whether it must run its course. But I do say that if it cannot be cured, it will continue to erode the safeguards against despotism, and the failure of the West may be such that freedom will be lost and will not be restored again except by another revolution.

From *The Public Philosophy* (1955), ch. II, 'The Derangement of Powers'.

'THE TIMES', *The Democratic Case Analysed*

MAJORITY RULE

An article by Mr Max Beloff in *The Fortnightly* reached the striking conclusion that the time has come for a serious inquiry into the extent to which the principle 'of majority rule under a regime of universal suffrage is an adequate method of dealing with the ever more intricate and technical problems of a modern industrial society in a competitive world'. The twentieth century has seen the cardinal principles of the British system of government removed, to an extent almost unparalleled, from the healthy impact of radical but well-intentioned criticism. Democracy has had its enemies, but they have for the most part been men who also repudiated the whole heritage of liberal civilisation. In the zeal with which it has rejected their counsel, public opinion has come near to accepting the belief that it is impossible to be sceptical of the infallibility of majorities and of any of the forms which the constitution has assumed in the last fifty years without at the same time repudiating the cause of liberty and all the settled conventions of decency in the conduct of public affairs. It is a salutary experiment, therefore, to follow Mr Beloff's example in turning back to the great Victorian political thinkers, who, though they were generally men with a stout faith in liberty, viewed with almost unqualified gloom the steady advance towards universal suffrage which they knew to be inevitable.

Mr Beloff finds, in particular, that the forebodings of John Stuart Mill, the most eminent of these liberal critics of democracy, have in part been justified. Mill was obsessed by the fear that, under democracy, the State might become the instrument of the most numerous and least gifted class in the community, and as such be employed in an indiscriminate campaign of expropriation leading to national bankruptcy. Like most of the

Victorians, he appreciated and perhaps exaggerated the importance to the welfare of society as a whole of the enterprise and talent of the few, and he held that organised mediocrity was the most formidable enemy alike of liberty and prosperity. The pages of Lecky's *Democracy and Liberty*, that diffuse but incredibly illuminating product of a mind formed equally by history and the close observation of contemporary affairs, are replete with more detailed prophecies of the same kind. Investigations into the results of recent General Elections have shown the probably unprecedented extent to which voting reflects the class structure of society. Drastic changes in the composition of the House of Commons may occur, but they are brought about by the minority of voters, often revealingly described as 'politically unstable', who retain the habit of empirical choice. In practice the Conservatives must look mainly for support to that large and highly variegated section of the community 'the middle classes', whose limits are set at one extreme by the victims of supertax and which, at the other, passes indistinctly into the ranks of the skilled workers; while the Socialists depend chiefly on a vast class of weekly wage-earners to whom voting Labour has become a fixed habit. Both classes are sufficiently comprehensive to make political extremism unprofitable for either party. So the paradoxical effect is produced that both parties are very largely obliged to recommend the same kind of policy firmly grounded on the maintenance of the social services but generally evading the acute financial difficulties which that aim presents. Hence arises the common complaint, which must be admitted to have much substance, that both parties tend to avoid the more unpalatable courses of action until they become absolutely necessary.

This is a state of affairs which the Victorians foresaw. The original advocates of majority rule in this country, the Utilitarians, conceived it as operating in a fluid society in which individuals would consult their own interests rather than those of a class in casting their votes. They believed that the composition of majorities would perpetually change so that in the course of a lifetime every individual would sometimes find himself 'in power'. These were not very inspiring arguments—the merit of the Utilitarians was precisely their honest realism—but they did afford some rational justification for majority rule on the basis of the accepted philosophy of the day. Later, democracy came to be defended by the neo-Hegelians like T. H. Green as a means of associating every citizen consciously and intelligently with the life of the community, as an education in patriotism, and as a method of discovering by an appeal to the moral insight of common humanity answers to questions which were always in part moral. It was theories such as these which led Britain to repudiate the principle by which the unreformed parliamentary system of the pre-1832 era was defended, the principle that Parliament should reflect a balanced variety of class interests and that, recognising the importance of class, the constitution should aim at preserving a rough equilibrium in the distribution of power between the classes.

What must be remembered is that democracy in Britain has a comparatively short history. Those who established it believed that its effectiveness would depend on certain clearly defined conditions, and it is to these conditions that public attention must now be addressed. They believed not in snap decisions by the majority but in the supremacy of a deliberate public opinion and they looked to a second Chamber to provide that element of deliberateness. To do this, however, the House of Lords must not only be equipped with adequate delaying powers; its composition must be such as to command the respect and confidence of the electorate, and it is a major tragedy that Lords Reform, the need for which is universally admitted, should have been so long delayed. The position of the House of Lords is at present the most serious mechanical defect in the constitution, yet even if this defect were removed the most important requirement of democracy, an advanced state of political education, would remain to be supplied. That task implies, what the Victorians always assumed, constant and candid political leadership which, despising the easy road to popularity, focuses public opinion fearlessly on the full implications of decisions which it has to take. The electorate has more than once shown that it responds to such leadership; but leadership of this kind can become a permanent factor in Britain's political life only if the main parties have—transcending their doctrinal feuds—a corporate sense of responsibility for the guidance and education of the electorate.

From *The Times* (2 Feb. 1953).

SECTION C

LIBERTY

JOHN STUART MILL, *Limits of Authority: A Liberal View*

What, then, is the rightful limit to the sovereignty of the individual over himself? Where does the authority of society begin? How much of human life should be assigned to individuality, and how much to society?

Each will receive its proper share, if each has that which more particularly concerns it. To individuality should belong the part of life in which it is chiefly the individual that is interested; to society, the part which chiefly interests society.

Though society is not founded on a contract, and though no good purpose is answered by inventing a contract in order to deduce social obligations from it, every one who receives the protection of society owes a return for the benefit, and the fact of living in society renders it indispensable that each should be bound to observe a certain line of conduct towards the rest. This conduct consists, first, in not injuring the interests of one another; or rather certain interests, which, either by express legal provision or by tacit understanding, ought to be considered as rights; and secondly, in each person's bearing his share (to be fixed on some equitable principle) of the labours and sacrifices incurred for defending the society or its members from injury and molestation. These conditions society is justified in enforcing, at all costs to those who endeavour to withhold fulfilment. Nor is this all that society may do. The acts of an individual may be hurtful to others, or wanting in due consideration for their welfare, without going to the length of violating any of their constituted rights. The offender may then be justly punished by opinion, though not by law. As soon as any part of a person's conduct affects prejudicially the interests of others, society has jurisdiction over it, and the question whether the general welfare will or will not be promoted by interfering with it, becomes open to discussion. But there is no room for entertaining any such question when a person's conduct affects the interests of no person besides himself, or needs not affect them unless they like (all the persons concerned being of full age, and the ordinary amount of understanding). In all such cases, there should be perfect freedom, legal and social, to do the action and stand the consequences.

It would be a great misunderstanding of this doctrine, to suppose that it is one of selfish indifference, which pretends that human beings have no business with each other's conduct in life, and that they should not concern themselves about the well-doing or well-being of one another, unless their own interest is involved. Instead of any diminution, there is need of a great increase of disinterested exertion to promote the good of others. But disinterested benevolence can find other instruments to persuade people to their good, than whips and scourges, either of the literal or the metaphorical sort. I am the last person to undervalue the self-regarding virtues; they are only second in importance, if even second, to the social. It is equally the business of education to cultivate both. But even education works by conviction and persuasion as well as by compulsion, and it is by the former only that, when the period of education is passed, the self-regarding virtues should be inculcated. Human beings owe to each other help to distinguish the better from the worse, and encouragement to choose the former and avoid the latter. They should be for ever stimulating each other to increased exercise of their higher faculties, and increased direction of their feelings and aims towards wise instead of foolish, elevating instead of degrading, objects and contemplations. But neither one person, nor any number of persons, is warranted in saying to another human creature of ripe years, that he shall not do with his life for his own benefit what he chooses to do with it. He is the person most interested in his own well-being; the interest which any other person, except in cases of strong personal attachment, can have in it, is trifling, compared with that which he himself has; the interest which society has in him individually (except as to his conduct to others) is fractional, and altogether indirect: while with respect to his own feelings and circumstances, the most ordinary man or woman has means of knowledge immeasurably surpassing those that can be possessed by any one else. The interference of society to overrule his judgment and purposes in what only regards himself, must be grounded on general presumptions; which may be altogether wrong, and even if right, are as likely as not to be misapplied to individual cases, by persons no better acquainted with the circumstances of such cases than those are who look at them merely from without. In this department, therefore, of human affairs, Individuality has its proper field of action. In the conduct of human beings towards one another, it is necessary that general rules should for the most part be observed, in order that people may know what they have to expect: but in each person's own concerns, his individual spontaneity is entitled to free exercise. Considerations to aid his judgment, exhortations to strengthen his will, may be offered to him, even obtruded on him, by others; but he himself is the final judge. All errors which he is likely to commit against advice and warning, are far outweighed by the evil of allowing others to constrain him to what they deem his good.

I do not mean that the feelings with which a person is regarded by others, ought not to be in any way affected by his self-regarding qualities or deficiencies. This is neither possible nor desirable. If he is eminent in any of the qualities which conduce to his own good, he is, so far, a proper object of admiration. He is so much the nearer to the ideal perfection of human nature. If he is grossly deficient in those qualities, a sentiment the opposite of admiration will follow. There is a degree of folly, and a degree of what may be called (though the phrase is not unobjectionable) lowness or depravation of taste, which, though it cannot justify doing harm to the person who manifests it, renders him necessarily and properly a subject of distaste, or, in extreme cases, even of contempt: a person could not have the opposite qualities in due strength without entertaining these feelings. Though doing no wrong to any one, a person may so act as to compel us to judge him, and feel to him, as a fool, or as a being of an inferior order: and since this judgment and feeling are a fact which he would prefer to avoid, it is doing him a service to warn him of it beforehand, as of any other disagreeable consequence to which he exposes himself. It would be well, indeed, if this good office were much more freely rendered than the common notions of politeness at present permit, and if one person could honestly point out to another that he thinks him in fault, without being considered unmannerly or presuming. We have a right, also, in various ways, to act upon our unfavourable opinion of any one, not to the oppression of his individuality, but in the exercise of ours. We are not bound, for example, to seek his society; we have a right to avoid it (though not to parade the avoidance), for we have a right to choose the society most acceptable to us. We have a right, and it may be our duty, to caution others against him, if we think his example or conversation likely to have a pernicious effect on those with whom he associates. We may give others a preference over him in optional good offices, except those which tend to his improvement. In these various modes a person may suffer very severe penalties at the hands of others, for faults which directly concern only himself; but he suffers these penalties only in so far as they are the natural, and, as it were, the spontaneous consequences of the faults themselves, not because they are purposely inflicted on him for the sake of punishment. A person who shows rashness, obstinacy, self-conceit—who cannot live within moderate means—who cannot restrain himself from hurtful indulgences—who pursues animal pleasures at the expense of those of feeling and intellect—must expect to be lowered in the opinion of others, and to have a less share of their favourable sentiments; but of this he has no right to complain, unless he has merited their favour by special excellence in his social relations, and has thus established a title to their good offices, which is not affected by his demerits towards himself.

What I contend for is, that the inconveniences which are strictly inseparable from the unfavourable judgment of others, are the only ones to which a person should ever be subjected for that portion of his conduct and character which concerns his own good, but which does not affect the interests of others in their relations with him. Acts injurious to others require a totally different treatment. Encroachment on their rights; infliction on them of any loss or damage not justified by his own rights; falsehood or duplicity in dealing with them; unfair or ungenerous use of advantages over them; even selfish abstinence from defending them against injury—these, are fit objects of moral reprobation, and, in grave cases, of moral retribution and punishment. And not only these acts, but the dispositions which lead to them, are properly immoral, and fit subjects of disapprobation which may rise to abhorrence. Cruelty of disposition; malice and ill-nature; that most anti-social and odious of all passions, envy; dissimulation and insincerity; irascibility on insufficient cause, and resentment disproportioned to the provocation; the love of domineering over others; the desire to engross more than one's share of advantages . . . ; the pride which derives gratification from the abasement of others; the egotism which thinks self and its concerns more important than everything else, and decides all doubtful questions in its own favour;—these are moral vices, and constitute a bad and odious moral character: unlike the self-regarding faults previously mentioned, which are not properly immoralities, and to whatever pitch they may be carried, do not constitute wickedness. They may be proofs of any amount of folly, or want of personal dignity and self-respect; but they are only a subject of moral reprobation when they involve a breach of duty to others, for whose sake the individual is bound to have care for himself. What are called duties to ourselves are not socially obligatory, unless circumstances render them at the same time duties to others. The term duty to oneself, when it means anything more than prudence, means self-respect or self-development; and for none of these is any one accountable to his fellow-creatures, because for none of them is it for the good of mankind that he be held accountable to them.

The distinction between the loss of consideration which a person may rightly incur by defect of prudence or of personal dignity, and the reprobation which is due to him for an offence against the rights of others, is not a merely nominal distinction. It makes a vast difference both in our feelings and in our conduct towards him, whether he displeases us in things in which we think we have a right to control him, or in things in which we know that we have not. If he displeases us, we may express our distaste, and we may stand aloof from a person as well as from a thing that displeases us; but we shall not therefore feel called on to make his life uncomfortable. We shall reflect that he already bears, or will bear, the whole penalty of his error; if he spoils his life by mismanagement, we shall not, for that reason, desire to spoil it still further: instead of wishing to punish him, we shall rather endeavour to alleviate his punishment, by showing him how he may avoid or cure the evils his conduct tends to bring upon him. He may be to us an object of pity, perhaps of dislike, but not of anger or resentment; we shall not treat him like an enemy of society; the worst we shall think ourselves justified in doing is leaving him to himself, if we do not interfere benevolently by showing interest or concern for him. It is far otherwise if he has infringed the rules necessary for the protection of his fellow-creatures, individually or collectively. The evil consequences of his acts do not then fall on himself, but on others; and society, as the protector of all its members, must retaliate on him; must inflict pain on him for the express purpose of punishment, and must take care that it be sufficiently severe. In the one case, he is an offender at our bar, and we are called on not only to sit in judgment on him, but, in one shape or another, to execute our own sentence: in the other case, it is not our part to inflict any suffering on him, except what may incidentally follow from our using the same liberty in the regulation of our own affairs, which we allow to him in his.

The distinction here pointed out between the part of a person's life which concerns only himself, and that which concerns others, many persons will refuse to admit. How (it may be asked) can any part of the conduct of a member of society be a matter of indifference to the other members? No person is an entirely isolated being; it is impossible for a person to do anything seriously or permanently hurtful to himself, without mischief reaching at least to his near connections, and often far beyond them. If he injures his property, he does harm to those who directly or indirectly derived support from it, and usually diminishes, by a greater or less amount, the general resources of the community. If he deteriorates his bodily or mental faculties, he not only brings evil upon all who depended on him for any portion of their happiness, but disqualifies himself for rendering the services which he owes to his fellow creatures generally; perhaps becomes a burthen on their affection or benevolence; and if such conduct were very frequent, hardly any offence that is committed would detract more from the general sum of good. Finally, if by his vices or follies a person does no direct harm to others, he is nevertheless (it may be said) injurious by his example; and ought to be compelled to control himself, for the sake of those whom the sight or knowledge of his conduct might corrupt or mislead.

And even (it will be added) if the consequences of misconduct could be confined to the vicious or thoughtless individual, ought society to abandon to their own guidance those who are manifestly unfit for it? If protection against themselves is confessedly due to children and persons under age, is not society equally bound to afford it to persons of mature years who are equally incapable of self-government? If gambling, or drunkenness, or incontinence, or idleness, or uncleanliness, are as injurious to happiness, and as great a hindrance to improvement, as many or most of the acts prohibited by law, why (it may be asked) should not law, so far as is consistent with practicability and social convenience, endeavour to repress these also? And as a supplement to the unavoidable imperfections of law, ought not opinion at least to organise a powerful police against these vices, and visit rigidly with social penalties those who are known to practise them? There is no question here (it may be said) about restricting individuality, or impeding the trial of new and original experiments in living. The only things it is sought to prevent are things which have been tried and condemned from the beginning of the world until now; things which experience has shown not to be useful or suitable to any person's individuality. There must be some length of time and amount of experience, after which a moral or prudential truth may be regarded as established: and it is merely desired to prevent generation after generation from falling over the same precipice which has been fatal to their predecessors.

I fully admit that the mischief which a person does to himself may seriously affect, both through their sympathies and their interests, those nearly connected with him, and in a minor degree, society at large. When, by conduct of this sort, a person is led to violate a distinct and assignable obligation to any other person or persons, the case is taken out of the self-regarding class, and becomes amenable to moral disapprobation in the proper sense of the term. If, for example, a man, through intemperance or extravagance, becomes unable to pay his debts, or, having undertaken the moral responsibility of a family, becomes from the same cause incapable of supporting or educating them, he is deservedly reprobated, and might be justly punished; but it is for the breach of duty to his family or creditors, not for the extravagance. If the resources which ought to have been devoted to them, had been diverted from them for the most prudent investment, the moral culpability would have been the same. George Barnwell murdered his uncle to get money for his mistress, but if he had done it to set himself up in business, he would equally have been hanged. Again, in the frequent case of a man who causes grief to his family by addiction to bad habits, he deserves reproach for his unkindness or ingratitude; but so he may for cultivating habits not in themselves vicious, if they are painful to those with whom he passes his life, or who from personal ties are dependent on him for their comfort. Whoever fails in the consideration generally due to the interests and feelings of others, not being compelled by some more imperative duty, or justified by allowable self-preference, is a subject of moral disapprobation for that failure, but not for the cause of it, nor for the errors, merely personal to himself, which may have remotely led to it. In like manner, when a person disables himself, by conduct purely self-regarding, from the performance of some definite duty incumbent on him to the public, he is guilty of a social offence. No person ought to be punished simply for being drunk; but a soldier or a policeman should be punished for being drunk on duty. Whenever, in short, there is a definite damage, or a definite risk of damage, either to an individual or to the public, the case is taken out of the province of liberty, and placed in that of morality or law.

But with regard to the merely contingent, or, as it may be called, constructive injury which a person causes to society, by conduct which neither violates any specific duty to the public, nor occasions perceptible hurt to any assignable individual except himself; the inconvenience is one which society can afford to bear, for the sake of the greater good of human freedom. If grown persons are to be punished for not taking proper care of themselves, I would rather it were for their own sake, than under pretence of preventing them from impairing their capacity of rendering to society benefits which society does not pretend it has a right to exact. But I cannot consent to argue the point as if society had no means of bringing its weaker members up to its ordinary standard of rational conduct, except waiting till they do something irrational, and then punishing them, legally or morally for it. Society has had absolute power over them during all the early portion of their existence: it has had the whole period of childhood and nonage in which to try whether it could make them capable of rational conduct in life. The existing generation is master both of the training and the entire circumstances of the generation to come; it cannot indeed make them perfectly wise and good, because it is itself so lamentably deficient in goodness and wisdom; and its best efforts are not always, in individual cases, its most successful ones; but it is perfectly well able to make the rising generation, as a whole, as good as, and a little better than, itself. If society lets any considerable number of its members grow up mere children, incapable of being acted on by rational consideration of distant motives, society has itself to blame for the consequences. Armed not only with all the powers of education, but with the ascendancy which the authority of a received opinion always exercises over the minds who are least fitted to judge for themselves; and aided by the *natural* penalties which cannot be prevented from falling on those who incur the distaste or the contempt of those who know them; let not society pretend that it needs, besides all this, the power to issue commands and enforce obedience in the personal concerns of individuals, in which, on all principles of justice and policy, the decision ought to rest with those who are to abide the consequences. Nor is there anything which tends more to discredit and frustrate the better means of influencing conduct, than a resort to the worse. If there be among those whom it is attempted to coerce into prudence or temperance, any of the material of which vigorous and independent characters are made, they will infallibly rebel against the yoke. No such person will ever feel that others have a right to control him in his concerns, such as they have to prevent him from injuring them in theirs; and it easily comes to be considered a mark of spirit and courage to fly in the face of such usurped authority, and do with ostentation the exact opposite of what it enjoins; as in the fashion of grossness which succeeded, in the time of Charles II, to the fanatical moral intolerance of the Puritans. With respect to what is said of the necessity of protecting society from the bad example set to others by the vicious or the self-indulgent; it is true that bad example may have a pernicious effect, especially the example of doing wrong to others with impunity to the wrongdoer. But we are now speaking of conduct which, while it does no wrong to others, is supposed to do great harm to the agent himself: and I do not see how those who believe this, can think otherwise than that the example, on the whole, must be more salutary than hurtful, since, if it displays the misconduct, it displays also the painful or degrading consequences which, if the conduct is justly censured, must be supposed to be in all or most cases attendant on it.

But the strongest of all the arguments against the interference of the public with purely personal conduct, is that when it does interfere, the odds are that it interferes wrongly, and in the wrong place. On questions of social morality, of duty to others, the opinion of the public, that is, of an overruling majority, though often wrong, is likely to be still oftener right; because on such questions they are only required to judge of their own interests; of the manner in which some mode of conduct, if allowed to be practised, would affect themselves. But the opinion of a similar majority, imposed as a law on the minority, on questions of self-regarding conduct, is quite as likely to be wrong as right; for in these cases public opinion means, at the best, some people's opinion of what is good or bad for other people; while very often it does not even mean that; the public, with the most perfect indifference, passing over the pleasure or convenience of those whose conduct they censure, and considering only their own preference. There are many who consider as an injury to themselves any conduct which they have a distaste for, and resent it as an outrage to their feelings; as a religious bigot, when charged with disregarding the religious feelings of others, has been known to retort that they disregard his feelings, by persisting in their abominable worship or creed. But there is no parity between the feeling of a person for his own opinion, and the feeling of another who is offended at his holding it; no more than between the desire of a thief to take a purse, and the desire of the right owner to keep it. And a person's taste is as much his own peculiar concern as his opinion or his purse. It is easy for any one to imagine an ideal public, which leaves the freedom and choice of individuals in all uncertain matters undisturbed, and only requires them to abstain from modes of conduct which universal experience has condemned. But where has there been seen a public which set any such limit to its censorship? or when does the public trouble itself about universal experience? In its interferences with personal conduct it is seldom thinking of anything but the enormity of acting or feeling differently from itself; and this standard of judgment, thinly disguised, is held up to mankind as the dictate of religion and philosophy, by nine-tenths of all moralists and speculative writers. These teach that things are right because they are right; because we feel them to be so. They tell us to search in our own minds and hearts for laws of conduct binding on ourselves and on all others. What can the poor public do but apply these instructions, and make their own personal feelings of good and evil, if they are tolerably unanimous in them, obligatory on all the world?

From *On Liberty* (1859).

FITZJAMES STEPHEN, *A Critic of Liberalism on Liberty*

So far I have considered the theoretical grounds of Mr Mill's principle and its practical application to liberty of thought and discussion. I now proceed to consider its application to morals. It may be well to restate it for fear that I may appear to be arguing with an imaginary opponent.

> The object of this essay is to assert one very simple principle as entitled to govern absolutely all the dealings of society with the individual in the way of compulsion and control, whether the means used be physical force or the moral coercion of public opinion. That principle is, that the sole end for which mankind are warranted, individually or collectively, in interfering with the liberty of action of any of their number is self-protection.

A little further on we are told that

> from the liberty of each individual follows the liberty within the same limits of combination among individuals—freedom to unite for any purpose not involving harm to others.

The following consequences would flow legitimately from this principle. A number of persons form themselves into an association for the purpose of countenancing each other in the practice of seducing women, and giving the widest possible extension to the theory that adultery is a good thing. They carry out these objects by organising a system for the publication and circulation of lascivious novels and pamphlets calculated to inflame the passions of the young and inexperienced. The law of England would treat this as a crime. It would call such books obscene libels, and a combination for such a purpose a conspiracy. Mr Mill, apparently, would not only regard this as wrong, but he would regard it as an act of persecution if the newspapers were to excite public indignation against the parties concerned by language going one step beyond the calmest discussion of the expediency of such an 'experiment in living'. Such an association would be impossible in this country, because if the law of the land did not deal with it, lynch law infallibly would. This Mr Mill ought in consistency to regard as a lamentable proof of our bigotry and want of acquaintance with the true principles of liberty.

The manner in which he discusses an illustration closely analogous to this, and in which he attempts to answer an objection which must suggest itself to every one, throws the strongest possible light on the value of his own theory. His illustration is as follows: 'Fornication must be tolerated and so must gambling; but should a person be free to be a pimp or to keep a gambling house?' He puts the arguments on each side without drawing any conclusion, and the strongest of them are as follows:

> On the side of toleration it may be said that if the principles which we have hitherto defended are true, society has no business as society to decide anything to be wrong which concerns only the individual; that it cannot go beyond persusaion, and that one person should be as free to persuade as another to dissuade. In opposition to this it may be contended that, although the public or the state are not warranted in authoritatively deciding for purposes of repression or punishment that such or such conduct affecting only the interests of the individual is good or bad, they are fully justified in assuming, if they regard it as bad, that its being so or not is at least a disputable question; that this being supposed they cannot be acting wrongly in endeavouring to exclude the influence of solicitations which are not disinterested, of instigators who cannot possibly be impartial, who have a direct personal interest on one side, and that the side which the state believes to be wrong, and who confessedly promote it for personal objects only.

There is a kind of ingenuity which carries its own refutation on its face. How can the state or the public be competent to determine any question whatever if it is not competent to decide that gross vice is a bad thing? I do not think the state ought to stand bandying compliments with pimps. 'Without offence to your better judgment, dear sir, and without presuming to set up my opinion against yours, I beg to observe that I am entitled for certain purposes to treat the question whether your views of life are right as one which admits of two opinions. I am far from expressing absolute condemnation of an experiment in living from which I dissent (I am sure that mere dissent will not offend a person of your liberality of sentiment), but still I am compelled to observe that you are not altogether unbiased by personal considerations in the choice of the course of life which you have adopted (no doubt for reasons which appear to you satisfactory, though they do not convince me). I venture accordingly, though with the greatest deference, to call upon you not to exercise your profession; at least I am not indisposed to think that I may, upon full consideration, feel myself compelled to do so'. My feeling is that if society gets its grip on the collar of such a fellow it should say to him, 'You dirty rascal, it may be a question whether you should be suffered to remain in your native filth untouched, or whether my opinion about you should be printed by the lash on your bare back. That question will be determined without the smallest reference to your wishes or feelings; but as to the nature of my opinion about you, there can be no question at all'.

From *Liberty, Equality, Fraternity* (1874), ch. IV, 'The Doctrine of Liberty in its Application to Morals'.

LORD HUGH CECIL, *A Conservative View*

It was asked of old, 'Did the owl come out of the egg or the egg out of the owl?' Which is first, the embryo out of which the perfect organism is evolved, or the perfect organism from which is born the embryo? A somewhat similar question might be put about the state and the individual. Are we to think of the state as something built up by individuals for their own ends, like a house in which they may dwell, or a temple in which they may serve God? If so, we are face to face with the difficulty that the individual as we know him is largely the creation of the state. Not only almost all his wealth, but much of what is closer to his personality, depends upon the action of the state. It is the state and what depends on the state, that makes the difference between civilisation and savagery. Without the state, therefore, physical health would have to conform to quite different conditions and intellectual cultivation would scarcely exist at all. Probably the great majority of the population have become by long ages of civilised life, in which they and their forefathers for many generations have lived, too weakly to stand the strain and the exposure which would be involved by a return to barbarism or even to the conditions of the first stages of national progress. The rise in the standard of comfort has been so great that what were deemed comforts or even luxuries are now necessaries indispensable to life and health. The hardiest labourer could not now live as a Saxon noble used to do. And men are not only less robust, they are also dependent for the conditions of existence on complicated and artificial organisation. Such events as the recent railway strike bring home to us how essentially artificial the existence of a civilised man is. Highly organised means of communication are only one part of what has grown up under the protection and superintendence of the state. Yet if these means of communication be interrupted for even a short time, the greater part of the population is in danger of actual starvation, and the hindrance and injury to trade and commerce defy reckoning and almost imagination. Nor is it only the material resources upon which human life depends over which the state and its civilising action exert a powerful influence. The mind itself is largely formed and guided by the environment of civilisation. If we could imagine ourselves transported back to some ruder age when civilisation was still undeveloped and incomplete, we should find the roughness of surroundings producing a harshness and coarseness in human nature, to our temperaments almost intolerable. Doubtless there would be some counterbalancing elements of strength and virtue which tend to die away in circumstances of luxury. But the experience would make it impossible to deny that ordinary human nature has been very deeply affected by the security and amenity of civilisation, and that therefore mankind can truly be said to have been changed even in its inner being by the consequences of state action. Yet to this general proposition an important reservation must be made. It is true that if we look at humanity in the large, if we think of the ordinary man, we must rate the power of the state and of civilisation very high. But if we look at individual character at its best, even in uncivilised surroundings, we find ourselves in the presence of something in creating which the state plays no part, of an unearthly element in human character which even in the least favourable circumstances, transcending all mundane hindrances, achieves amidst the rudest savagery as amidst the most finished culture, the shining splendour of a saint. But with this exception, which affects the spiritual rather than the mental or physical side of human nature, we may say that the well-being of mankind so largely depends on the action of the state that one might almost decide that the state makes the individual.

And yet the opposite theory is more obvious and not less true. It is plain that historically the individual is prior to the state, and that he slowly developed the state in order to meet his needs. It is plain also that even today the individuals who form a state not only consciously work its mechanism, but less consciously determine by the influence of their characters the general mental and moral atmosphere that prevails in the community. The state is in short the sum of the individuals who make it up, if it be thought of either as an instrument ministering to human needs or as creating an environment in which human character develops. And actually, not merely from age to age, but from year to year and even from month to month, the social life of a community changes with the changing standard that prevails in the region of individual virtue, self-control and responsibility.

So far, we seem equally able to follow unanswerable lines of argument leading in different, if not opposite, directions. But if we think of the subject in a less abstract vein and mainly with a view of solving the problems of politics, we come upon a consideration which is of crucial practical importance. In many respects, as we have seen, the individual is as much derived from the state as the state is from the individual. His health and strength, his mental outlook, even so much of his character as depends on environment, have been largely affected by what the state has done. But there is a centre of spiritual life in human nature which lies beyond the sphere of the state. And this life has sometimes power to be independent of all surrounding conditions. Almost everything in the mind and the body have been modified by civilisation; but examples of human virtue and sanctity are to be found in circumstances untouched by the hand of the state as they are in the most civilised surroundings. Very few citizens of London today, depending for their wealth, their sustenance and their mental atmosphere on what the state does and has done, are better or so good as St John the Baptist who lived in the wilderness and fed on locusts and wild honey. This is indeed only an illustration of what has earlier been pointed out, that the spiritual life of a Christian is essentially individual, and that, though it expresses itself in political and social action, it exists and is subject to the power of grace only within the individual soul. When, therefore, we are judging, as we are bound to do, political action by a moral standard, the state has to conform to the individual's code. We are obliged to regard the state as an aggregation of individuals acting in accordance with the moral obligations which control those individuals. We feel obliged to reject 'reason of state', whether in home or foreign affairs, if by that expression is meant the supersession in matters of state of the ordinary obligations of individuals by another moral code. We find we must decide all moral issues, and therefore ultimately all the fundamental principles of politics, by reference to individual duty. Morality is an individual matter, and this gives a primacy to the individual over the state. To adapt a well-known phrase to a new purpose: the individual is the sun and the state is the moon which shines with borrowed light.

From *Conservatism* (1912), ch. VI,
'The State and the Individual'.

BERTRAND RUSSELL, *The Competition of Ideas*

Uniformity, which is a natural result of state control, is desirable in some things and undesirable in others. In Florence, in the days before Mussolini, there was one rule of the roads in the town and the opposite rule in the surrounding country. This kind of diversity was inconvenient, but there were many matters in which Fascism suppressed a *desirable* kind of diversity. In matters of opinion it is a good thing if there is vigorous discussion between different schools of thought. In the mental world there is everything to be said in favour of a struggle for existence, leading, with luck, to a survival of the fittest. But if there is to be mental competition, there must be ways of limiting the means to be employed. The decision should not be by war, or by assassination, or by imprisonment of those holding certain opinions, or by preventing those holding unpopular views from earning a living. Where private enterprise prevails, or where there are many small states, as in Renaissance Italy and eighteenth-century Germany, these conditions are to some extent fulfilled by rivalry between different possible patrons. But when, as has tended to happen throughout Europe, states become large and private fortunes small, traditional methods of securing intellectual diversity fail. The only method that remains available is for the state to hold the ring and establish some sort of Queensberry rules by which the contest is to be conducted.

From *Authority and the Individual*, Reith Lectures, 1948-9.

SIR ALFRED DENNING, *Rule of Law*

A FAIR TRIAL

Every country which is under the rule of law must have courts to try persons who offend against the law. It cannot allow private individuals to take the law into their own hands. This applies to all modern countries: East as well as West, North as well as South. Each of them is under the rule of law in this sense, that each has an organised government which keeps order among the people by means of laws which must be observed. Soviet Russia has laws against murder, rape and theft just as England has. No private individual is allowed to take the law into his own hands and exact his own private vengeance for the wrong done to him. If order is to be kept in any country it is fundamental that any person who is accused of an offence must be brought before the courts of the land and tried and punished by those courts, and not by the relatives or friends of the person whom he has murdered, raped or robbed. The so called 'lynch law', whereby a gang of people summarily put an offender to death without trial, is no law at all. It is the negation of law, and is not permitted in any modern country, because of the disorders which would ensue. If people were allowed to exact their own private vengeance for real wrongs, they would soon exact it for supposed wrongs and the country would be in a state of anarchy.

There is, however, another sense in which we say that a country is under the rule of law: and that is when not only private individuals, but also the police and even the Government departments themselves, are not allowed to take the law into their own hands, but must bring to trial every person whom they accuse. Most modern countries recognise this rule so far as ordinary crimes are concerned. Even if the police catch a man red-handed, they are not allowed to punish him without trial. Even if he has been seen to commit a murder, the police must not shoot him dead. They must only arrest him and bring him for trial. The only exception is when there is no other way to arrest him but to shoot him dead. The reason for this rule is the fundamental principle of natural justice that no man can be a judge in his own cause. The police in such cases are the accusers and cannot therefore also be judges. They must bring the accused person for trial before the courts of the land and not punish him summarily themselves.

POLITICAL OFFENCES

It is when we come to political offences, such as treason or sedition, that we find the great difference. These are offences against the Government itself, and according to the principles of natural justice they ought to be tried by independent judges and not by the Government, which is an interested party. The Government cannot be a judge in its own cause any more than anyone else. But here is the point where divergent political philosophies come into play. The totalitarian philosophy puts the safety of the Government above all else and says that the police and judges are only instruments to secure its safety and to carry out the Government policy. The individualist philosophy regards human personality as the supreme value and says that every individual in the country is entitled to be protected by the judges against arbitrary action on the part of the Government. Everyone is entitled therefore to a fair trial even when he is accused of a political offence: and he can only be assured of this if the judges are independent of the Government.

The totalitarian countries pay, however, a delicate tribute to the individualist philosophy in that they often go to the trouble of putting political offenders on trial. They go through the form of a trial even though the result is a foregone conclusion in which the judges have been told by the Government what they are to do. The totalitarian countries thus implicitly recognise that no man should be condemned without a trial, even when he is accused by the Government. But when they hold a trial, we who stand by may well ask, What is the use of any trial unless it is a fair trial? An unfair trial condemns those who hold it; and not those who are condemned by it. Individualist countries have been known, however, to return the compliment by adopting sometimes totalitarian methods. They have allowed their agents to adopt inquisitorial methods and to condemn men for their political past without going through the formalities of a trial—without indeed any specific charge being made against them. I venture to assert that nothing is more important in our civilisation today than that we should insist on this fundamental principle that no one should be condemned without a trial, by which I mean of course a fair trial.

From *The Road to Justice* (1955).

SECTION D

LIBERTY AND ECONOMIC JUSTICE

F. A. Hayek, *Liberal-Individualism*

The liberal argument is in favour of making the best possible use of the forces of competition as a means of co-ordinating human efforts, not an argument for leaving things just as they are. It is based on the conviction that where effective competition can be created, it is a better way of guiding individual efforts than any other. It does not deny, but even emphasises, that, in order that competition should work beneficially, a carefully thought-out legal framework is required, and that neither the existing nor the past legal rules are free from grave defects. Nor does it deny that where it is impossible to create the conditions necessary to make competition effective, we must resort to other methods of guiding economic activity. Economic liberalism is opposed, however, to competition being supplanted by inferior methods of co-ordinating individual efforts. And it regards competition as superior not only because it is in most circumstances the most efficient method known, but even more because it is the only method by which our activities can be adjusted to each other without coercive or arbitrary intervention of authority. Indeed, one of the main arguments in favour of competition is that it dispenses with the need for 'conscious social control' and that it gives the individuals a chance to decide whether the prospects of a particular occupation are sufficient to compensate for the disadvantages and risks connected with it.

The successful use of competition as the principle of social organisation precludes certain types of coercive interference with economic life, but it admits of others which sometimes may very considerably assist its work and even requires certain kinds of government action. But there is good reason why the negative requirements, the points where coercion must not be used, have been particularly stressed. It is necessary in the first instance that the parties in the market should be free to sell and buy at any price at which they can find a partner to the transaction, and that anybody should be free to produce, sell, and buy anything that is produced or sold at all. And it is essential that the entry into the different trades should be open to all on equal terms, and that the law should not tolerate any attempts by individuals or groups to restrict this entry by open or concealed force. Any attempt to control prices or quantities of particular commodities deprives competition of its power of bringing about an effective co-ordination of individual efforts, because price changes then cease to register all the relevant changes in circumstances and no longer provide a reliable guide for the individual's actions.

This is not necessarily true, however, of measures merely restricting the allowed methods of production, so long as these restrictions affect all potential producers equally and are not used as an indirect way of controlling prices and quantities. Though all such controls of the methods of production impose extra costs, *i.e.* make it necessary to use more resources to produce a given output, they may be well worth while. To prohibit the use of certain poisonous substances, or to require special precautions in their use, to limit working hours or to require certain sanitary arrangements, is fully compatible with the preservation of competition. The only question here is whether in the particular instance the advantages gained are greater than the social costs which they impose. Nor is the preservation of competition incompatible with an extensive system of social services—so long as the organisation of these services is not designed in such a way as to make competition ineffective over wide fields.

It is regrettable, though not difficult to explain, that much less attention than to these negative points has in the past been given to the positive requirements of a successful working of the competitive system. The functioning of competition not only requires adequate organisation of certain institutions like money, markets, and channels of information—some of which can never be adequately provided by private enterprise—but it depends above all on the existence of an appropriate legal system, a legal system designed both to preserve competition and to make it operate as beneficially as possible. It is by no means sufficient that the law should recognise the principle of private property and freedom of contract; much depends on the precise definition of the right of property as applied to different things. The systematic study of the forms of legal institutions which will make the competitive system work efficiently has been sadly neglected; and strong arguments can be advanced that serious shortcomings here, particularly with regard to the law of corporations and of patents, have not only made competition work much more badly than it might have done, but have even led to the destruction of competition in many spheres.

There are, finally, undoubted fields where no legal arrangements can create the main condition on which the usefulness of the system of competition and private property depends: namely, that the owner benefits from all the useful services rendered by his property and suffers for all the damages caused to others by its use. Where, for example, it is impracticable to make the enjoyment of certain services dependent on the payment of a price, competition will not produce the services; and the price system becomes similarly ineffective when the damage caused to others by certain uses of property cannot be effectively charged to the owner of that property. In all these instances there is a divergence between the items which enter into private calculation and those which affect social welfare; and whenever this divergence becomes important some method other than competition may have to be found to supply the services in question. Thus neither the provision of signposts on the roads, nor, in most circumstances, that of the roads themselves, can be paid for by every individual user. Nor can certain harmful effects of deforestation, or of some methods of farming, or of the smoke and noise of factories, be confined to the owner of the property in question or to those who are willing to submit to the damage for an agreed compensation. In such instances we must find some substitute for the regulation by the price mechanism. But the fact that we have to resort to the substitution of direct regulation by authority where the conditions for the proper working of competition cannot be created, does not prove that we should suppress competition where it can be made to function.

To create conditions in which competition will be as effective as possible, to supplement it where it cannot be made effective, to provide the services which, in the words of Adam Smith, 'though they may be in the highest degree advantageous to a great society, are, however, of such a nature, that the profit could never repay the expense to any individual or small number of individuals', these tasks provide indeed a wide and unquestioned field for state activity. In no system that could be rationally defended would the state just do nothing. An effective competitive system needs an intelligently designed and continuously adjusted legal framework as much as any other. Even the most essential prerequisite of its proper functioning, the prevention of fraud and deception (including exploitations of ignorance) provides a great and by no means yet fully accomplished object of legislative activity.

The task of creating a suitable framework for the beneficial working of competition had, however, not yet been carried very far when states everywhere turned from it to that of supplanting competition by a different and irreconcilable principle. The question was no longer one of making competition work and of supplementing it, but of displacing it altogether. It is important to be quite clear about this: the modern movement for planning is a movement against competition as such, a new flag under which all the old enemies of competition have rallied. And although all sorts of interests are now trying to re-establish under this flag privileges which the liberal era swept away, it is socialist propaganda for planning which has restored to respectability among liberal-minded people opposition to competition, and which has effectively lulled the healthy suspicion which any attempt to smother competition used to arouse. What in effect unites the socialists of the Left and the Right is this common hostility to competition and their common desire to replace it by a directed economy. Though the terms capitalism and socialism are still generally used to describe the past and the future forms of society, they conceal rather than elucidate the nature of the transition through which we are passing.

Yet, though all the changes we are observing tend in the direction of a comprehensive central direction of economic activity, the universal struggle against competition promises to produce in the first instance something in many respects even worse, a state of affairs which can satisfy neither planners nor liberals: a sort of syndicalist or 'corporative' organisation of industry, in which competition is more or less suppressed by planning, is left in the hands of the independent monopolies of the separate industries. This is the inevitable first result of a situation in which the people are united in their hostility to competition but agree on little else. By destroying competition in industry after industry, this policy puts the consumer at the mercy of the joint monopolist action of capitalists and workers in the best organised industries. Yet, although this is a state of affairs which in wide fields has already existed for some time, and although much of the muddled (and most of the interested) agitation for planning aims at it, it is not a state which is likely to persist or can be rationally justified. Such independent planning by industrial monopolies would, in fact, produce effects opposite to those at which the argument for planning aims. Once this stage is reached the only alternative to a return to competition is the control of the monopolies by the state, a control which, if it is to be made effective, must become progressively more complete and more detailed. It is this stage we are rapidly approaching. When, shortly before the war, one of the weeklies pointed out that there were 'many signs that British leaders are growing accustomed to thinking in terms of national development by controlled monopolies', this was probably a true estimate of the position as it then existed. Since then this process has been greatly accelerated by the war, and its grave defects and dangers will become increasingly obvious as time goes on.

The idea of complete centralisation of the direction of economic activity still appals most people, not only because of the stupendous difficulty of the task, but even more because of the horror inspired by the idea of everything being directed from a single centre. If we are nevertheless rapidly moving towards such a state this is largely because most people still believe that it must be possible to find some Middle Way between 'atomistic' competition and central direction. Nothing indeed seems at first more plausible, or is more likely to appeal to reasonable people, than the idea that our goal must be neither the extreme decentralisation of free competition, nor the complete centralisation of a single plan, but some judicious mixture of the two methods. Yet mere common sense proves a treacherous guide in this field. Although competition can bear some admixture of regulation, it cannot be combined with planning to any extent we like without ceasing to operate as an effective guide to production. Nor is 'planning' a medicine which, taken in small doses, can produce the effects for which one might hope from its thoroughgoing application. Both competition and central direction become poor and inefficient tools if they are incomplete;

they are alternative principles used to solve the same problem, and a mixture of the two means that neither will really work and that the result will be worse than if either system had been consistently relied upon. Or, to express it differently, planning and competition can be combined only by planning for competition, but not by planning against competition.

From *The Road to Serfdom* (1944), ch. III, 'Individualism and Collectivism'.

R. H. TAWNEY, *Economic Liberty as seen by a Socialist*

Liberty and equality have usually in England been considered antithetic; and, since fraternity has rarely been considered at all, the famous trilogy has been easily dismissed as a hybrid abortion. Equality implies the deliberate acceptance of social restraints upon individual expansion. It involves the prevention of sensational extremes of wealth and power by public action for the public good. If liberty means, therefore, that every individual shall be free, according to his opportunities, to indulge without limit his appetite for either, it is clearly incompatible, not only with economic and social, but with civil and political, equality, which also prevent the strong exploiting to the full the advantages of their strength, and, indeed, with any habit of life save that of the Cyclops. But freedom for the pike is death for the minnows. It is possible that equality is to be contrasted, not with liberty, but only with a particular interpretation of it.

The test of a principle is that it can be generalised, so that the advantages of applying it are not particular, but universal. Since it is impossible for every individual, as for every nation, simultaneously to be stronger than his neighbours, it is a truism that liberty, as distinct from the liberties of special persons and classes, can exist only in so far as it is limited by rules, which secure that freedom for some is not slavery for others. The spiritual energy of human beings, in all the wealth of their infinite diversities, is the end to which external arrangements, whether political or economic, are merely means. Hence institutions which guarantee to men the opportunity of becoming the best of which they are capable are the supreme political good, and liberty is rightly preferred to equality, when the two are in conflict. The question is whether, in the conditions of modern society, they conflict or not. It is whether the defined and limited freedom, which alone can be generally enjoyed, is most likely to be attained by a community which encourages violent inequalities, or by one which represses them.

Inequality of power is not necessarily inimical to liberty. On the contrary, it is the condition of it. Liberty implies the ability to act, not merely to resist. Neither society as a whole, nor any group within it, can carry out its will except through organs; and, in order that such organs may function with effect, they must be sufficiently differentiated to perform their varying tasks, of which direction is one and execution another. But, while inequality of power is the condition of liberty, since it is the condition of any effective action, it is also a menace to it, for power which is sufficient to use is sufficient to abuse. Hence, in the political sphere, where the danger is familiar, all civilised communities have established safeguards, by which the advantages of differentiation of function, with the varying degrees of power which it involves, may be preserved, and the risk that power may be tyrannical, or perverted to private ends, averted or diminished. They have endeavoured, for example, as in England, to protect civil liberty by requiring that, with certain exceptions, the officers of the state shall be subject to the ordinary tribunals, and political liberty by insisting that those who take decisions on matters affecting the public shall be responsible to an assembly chosen by it. The precautions may be criticised as inadequate, but the need for precautions is not today disputed. It is recognised that political power must rest ultimately on consent, and that its exercise must be limited by rules of law.

The dangers arising from inequalities of economic power have been less commonly recognised. They exist, however, whether recognised or not. For the excessive abuse of power, and its divorce from responsibility, which results in oppression, are not confined to the relations which arise between men as members of a state. They are not a malady which is peculiar to political systems, as was typhus to slums, and from which other departments of life can be regarded as immune. They are a disease, not of political organisation, but of organisation. They occur, in the absence of preventive measures, in political associations, because they occur in all forms of association in which large numbers of individuals are massed for collective action. The isolated worker may purchase security against exploitation at the cost of poverty, as the hermit may avoid the corruptions of civilisation by forgoing its advantages. But, as soon as he is associated with his fellows in a common undertaking, his duties must be specified and his rights defined; and, in so far as they are not, the undertaking is impeded. The problem of securing a livelihood ceases to be merely economic, and becomes social and political. The struggle with nature continues, but on a different plane. Its efficiency is heightened by co-operation. Its character is complicated by the emergence of the question of the terms on which co-operation shall take place.

In an industrial civilisation, when its first phase is over, most economic activity is corporate activity. It is carried on, not by individuals, but by groups, which are endowed by the state with a legal status, and the larger of which, in size, complexity, specialisation of functions and unity of control, resemble less the private enterprise of the past than a public department. As far as certain great industries are concerned, employment must be found in the service of these corporations, or not at all. Hence the mass of mankind pass their working lives under the direction of a hierarchy, whose heads define, as they think most profitable, the lines on which the common enterprise is to proceed, and determine, subject to the intervention of the state and voluntary organisations, the economic, and to a considerable, though diminishing, extent, the social environment of their employees. Possessing the reality of power, without the decorative trappings—unless, as in England is often the case, it thinks it worth while to buy them—this business oligarchy is the effective aristocracy of industrial nations, and the aristocracy of tradition and prestige, when such still exists, carries out its wishes and courts its favours. In such conditions, authority over human beings is exercised, not only through political, but through economic, organs. The problem of liberty, therefore, is necessarily concerned, not only with political, but also with economic, relations.

It is true, of course, that the problems are different. But to suppose that the abuses of economic power are trivial, or that they are automatically prevented by political democracy, is to be deceived by words. Freedom is always, no doubt, a matter of degree; no man enjoys all the requirements of full personal development, and all men possess some of them. It is not only compatible with conditions in which all men are fellow-servants, but would find in such conditions its most perfect expression. What it excludes is a society where only some are servants, while others are masters.

For, whatever else the idea involves, it implies at least, that no man shall be amenable to an authority which is arbitrary in its proceedings, exorbitant in its demands, or incapable of being called to account when it abuses its office for personal advantage. In so far as his livelihood is at the mercy of an irresponsible superior, whether political or economic, who can compel his reluctant obedience by *force majeure*, whose actions he is unable to modify or resist, save at the cost of grave personal injury to himself and his dependents, and whose favour he must court, even when he despises it, he may possess a profusion of more tangible blessings, from beer to motor-bicycles, but he cannot be said to be in possession of freedom. In so far as an economic system grades mankind into groups, of which some can wield, if unconsciously, the force of economic duress for their own profit or convenience, whilst others must submit to it, its effect is that freedom itself is similarly graded. Society is divided, in its economic and social relations, into classes which are ends, and classes which are instruments. Like property, with which in the past it has been closely connected, liberty becomes the privilege of a class, not the possession of a nation.

Political principles resemble military tactics; they are usually designed for a war which is over. Freedom is commonly interpreted in England in political terms, because it was in the political arena that the most resounding of its recent victories were won. It is regarded as belonging to human beings as citizens, rather than citizens as human beings; so that it is possible for a nation, the majority of whose members have as little influence on the decisions that determine their economic destinies as on the motions of the planets, to applaud the idea with self-congratulatory gestures of decorous enthusiasm, as though history were of the past, but not of the present. If the attitude of the ages from which it inherits a belief in liberty had been equally ladylike, there would have been, it is probable, little liberty to applaud.

For freedom is always relative to power, and the kind of freedom which at any moment it is most urgent to affirm depends on the nature of the power which is prevalent and established. Since political arrangements may be such as to check excesses of power, while economic arrangements permit or encourage them, a society, or a large part of it, may be both politically free and economically the opposite. It may be protected against arbitrary action by the agents of government, and be without the security against economic oppression which corresponds to civil liberty. It may possess the political institutions of an advanced democracy, and lack the will and ability to control the conduct of those powerful in its economic affairs, which is the economic analogy of political freedom.

The extension of liberty from the political to the economic sphere is evidently among the most urgent tasks of industrial societies. It is evident also, however, that, in so far as this extension takes place, the traditional antithesis between liberty and equality will no longer be valid. As long as liberty is interpreted as consisting exclusively in security against oppression by the agents of the state, or as a share in its government, it is plausible, perhaps, to dissociate it from equality; for, though experience suggests that, even in this meagre and restricted sense, it is not easily maintained in the presence of extreme disparities of wealth and influence, it is possible for it to be enjoyed, in form at least, by pauper and millionaire. Such disparities, however, though they do not enable one group to become the political master of another, necessarily cause it to exercise a preponderant influence on the economic life of the rest of society.

Hence, when liberty is construed, realistically, or implying, not merely a minimum of civil and political rights, but securities that the economically weak will not be at the mercy of the economically strong, and that the control of those aspects of economic life by which all are affected will be amenable, in the last resort, to the will of all, a large measure of equality, so far from being inimical to liberty, is essential to it. In conditions which impose co-operative, rather than merely individual, effort, liberty is, in fact, equality in action, in the sense, not that all men perform identical functions or wield the same degree of power, but that all men are equally protected against the abuse of power, and equally entitled to insist that power shall be used, not for personal ends, but for the general advantage. Civil and political liberty obviously imply, not that all men shall be members of parliament, cabinet ministers, or civil servants, but the absence of such civil and political inequalities as enable one class to impose its will on another by legal coercion. It should be not less obvious that economic liberty implies, not that all men shall initiate, plan, direct, manage, or administer, but the absence of such economic inequalities as can be used as a means of economic constraint.

The danger to liberty which is caused by inequality varies with differences of economic organisation and public policy. When the mass of the population are independent producers, or when, if they are dependent on great undertakings, the latter are subject to strict public control, it may be absent or remote. It is seen at its height when important departments of economic activity are the province of large organisations, which, if they do not themselves, as sometimes occurs, control the state, are sufficiently powerful to resist control by it. Among the numerous interesting phenomena which impress the foreign observer of American economic life, not the least interesting is the occasional emergence of industrial enterprises which appear to him, and, indeed, to some Americans, to have developed the characteristics, not merely of an economic undertaking, but of a kind of polity. Their rule may be a mild and benevolent paternalism, lavishing rest-rooms, schools, gymnasia, and guarantees for constitutional behaviour on care-free employees; or it may be a harsh and suspicious tyranny. But, whether as amiable as Solon, or as ferocious as Lycurgus, their features are cast in a heroic mould. Their gestures are those of the sovereigns of little commonwealths rather than of mere mundane employers.

American official documents have, on occasion, called attention to the tendency of the bare stem of business to burgeon, in a favourable environment, with almost tropical exuberance, so that it clothes itself with functions that elsewhere are regarded as belonging to political authorities. The corporations controlled by six financial groups, stated the Report of the United States Commission on Industrial Relations some twenty years ago, employ 2,651,684 wage-earners, or 440,000 per group. Some of these companies own, not merely the plant and equipment of industry, but the homes of the workers, the streets through which they pass to work, and the halls in which, if they are allowed to meet, their meetings must be held. They employ private spies and detectives, private police and, sometimes, it appears, private troops, and engage, when they deem it expedient, in private war. While organised themselves, they forbid organisation among their employees, and enforce their will by evicting malcontents from their homes, and even, on occasion, by the use of armed force. In such conditions business may continue in its modesty, since its object is money, to describe itself as business; but, in fact, it is a tyranny. The main objection to the large corporation, remarks Mr Justice Brandeis, who, as a judge of the Supreme Court, should know the facts, is that it makes possible—and in many cases makes inevitable—the exercise of industrial absolutism. Property in capital, thus inflated and emancipated, acquires attributes analogous to those of property in land in a feudal society. It carries with it the disposal, in fact, if not in law, of an authority which is quasi-governmental. Its owners possess what would have been called in the ages of darkness a private jurisdiction, and their relations to their dependents, though contractual in form, resemble rather those of ruler and subject than of equal parties to a commercial venture. The liberty which they defend against the encroachments of trade unionism and the state is most properly to be regarded, not as freedom, but as a franchise.

The conventional assertion that inequality is inseparable from liberty is obviously, in such circumstances, unreal and unconvincing; for the existence of the former is a menace to the latter, and the latter is most likely to be secured by curtailing the former. It is true that in England, where three generations of trade unionism and state intervention have done something to tame it, the exercise of economic power is, at ordinary times, less tyrannical than it once was. It still remains, nevertheless, a formidable menace to the freedom of common men. The pressure of such power is felt by the consumer, when he purchases necessaries which directly or indirectly, are controlled by a monopoly. It is felt in the workshop, where, within the limits set by industrial legislation and collective agreements, the comfort and amenity of the wage-earners' surroundings, the discipline and tone of factory life, the security of employment and methods of promotion, the recruitment and dismissal of workers, the degree to which successive relays of cheap juvenile labour are employed, the opportunity to secure consideration for grievances, depend ultimately upon the policy pursued by a board of directors, who may have little love, indeed, for their shareholders, but who represent, in the last resort, their financial interests, and who, in so far as they are shareholders themselves, are necessarily judges in their own cause.

The effects of such autocracy are even graver in the sphere of economic strategy, which settles the ground upon which these tactical issues are fought out, and, in practice, not infrequently determines their decision before they arise. In such matters as the changes in organisation most likely to restore prosperity to an embarrassed industry, and, therefore, to secure a tolerable livelihood to the workers engaged in it; methods of averting or meeting a depression; rationalisation, the closing of plants and the concentration of production; the sale of a business on which a whole community depends or its amalgamation with a rival—not to mention the critical field of financial policy, with its possibilities, not merely of watered capital and of the squandering in dividends of resources which should be held as reserves, but of a sensational redistribution of wealth and widespread unemployment as a result of decisions taken by bankers—the diplomacy of business, like that of governments, before 1914, is still commonly conducted over the heads of those most affected by it. The interests of the public, as workers and consumers, may receive consideration when these matters are determined; but the normal organisation of economic life does not offer reliable guarantee that they will be considered. Nor can it plausibly be asserted that, if they are not, those aggrieved can be certain of any redress.

Power over the public is public power. It does not cease to be public merely because private persons are permitted to buy and sell, own and bequeath it, as they deem most profitable. To retort that its masters are themselves little more than half-conscious instruments, whose decisions register and transmit the impact of forces that they can neither anticipate nor control, though not wholly unveracious, is, nevertheless, superficial. The question is not whether there are economic movements which elude human control, for obviously there are. It is whether the public possesses adequate guarantees that those which are controllable are controlled in the general interest, not in that of a minority. Like the gods of Homer, who were subject themselves to a fate behind the fates, but were not thereby precluded from interfering at their pleasure in the affairs of men, the potentates of the economic world exercise discretion, not, indeed, as to the situation which they will meet, but as to the manner in which they will meet it. They hold the initiative, have such freedom to manoeuvre as circumstances allow, can force an issue or postpone it, and, if open conflict seems inevitable or expedient, can choose, as best suits themselves, the ground where it shall take place.

'Even if socialism were practicable without the destruction of freedom', writes Lord Lothian, 'would there be any advantage in converting the whole population into wage or salary earners, directed by the relatively few, also salaried, officials, who by ability, or promotion, or "pull", could work their way to the top of the political machine or the permanent bureaucracy? . . . Is not that community the best, and, in the widest sense of the word, the most healthy, which has the largest proportion of citizens who have the enterprise, and energy, and initiative, to create new things and new methods for themselves, and not merely to wait to carry out the orders of somebody "higher up"?' In view of the practice, of some parts, at least, of the business world, the less said about 'pull', perhaps, the better. But how true in substance! And how different the liner looks from the saloon-deck and the stoke-hold! And how striking that the conditions which Lord Lothian deplores as a hypothetical danger should be precisely those which ordinary men experience daily as an ever-present fact!

For, in England at any rate, as a glance at the Registrar-General's report would have sufficed to show him, not only the majority of the population, but the great majority, are today 'wage or salary earners', who, for quite a long time, have been 'directed by the relatively few', and who, if they did not 'wait to carry out the orders of somebody higher up', would be sent about their business with surprising promptitude. Unless Lord Lothian proposes to abolish, not only a particular political doctrine, but banks, railways, coal-mines, and cotton-mills, the question is not whether orders shall be given, but who shall give them; whether there shall be guarantees that they are given in the general interest; and whether those to whom they are given shall have a reasonable security that, when their welfare is at stake, their views will receive an unbiased consideration.

Freedom may be, as he insists, more important than comfort. But is a miner, who is not subject to a bureaucracy, or at least, to a bureaucracy of the kind which alarms Lord Lothian, conspicuously more free than a teacher, who is? If a man eats bread made of flour produced to the extent of forty per cent by two milling combines and meat supplied by an international meat trust, and lives in a house built of materials of which twenty-five per cent are controlled by a ring, and buys his tobacco from one amalgamation, and his matches from another, while his wife's sewing-thread is provided by a third, which has added eight millionaires to the national roll of honour in the last twenty years, is he free as a consumer? Is he free as a worker, if he is liable to have his piece-rates cut at the discretion of his employer, and, on expressing his annoyance, to be dismissed as an agitator, and to be thrown on the scrap-heap without warning because his employer had decided to shut down a plant, or bankers to restrict credit, and to be told, when he points out that the industry on which his livelihood depends is being injured by mismanagement, that his job is to work, and that the management in question will do his thinking for him? And if, in such circumstances, he is but partially free as a consumer and a worker, is not his freedom as a citizen itself also partial, rather than, as Lord Lothian would desire, unqualified and complete?

Lord Lothian is misled as to liberty, because he has omitted to consider the bearing upon it of another phenomenon, the phenomenon of inequality. The truth is that, when the economic scales are so unevenly weighted, to interpret liberty as a political principle, which belongs to one world, the world of politics and government, while equality belongs—if, indeed, it belongs anywhere—to another world, the world of economic affairs, is to do violence to realities. Governments, it is true, exercise powers of a great and special kind, and freedom requires that they should be held strictly to account. But the administration of things is not easily distinguished, under modern conditions of mass organisations, from the control of persons, and both are in the hands, to some not inconsiderable degree, of the minority who move the levers of the economic mechanism. The truth of the matter is put by Professor Pollard in his admirable study *The Evolution of Parliament.*

> There is only one solution [he writes] of the problem of liberty, and it lies in equality . . . . Men vary in physical strength; but so far as their social relations go that inequality has been abolished . . . . Yet there must have been a period in social evolution when this refusal to permit the strong man to do what he liked with his own physical strength seemed, at least to the strong, an outrageous interference with personal liberty . . . There is, in fact, no more reason why a man should be allowed to use his wealth or his brain than

his physical strength as he likes . . . . The liberty of the weak depends upon the restraint of the strong, that of the poor upon the restraint of the rich, and that of the simpler-minded upon the restraint of the sharper. Every man should have this liberty and no more, to do unto others as he would that they should do unto him; upon that common foundation rest liberty, equality, and morality.

From *Equality* (1931).

Barbara Wootton, *Freedom and Planning*

In the preceding chapters I have tried to show that there is nothing in the conscious planning of economic priorities which is inherently incompatible with the freedoms which mean most to the contemporary Englishman or American. Civil liberties are quite unaffected. We can, if we wish, deliberately plan so as to give the fullest possible scope for the pursuit by individuals and social groups of cultural ends which are in no way state determined. The consumer can enjoy the pleasure of comparing prices and qualities, and spending money that is freely available to the limit of his income, just as and when he thinks fit. Industrial direction and industrial conscription are unnecessary. Planning need not even be the death-warrant of all private enterprise; and it is certainly not the passport of political dictatorship. It is true (and indeed obvious) that the same part of the economic pattern cannot both be deliberately planned, and left to emerge as the result of the uncoordinated actions of thousands of consumers. But consumers' sovereignty, in any meaningful and defensible sense, seems to be quite unattainable and certainly never to have been attained outside the covers of an academic textbook; and there is the less cause for tears on this account, inasmuch as no ordinary consumer would be conscious whether he enjoyed that sovereignty or not. It is true also that the preservation of free choice of employment under planning would be impossible if wages were to be settled by a private tug-of-war between employers and employed, in which each party exploited its full economic strength. But against this must be set the fact that free choice of employment will never be a reality without planning, since legal freedom of choice is a mockery if economic pressure compels the chooser to accept the first available job. The right of effective choice of employment is the one great freedom which the pre-war Englishman, or American, or Continental European outside Russia, has never enjoyed. Planning could give it to him.

From *Freedom under Planning* (1945), ch. VIII, 'Who is to Plan the Planners?'

Labour Party Manifesto, 1945, Socialism in Action

JOBS FOR ALL

All parties pay lip service to the idea of jobs for all. All parties are ready to promise to achieve that end by keeping up the national purchasing power and controlling changes in the national expenditure through Government action. Where agreement ceases is in the degree of control of private industry that is necessary to achieve the desired end.

In hard fact, the success of a full employment programme will certainly turn upon the firmness and success with which the Government fits into that programme the investment and development policies of private as well as public industry.

Our opponents would be ready to use state action to do the best they can to bolster up private industry whenever it plunges the nation into heavy unemployment. But if the slumps in uncontrolled private industry are too severe to be balanced by public action—as they will certainly prove to be—our opponents are not ready to draw the conclusion that the sphere of public action must be extended.

They say, 'Full employment. Yes! If we can get it without interfering too much with private industry'. We say, 'Full employment in any case, and if we need to keep a firm public hand on industry in order to get jobs for all, very well. No more dole queues, in order to let the Czars of Big Business remain kings in their own castles. The price of so-called 'economic freedom' for the few is too high if it is bought at the cost of idleness and misery for millions?'

What will the Labour Party do?

First, the whole of the national resources, in land, material and labour must be fully employed. Production must be raised to the highest level and related to purchasing power. Over-production is not the cause of depression and unemployment; it is under-consumption that is responsible. It is doubtful whether we have ever, except in war, used the whole of our productive capacity. This must be corrected because, upon our ability to produce and organise a fair and generous distribution of the product, the standard of living of our people depends.

Secondly, a high and constant purchasing power can be maintained through good wages, social services and insurance, and taxation which bears less heavily on the lower-income groups. But everybody knows that money and savings lose their value if prices rise, so rents and the prices of the necessities of life will be controlled.

Thirdly, planned investment in essential industries and on houses, schools, hospitals and civic centres will occupy a large field of capital expenditure. A National Investment Board will determine social priorities and promote better timing in private investment. In suitable cases we would transfer the use of efficient Government factories from war production to meet the needs of peace. The location of new factories will be suitably controlled, and where necessary the Government will itself build factories. There must be no depressed areas in the New Britain.

Fourthly, the Bank of England with its financial powers must be brought under public ownership, and the operations of the other banks harmonised with industrial needs.

By these and other means full employment can be achieved. But a policy of Jobs for All must be associated with a policy of general economic expansion and efficiency as set out in the next section of this Declaration. Indeed, it is not enough to ensure that there are jobs for all. If the standard of life is to be high—as it should be—the standard of production must be high. This means that industry must be thoroughly efficient if the needs of the nation are to be met.

INDUSTRY IN THE SERVICE OF THE NATION

By the test of war some industries have shown themselves capable of rising to new heights of efficiency and expansion. Others, including some of our older industries fundamental to our economic structure, have wholly or partly failed.

Today we live alongside economic giants—countries where science and technology take leaping strides year by year.

Britain must match those strides—and we must take no chances about it. Britain needs an industry organised to enable it to yield the best that human knowledge and skill can provide. Only so can our people reap the full benefits of this age of discovery, and Britain keep her place as a Great Power.

The Labour Party intends to link the skill of British craftsmen and designers to the skill of British scientists in the service of our fellow men. The genius of British scientists and technicians who have produced radio-location, jet propulsion, penicillin, and the Mulberry Harbours in wartime, must be given full rein in peacetime too.

Each industry must have applied to it the test of national service. If it serves the nation, well and good; if it is inefficient and falls down on its job, the nation must see that things are put right.

These propositions seem indisputable, but for years before the war anti-Labour Governments set them aside, so that British industry over a large field fell into a state of depression, muddle and decay. Millions of working and middle-class people went through the horrors of unemployment and insecurity. It is not enough to sympathise with these victims: we must develop an acute feeling of national shame—and act.

The Labour Party is a Socialist Party, and proud of it. Its ultimate purpose at home is the establishment of the Socialist Commonwealth of Great Britain—free, democratic, efficient, progressive, public-spirited, its material resources organised in the service of the British people.

But Socialism cannot come overnight, as the product of a weekend revolution. The members of the Labour Party, like the British people, are practical-minded men and women.

There are basic industries ripe and over-ripe for public ownership and management in the direct service of the nation. There are many smaller businesses rendering good service which can be left to go on with their useful work.

There are big industries not yet ripe for public ownership which must nevertheless be required by constructive supervision to further the nation's needs and not to prejudice national interests by restrictive anti-social monopoly or cartel agreements—caring for their own capital structures and profits at the cost of a lower standard of living for all.

In the light of these considerations, the Labour Party submits to the nation the following industrial programme:

(1) Public ownership of the fuel and power industries.
(2) Public ownership of inland transport.
(3) Public ownership of iron and steel.
(4) Public supervision of monopolies and cartels.
(5) A firm and clear-cut programme for the export trade.
(6) The shaping of suitable economic and price controls.
(7) The better organisation of Government departments.

From *Labour Party Manifesto, 1945*, §§ iii, iv.

The Conservative Case

(1) Lord Hailsham

Political liberty is nothing else but the diffusion of power. All power tends to corrupt, absolute power to corrupt absolutely. It follows that political liberty is impossible to the extent that power is concentrated in the hands of a few men. It does not matter whether these be popularly elected or no. Give men power and they will misuse it. Give them absolute power, that is, concentrate in their hands all the various kinds and degrees of power, and they will abuse it absolutely. If power is not to be abused it must be spread as widely as possible throughout the community.

Thus, although Conservatives have always supported a strong central authority when the danger to order has consisted in too much decentralisation, today they believe that it would be an evil day for Britain, and for freedom, if all power fell into the hands of the Cabinet. For since political liberty is nothing else than the diffusion of power, the splitting up of political and legal power into different parcels is the essential means of securing it.

Conservatives see no inconsistency in having opposed Liberals and Whigs in the name of authority, Socialists in the name of freedom. The ground is the same, but it is being attacked from a different direction. The great heresy of the nineteenth century was self-interest. But today the boot is on the other foot. When the predominant left wing philosophy was Liberalism, the danger was too much liberty—in the political sphere creating chaos, in the economic sphere producing alternate boom and slump, and creating mass unemployment.

But today the predominant theory of the left is Socialism, and the danger is not too much but too little freedom. The great heresy of our age is no longer self-interest, it is State Worship, and instead of the altars being ablaze in honour of Mammon, we make our children pass through the fire to Moloch.

In each fight Conservatives have taken the same stand. Abused and traduced as reactionaries and out of touch with the times, they opposed the excessive individualism of the Liberals in the name of the same principle as that in defence of which they now oppose Socialism—the Rule of Law, the enemy alike of dictatorship and anarchy, the friend by whose good offices authority and liberty can alone be reconciled.

There are some who tend to deny the value of freedom. What is freedom, they ask, under Capitalism but freedom to starve? It is not enough to enjoy a political democracy; it is necessary to have an economic democracy as well.

In a sense, these critics are right.

But what is meant by economic freedom or economic democracy? Conservatives are tempted to reply in a single sentence.

Just as political democracy and political freedom mean the diffusion, the sharing of political power, so economic democracy, economic freedom, means the sharing, the diffusion, of economic power, that is property, as widely as possible throughout the community. This diffusion Conservatives regard as the very antithesis of Socialism.

Conservatives therefore wish to see economic democracy, but they can find no meaning in the phrase unless it implies the sharing of property as widely as possible. Economic democracy is, and is nothing else than, the 'property-owning democracy' called for by Mr Anthony Eden. Such a property-owning democracy, although it is inconsistent with the co-existence of great wealth coupled with great poverty, is not inconsistent with the existence of large independent fortunes held either by Corporations or by individuals. Such independent fortunes, properly controlled by law, form, in our view, a valuable, indeed an indispensable, counterpoise to the vast complex of economic power controlled by the modern state.

Conservatives therefore consider it an essential part of economic democracy to see wealth shared as widely as possible by individuals. They desire to see wealth also shared by groups. They rejoice to see it shared by great Trade Unions so long as these are neither subservient to the interests of a single political party nor ambitious to control the political machinery of the state. Conservatives also wish property to be shared by traders and trading companies and by local authorities. But, above all, they want to see property in the family, and the family itself an independent centre of power enjoying its own franchises and prerogatives and occupying its true position as the foundation of civilised society.

In all this the Conservatives find an unanswerable case against Socialism, under which name they include all forms of state worship, in all the forms in which it has been present, Leninist, Marxist, Fascist, or Transport House (and each of these can by this test be regarded as Socialist, though not all are equally evil). Socialism aims at the concentration of power, political and economic, in the hands of a few political chiefs. The arguments for it are the arguments which have been used for dictatorship from time immemorial—efficiency, national crisis, the protection of the multitude of 'common men' against the power of the wealthy or influential, the efficient redistribution of wealth or the like.

The Socialist is not content with control. He must have ownership. That is to say, he is not satisfied with preventing wrongful action by the owners of industry; he demands to use industry as he desires himself in despite of those from whom he proposes to take it by force, and notwithstanding that their own use of it may be proved to be legitimate.

From *The Case for Conservatism* (*1947*), ch. x, 'Liberty'.

(2) Sir Winston Churchill

THE BASIC MINIMUM

The scheme of society for which we stand is the establishment and maintenance of a basic minimum standard of life and labour below which a man or woman of goodwill, however old and weak, will not be allowed to fall. The food they receive, the prices they have to pay for basic necessities, the homes they live in, must be the first care of the state, and must have priority over all other peace-time requirements. Once that standard is being faithfully and even rigorously worked for by all concerned, and without prejudice to it we propose if and when we have the power to set the people free as quickly as possible from the controls and restrictions which now beset their daily life. We propose to sweep away with sturdy strokes the vast encumbrances of regulations and penalties which are today preventing our people from making a good living in their island home. Once the basic standard has been established we shall liberate the energies, the genius, the contrivance of the British nation from the paralysing and humiliating thraldom in which they are now plunged. Above the minimum basic standard there will be free competition. Everyone will be free to make the best of himself without jealousy or spite by all the means that honour, and the long respected laws and customs of our country allow.

Conservative Party Conference, Brighton, 4 October 1947.

(3) *Conservative Party Manifesto, May 1955*

THE STATE HOLDING THE RING

If Britain is to seize the opportunities which our trade policy can open up, economic arrangements at home have got to be as modern, and go-ahead as we can possibly make them.

Conservatives neither minimise nor exaggerate the part that Governments can play in bringing these conditions about. It is for the state to give a lead, to provide incentive, support and advice, to protect the public interest and to restrain abuse. But it is certainly no proper function of the state in normal times to go into trade itself, to interfere in the day-to-day running of business, or to tell housewives how to do their shopping. Within broad but well-defined limits of basic public concern, we insist on freedom of action for producers and freedom of choice for consumers.

From *United for Peace and Progress* (May, 1955), page 16.

FRANÇOIS LAFITTE, *The Welfare State*

The new dimensions of the social budget are due to the fact that public social services are now in aim, though by no means always in practice, comprehensive and universalist. They are intimately concerned with the personal welfare of every citizen, not merely as in the past with the needs of special groups of citizens distinguished by criteria of status, such as destitution, income, occupation, or economic class. This universalism is the essence of the Welfare State. It marks a revolution, still in its very early stages, in the assumptions underlying social policy.

The Welfare State assumes that all citizens, not merely the abnormal, the poor, or the lower classes, have certain social needs which cannot be satisfactorily met from their personal earnings, from private or commercial services, from charity or voluntary clubbing together. It assumes that these needs—for education, medical care, income during illness and retirement, and much else—are best provided for by publicly organised services available to all by virtue simply of their citizenship, just as roads, fire brigades, and other communal facilities are used by all citizens. It assumes that for nearly all citizens the public social services, rather than the market or voluntary services, will be the normal way of securing the requisite satisfactions.

It assumes that the state must see to it that all important social needs 'from the cradle to the grave' are adequately provided for, either by public services or by public support and supplementation of voluntary facilities. In principle the Welfare State, far from viewing its social services as a regrettable burden, wants its citizens to use them for their own betterment or convenience, and strives to improve the services offered. It seeks to remove the causes of avoidable distress, above all by preventing unemployment; but it does not expect thereby to make social services less necessary but rather, by needing to spend less on relieving avoidable poverty or illness, to have more resources for constructive services such as education.

From *The New Outline of Modern Knowledge* (Gollancz, 1956), Section iv, 'Social Aims of the Contemporary State'.

SECTION E

DECENTRALISATION

BERTRAND RUSSELL, *Importance of the Group*

In a highly organised world, personal initiative connected with a group must be confined to a few unless the group is small. If you are a member of a small committee you may reasonably hope to influence its decisions. In national politics, where you are one of some twenty million voters, your influence is infinitesimal unless you are exceptional or occupy an exceptional position. You have, it is true, a twenty-millionth share in the government of others, but only a twenty-millionth share in the government of yourself. You are therefore much more conscious of being governed than of governing. The government becomes in your thoughts a remote and largely malevolent 'they', not a set of men whom you, in concert with others who share your opinions, have chosen to carry out your wishes. Your individual feeling about politics, in these circumstances, is not that intended to be brought about by democracy, but much more nearly what it would be under a dictatorship.

The sense of bold adventure, and of capacity to bring about results that are felt to be important, can only be restored if power can be delegated to small groups in which the individual is not overwhelmed by mere numbers. A considerable degree of central control is indispensable, if only for the reasons that we considered at the beginning of this lecture. But to the utmost extent compatible with this requisite, there should be devolution of the powers of the state to various kinds of bodies—geographical, industrial, cultural, according to their functions. The powers of these bodies should be sufficient to make them interesting, and to cause energetic men to find satisfaction in influencing them. They would need, if they were to fulfil their purpose, a considerable measure of financial autonomy. Nothing is so damping and deadening to initiative as to have a carefully thought out scheme vetoed by a central authority which knows almost nothing about it and has no sympathy with its objects. Yet this is what constantly happens in Britain under our system of centralised control. Something more elastic and less rigid is needed if the best brains are not to be paralysed. And it must be an essential feature of any wholesome system that as much as possible of the power should be in the hands of men who are interested in the work that is to be done.

From *Authority and the Individual* (1949).

BERTRAND DE JOUVENEL, *The Nostalgia for the Small Community*

We are not here employing the didactic method. Our approach to the subject being that of explorer, not schoolmaster, we have advanced, and brought the reader along with us, rather after the manner of ants which, on meeting an obstacle, look all around for a way past; after a necessary deviation, they go on again in the old direction. What we were seeking was a clear conception of the common good, which might serve the magistrate as a criterion for judging whether a particular decision accorded with or was repugnant to it. Such a criterion would certainly be within our grasp if we had received a vision of the ideal social state, which it was a question of maintaining or creating. But beyond all question every vision of this kind is a disastrous thing, which leads its visionaries on to taking total charge of society so that they may mould it closely to their desire; therein is tyranny.

The very varied benefits which men can in course of time confer on one another by mutual intercourse do not resemble, as has been increasingly borne in on us, a convergent series of which the formula can be found, but a divergent series which cannot be totalled. And the common good has seemed to us to consist in conditions which make possible the development of this indefinite series. Trustfulness between partners struck us as the most obvious of these conditions. But at that point we ran into grave difficulties, just when we were enjoying the satisfaction of joining up with a classical theory.

What we have met with is a contradiction between, on the one hand, the growth of this state of trustfulness and, on the other, the indefinite development of the relations between men, the enlargement of the area which they cover and the diversification of their content. The contradiction is one, clearly, between the effects sought and the condition necessary to their achievement. This contradiction has become steadily clearer; the quest for the climate of trustfulness raises in the mind the picture of a closed, narrow circle of neighbours who are very much alike, who value highly a type which each strives to realise and who are very proud of a common denominator which all wish to maintain. This picture, nourished by two sources, strikes our minds with extraordinary vividness. One source is the classical tradition: the state which almost every Greek and most Latin writers in their turn commended to our admiration was Sparta. It is unnecessary here to recall how, or to ask why, the state whose institutions took the place of battlements became the object of unstinted eulogies,[1] even in Athens which was then its enemy. This 'Laconomania'[2] is met in Plato, Xenophon, Polybius, Plutarch and many others in the 'classical heritage', which in time came to inspire generations of lycée-trained young men; a man like Saint-Just is an obvious product of it.[3]

Political writers and active politicians on both sides, the revolutionary and the reactionary, show affinities in common, the mention of which produces violent irritation in them or their disciples; at the root of these affinities is the vision of Sparta which haunts them all equally.

But we said that there were two sources for the dream of a closed, narrow community. One, as we have seen, is the classical tradition; the other is the psychological requirements of Everyman, who feels a nostalgia for the tribe. No one now agrees with the opinion expressed by Rousseau, that the human species was 'better, wiser and happier under its primitive constitution; as it gets away from it it becomes blind, wretched and evil'.[4] But almost everyone subconsciously wishes to recover the warmth of the primitive group. Psychoanalysts tell us that the unconscious longing of man is for his mother's breast; whether that is true or not, it is certain that he longs unconsciously for the social breast

[1] A most important book on this subject, which has received insufficient attention is: *Le Mirage Spartiate, Étude sur l'idéalisation de Sparta dans l'Antiquité grecque de l'Origine jusqu'aux Cyniques*, by F. Ollier, Paris, 1933. It throws a vivid light on the climate of opinion at Athens at the time of the Peloponnesian War.

[2] The word comes from Aristophanes: 'All the men were "Lacomanes", let their hair grow long, endured hunger, did not wash, did as Socrates did, carried clubs . . . ', quoted by Ollier, *op. cit.*, p. 211.

[3] Stendhal bears marked traces of it.

[4] *Rousseau juge de Jean-Jacques.* Third dialogue.

at which he was formed, for the small, closely-knit society which was the school of the species. This unavowed regret is the root of nearly all utopias, both revolutionary and reactionary, and every political heresy, left or right.

Perhaps it is relevant at this point to introduce the myth of Antaeus. This mythological person recovered his strength on touching the soil. And in like manner man, on finding himself again in a small, closely-knit community, displays extraordinary vigour. Therein is a principle common to successes of most varied kinds: those of communist cells, those also of the English aristocracy educated at schools in which the Spartan tradition lingers.

We are thus driven to three conclusions. The first is that the small society, as the milieu in which man is first bound, retains for him an infinite attraction; the next, that he undoubtedly goes to it to renew his strength; but, the last, that any attempt to graft the same features on a large society is Utopian[5] and leads to tyranny. With that admitted, it is clear that as social relations become wider and more various, the common good conceived as reciprocal trustfulness cannot be sought in methods which the model of a small, closed society inspires; such a model is, on the contrary, entirely misleading.

From *De la Souveraineté à la recherche du bien politique* (1955). (English translation in the press, for publication Autumn 1957 by Cambridge University Press and University of Chicago Press).

[5] In this respect Rousseau displayed a wisdom which his disciples missed: 'His object could not be to recall populous countries and large States to their primitive simplicity, but only to check, if possible, the progress of those whom smallness and situation had preserved from the same headlong rush to the perfection of society and the deterioration of the species.' *Ibid.*

SECTION F

INTERNATIONAL RELATIONS

THE ATLANTIC CHARTER, *Liberal*

... they [the signatory states] desire to see no territorial changes that do not accord with the freely expressed wishes of the peoples concerned.

... they respect the right of all peoples to choose the form of government under which they will live;

... they desire to bring about the fullest collaboration between all nations in the economic field, with the object of securing for all improved labour standards, economic advancement and social security.

... they hope to see established a peace which will afford to all nations the means of dwelling in safety within their own boundaries, and which will afford assurance that all the men in all the lands may live out their lives in freedom from fear and want.

... they believe all of the nations of the world, for realistic as well as spiritual reasons, must come to the abandonment of the use of force.

From *The Atlantic Charter* (1941).

GEORGE KENNAN, *Conservative-Empiricist*

As you have no doubt surmised, I see the most serious fault of our past policy formulation to lie in something that I might call the legalistic-moralistic approach to international problems. This approach runs like a red skein through our foreign policy of the last fifty years. It has in it something of the old emphasis on arbitration treaties, something of the Hague Conferences and schemes for universal disarmament, something of the more ambitious American concepts of the role of international law, something of the League of Nations and the United Nations, something of the Kellog Pact, something of the idea of a universal 'Article 51' pact, something of the belief in World Law and World Government. But it is none of these, entirely. Let me try to describe it.

It is the belief that it should be possible to suppress the chaotic and dangerous aspirations of governments in the international field by the acceptance of some system of legal rules and restraints. This belief undoubtedly represents in part an attempt to transpose the Anglo-Saxon concept of individual law into the international field and to make it applicable to governments as it is applicable here at home to individuals. It must also stem in part from the memory of the origin of our own political system —from the recollection that we were able, through acceptance of a common institutional and juridical framework, to reduce to harmless dimensions the conflicts of interest and aspiration among the original thirteen colonies and to bring them all into an ordered and peaceful relationship with one another. Remembering this, people are unable to understand that what might have been possible for the thirteen colonies in a given set of circumstances, might not be possible in the wider international field.

It is the essence of this belief, that instead of taking the awkward conflicts of national interest and dealing with them on their merits with a view to finding the solutions least unsettling to the stability of international life, it would be better to find some formal criteria of a juridical nature by which the permissible behaviour of states could be defined. There would then be judicial entities competent to measure the actions of governments against these criteria and to decide when their behaviour was acceptable and when unacceptable. Behind all this, of course, lies the American assumption that the things for which other peoples in this world are apt to contend are for the most part neither creditable nor important and might justly be expected to take second place behind the desirability of an orderly world, untroubled by international violence. To the American mind, it is implausible that people should have positive aspirations, and ones that they regard as legitimate, more important to them than the peacefulness and orderliness of international life. From this standpoint, it is not apparent why other peoples should not join us in accepting the rules of the game in international politics, just as we accept such rules in the competition of sport in order that the game may not become too cruel and too destructive and may not assume an importance we did not mean it to have.

If they were to do this, the reasoning runs, then the troublesome and chaotic manifestations of the national ego could be contained and rendered either unsubstantial or subject to easy disposal by some method familiar and comprehensible to our American usage. Departing from this background, the mind of American statesmanship, stemming as it does in so large a part from the legal profession in our country, gropes with unfailing persistence for some institutional framework which would be capable of fulfilling this function.

I cannot undertake in this short lecture to deal exhaustively with this thesis or to point out all the elements of unsoundness which I feel it contains. But some of its more outstanding weaknesses are worthy of mention.

In the first place, the idea of the subordination of a large number of states to an international juridical regime, limiting their possibilities for aggression and injury to other states, implies that these are all states like our own, reasonably content with their international borders and status, at least to the extent that they would be willing to refrain from pressing for change without international agreement. Actually, this has generally been true only of a portion of international society. We tend to underestimate the violence of national maladjustments and discontents elsewhere in the world if we think that they would always appear to other people as less important than the preservation of the juridical tidiness of international life.

Second, while this concept is often associated with a revolt against nationalism, it is a curious thing that it actually tends to confer upon the concept of nationality and national sovereignty an absolute value it did not have before. The very principle of 'one government, one vote', regardless of physical or political differences between states, glorifies the concept of national sovereignty and makes it the exclusive form of participation in international life. It envisages a world composed exclusively of sovereign national states with a full equality of status. In doing this, it ignores the tremendous variations in the firmness and soundness of national divisions: the fact is that origins of state borders and national personalities were in many instances fortuitous or at least poorly related to realities. It also ignores the law of change. The national state pattern is not, should not be, and cannot be a fixed and static thing. By nature, it is an unstable phenomenon in a constant state of change and flux. History has shown that the will and the capacity of individual peoples to contribute to their world environment is constantly changing. It is only logical that the organisational forms (and what else are such things as borders and governments?) should change with them. The function of a system of international relationships is not to inhibit this process of change by imposing a legal strait jacket upon it but rather to facilitate it: to ease its transitions, to temper the asperities to which it often leads, to isolate and moderate the conflicts to which it gives rise, and to see that these conflicts do not assume forms too unsettling for international life in general. But this is a task for diplomacy, in the most old-fashioned sense of the term. For this, law is too abstract, too inflexible, too hard to adjust to the demands of the unpredictable and the unexpected.

By the same token, the American concept of world law ignores those means of international offence—those means of the projection of power and coercion over other peoples—which by-pass institutional forms entirely or even exploit them against themselves: such things as ideological attack, intimidation, penetration, and disguised seizure of the institutional paraphernalia of national sovereignty. It ignores, in other words, the device of the puppet state and the set of techniques by which states can be converted into puppets with no formal violation of, or challenge to, the outward attributes of their sovereignty and their independence.

This is one of the things that have caused the peoples of the satellite countries of eastern Europe to look with a certain tinge of bitterness on the United Nations. The organisation failed so completely to save them from domination by a great neighbouring country, a domination no less invidious by virtue of the fact that it came into being by processes we could not call 'aggression'. And there is indeed some justification for their feeling, because the legalistic approach to international affairs ignores in general the international significance of political problems and the deeper sources of international instability. It assumes that civil wars will remain civil and not grow into international wars. It assumes the ability of each people to solve its own internal political problems in a manner not provocative of its international environment. It assumes that each nation will always be able to construct a government qualified to speak for it and cast its vote in the international arena and that this government will be acceptable to the rest of the international community in this capacity. It assumes, in other words, that domestic issues will not become international issues and that the world community will not be put in the position of having to make choices between rival claimants for power within the confines of the individual state.

Finally, this legalistic approach to international relations is faulty in its assumptions concerning the possibility of sanctions against offences and violations. In general, it looks to collective action to provide such sanction against the bad behaviour of states. In doing so, it forgets the limitations on the effectiveness of military coalition. It forgets that, as a circle of military associates widens in any conceivable political-military venture, the theoretical total of available military strength may increase, but only at the cost of compactness and ease of control. And the wider the coalition becomes, the more difficult it becomes to retain political unity and general agreement on the purposes and effects of what is being done. As we are seeing in the case of Korea, joint military operations against an aggressor have a different meaning for each participant and raise specific political issues for each one which are extraneous to the action in question and affect many other facets of international life. The wider the circle of military associates, the more cumbersome the problem of political control over their actions, and the more circumscribed the least common denominator of agreement. This law of diminishing returns lies so heavily on the possibilities for multilateral military action that it makes it doubtful whether the participation of smaller states can really add very much to the ability of the great powers to assure stability of international life. And this is tremendously important, for it brings us back to the realisation that even under a system of world law the sanction against destructive international behaviour might continue to rest basically, as it has in the past, on the alliances and relationships among the great powers themselves. There might be a state, or perhaps more than one state, which all the rest of the world community together could not successfully coerce into following a line of action to which it was violently averse. And if this is true, where are we? It seems to me that we are right back in the realm of the forgotten art of diplomacy from which we have spent fifty years trying to escape.

From *American Diplomacy 1900-1950* (1952),
ch. IV, 'Diplomacy in the Modern World'.

SECTION G

REPRESENTATIVE DEMOCRACY ON PAPER

ANIL CHANDRA BANERJEE, *The Constitution of the Indian Republic*

FUNDAMENTAL RIGHTS

The Indian Constitution contains the most elaborate declaration of fundamental rights so far recognised by any state in the world. Apart from its wide scope, three features of this chapter of the Constitution deserve particular notice. In the first place, Article 32 provides constitutional remedies for the enforcement of fundamental rights. The Supreme Court may be moved by appropriate proceedings for the enforcement of these rights, and that Court has been given power to issue directions or orders or writs for the enforcement of these rights. This provision for judicial control over the enforcement of fundamental rights is an excellent weapon in the armoury of the citizen. In India fundamental rights are not mere abstract declarations or pious wishes; they are definite privileges enforceable by law. Secondly, the fundamental rights are not absolute; the state is allowed to impose limitations on them in case of necessity. Thirdly, all laws inconsistent with or in derogation of the fundamental rights shall be void.

The fundamental rights enumerated in the Constitution fall under seven categories:

(1) *Right to Equality*

Equality before the law and equal protection of the laws are guaranteed. Discrimination on grounds of religion, race, caste, sex or place of birth is prohibited. Equality of opportunity in matters of public employment is guaranteed. Untouchability is abolished and the enforcement of any disability arising out of it is an offence punishable in accordance with law. All titles, except military or academic distinctions, are abolished.

(2) *Right to Freedom*

Article 19 confers on the citizen various rights (freedom of speech, freedom to acquire property, etc.) subject to certain necessary reservations. Article 20 protects him in some cases in respect of conviction for offences. Article 21 safeguards personal liberty. Article 22 guarantees protection against arrest and detention in certain cases. In this Article there is an attempt to strike a balance between the liberty of the subject and the safety of the state.

(3) *Right against Exploitation*

Traffic in human beings, forced labour and employment of children in hazardous occupations are prohibited.

(4) *Right to Freedom of Religion*

Freedom of conscience; free profession, practice and propagation of religion; freedom to manage religious affairs; freedom as to payment of taxes for promotion of any particular religion; freedom as to attendance at religious instruction or religious worship in educational institutions—these rights are guaranteed 'subject to public order, morality and health'. These provisions are quite in keeping with the spirit of secular democracy which it is India's aim to consolidate.

(5) *Cultural and Educational Rights*

The language, script, and culture of the minorities shall be protected. Their right to admission into state-managed or state-aided educational institutions and to establish and administer educational institutions of their choice is guaranteed.

(6) *Right to Property*

No person shall be deprived of his property save by authority of law. In case of compulsory acquisition of property compensation shall be paid.

(7) *Right to Constitutional Remedies*

Fundamental rights will be enforced by the Supreme Court (or by High Court or any other Court legally empowered to do so).

Directive Principles of State Policy

While the fundamental rights are enforceable through courts of law, the directive principles of state policy are extra-legal instructions issued to the Legislature and the Executive for their guidance. These principles are based on the political ideals embodied in the Preamble. Although not enforceable by any court, these principles are 'fundamental in the governance of the country and it shall be the duty of the state to apply these principles in making laws'. These principles give us an idea about the character and scope of the state which the Constitution aims at building up.

The main directive principles of state policy are the following:

(1) The state shall secure a just social order for the promotion of the welfare of the people.

(2) The state shall try to secure for all citizens (men and women equally) an adequate means of livelihood, to distribute the material resources of the community so as best to subserve the common good, to prevent harmful concentration of wealth and means of production, to provide equal pay for equal work for both men and women, to remove unhealthy conditions of work for men, women and children and to protect childhood and youth against exploitation.

(3) The state shall organise village panchayats.

(4) The state shall recognise, within the limits of its economic capacity, right to work, to education, and to public assistance in cases of unemployment, sickness, etc.

(5) The state shall secure just and humane conditions of work and maternity relief.

(6) The state shall secure living wage, decent standard of living, etc. for workers.

(7) The state shall enforce a uniform civil code throughout the country.

(8) The state shall provide, within a period of ten years from the commencement of the Constitution, free and compulsory education for all children below 14.

(9) The state shall promote the educational and economic interests of the Scheduled Castes, the Scheduled Tribes, etc.

(10) The state shall raise the level of nutrition, improve public health, and introduce prohibition.

(11) The state shall organise agriculture and animal husbandry on modern lines.

(12) The state shall protect monuments of artistic or historic interest.

(13) The state shall separate the judiciary from the executive.

(14) The state shall promote international peace and security and foster respect for international law and treaty obligation.

Dr Ambedkar said in the Constituent Assembly on 4 November 1948:

> If it is said that the Directive Principles have no legal force behind them, I am prepared to admit it. But I am not prepared to admit that they have no sort of binding force at all. Nor am I prepared to concede that they are useless because they have no binding force in law.
>
> The Directive Principles are like the Instrument of Instructions which were issued to the Governor-General and to the Governors of the Colonies and to those of India by the British Government under the 1935 Act... Wherever there is a grant of power in general terms for peace, order and good government, it is necessary that it should be accompanied by instructions regulating its existence.
>
> The inclusion of such instructions in a Constitution ... becomes justifiable for another reason. The ... Constitution ... only provides a machinery for the government of the country. It is not a contrivance to install any particular party in power as has been done in some countries. Who should be in power is left to be determined by the people, as it must be, if the system is to satisfy the tests of democracy. But whoever captures power will not be free to do what he likes to do with it. In the exercise of it, he will have to respect these instruments of instructions which are called Directive Principles. He cannot ignore them. He may not have to answer for their breach in a Court of Law. But he will certainly have to answer for them before the electorate at election time.

From *A Commentary on the Constitution of India* (1950).

PART II

COMMUNISM

INTRODUCTION

No theory of political organisation at the present time is so copiously or so self-consciously documented as Communism. The official texts, each with its own aura of sanctity, are legion. Certain works by Marx, Engels and Lenin, have become classics, and it is to these that any selection of documents of this kind must turn; for when dealing with a theory which has so clear a literary pedigree, it is the classic texts rather than the out-of-the-way quotations, which are useful to the general reader.

Marxism, however, is more than a political theory. As modified by Lenin and Stalin, and the present rulers of Russia, Marxism has become an official political theory in a sense which no other set of political propositions has been before: the theory which was evolved in the reading room at the British Museum and an upper room in Soho has been turned into a rule to live by in the Soviet Union. In the course of violent revolution and revolutionary improvisation, the official quest for orthodoxy was never lost, and the doctrines of the fathers were preserved and put forward as a coherent and watertight political philosophy, as well as an instrument of political power. Thus, Stalin and his co-authors, in the conclusion to the *History of the Communist Party of the Soviet Union (Bolsheviks)*, feel it necessary to write:

> The history of the Party teaches us that a party of the working class cannot perform the role of leader of its class, cannot perform the role of organiser and leader of the proletarian revolution, unless it has mastered the advanced theory of the working class movement, the Marxist-Leninist theory.
>
> The Marxist-Leninist theory must not be regarded as a collection of dogmas, as a catechism, as a symbol of faith, and the Marxists themselves as pedants and dogmatists. The Marxist-Leninist theory is the science of the development of society, the science of the working class movement, the science of the building of the Communist society. And as a science it does not and cannot stand still, but develops and perfects itself. Clearly, in its development it is bound to become enriched by new experience and new knowledge, and some of its propositions and conclusions are bound to change in the course of time, are bound to be replaced by new conclusions and propositions corresponding to the new historical conditions.
>
> Mastering the Marxist-Leninist theory does not at all mean learning all its formulas and conclusions by heart and clinging to their every letter. To

master the Marxist-Leninist theory we must first of all learn to distinguish between its letter and substance . . . .

The Marxist-Leninist theory is not a dogma, but a guide to action . . . .

It will be seen, therefore, that the political theory of Marxism can be regarded in two ways. As Stalin conceives it in the passage quoted here, it is a method of training the political sixth sense; flexible, pragmatic, ideological in the sense of a theory whose function is to be useful but not necessarily to enshrine truth. Thus regarded, it is a political weapon of the first order, a practical method of maintaining unity in a political party which is destined to lead the unthinking mass of a great people. It can be used to explain a sudden change of policy, or a sudden change of leadership, and train new members in the path of party truth. But the foundations of this political theory are also to be found in the Marxism expounded by Marx and Engels and Lenin, before theory was translated into state power. This political theory dealt with the universal subjects which have concerned other political philosophers—the nature of historical development, economic theory, the state—linking its conclusions on all these matters with a revolutionary theory of political action. What was to happen after the revolution remained vague and misty to Marx and Engels; Lenin's only concern was to capture state power—the problems of practical government he reduced in a fatuous passage in *The State and the Revolution* to a mere accounting process.

Accounting and control—that is the *main* thing required for the 'setting up' and correct functioning of the *first phase* of Communist society. *All* citizens are transformed into salaried employees of the state, which consists of armed workers. *All* citizens become employees and workers of a *single* national state 'syndicate'. All that is required is that they should work equally—do their proper share of work—and get paid equally. The accounting and control necessary for this have been *simplified* by capitalism to an extreme and reduced to the extraordinarily simple operation—which any literate person can perform—of checking and recording, knowledge of the four rules of arithmetic, and issuing receipts.

Marxism never set out to give a clear picture of how the proletarian state should be organised; it was content to show why there ought to be a revolution, and why it was historically necessary that there should be one.

It has often been pointed out that there is some confusion between the operation of historical laws, amoral and remorseless, on the one hand, and the geniune moral fervour with which

Marx sought to bring about the downfall of the capitalist exploiters whom he hated with an emotion which could not be described as scientific. Yet it seems essential to start any discussion of Communism with the theory of history known as historical materialism which—though by no means original—is one of Marx's most penetrating and pervasive contributions to political theory. Two passages quoted here—from the *Preface to the Critique of Political Economy* by Marx, and from *Anti-Dühring* by Engels, give with classic simplicity this explanation of human history and political organisation in economic terms.

In the social production which men carry on [wrote Marx] they enter into definite relations that are indispensable and independent of their will; these relations of production correspond to a definite stage of development of their material forces of production. The sum total of these relations of production constitutes the economic structure of society—the real foundation on which rises a legal and political superstructure and to which correspond definite forms of social consciousness. The mode of production determines the social and political life process in general.

And he went on with the famous phrase which is almost completely devoid of any precise meaning, but has a stirring ring to it, 'It is not the consciousness of men that determines their being, but on the contrary, their social being that determines their consciousness.' Leaving aside the ambiguities contained in phrases like 'the relations of production' and the textual criticism to which this passage and that from *Anti-Dühring* may be subjected, the theory of historical materialism offers an explanation of the rise of capitalism and links to the rise of this form of economic organisation, a destructive criticism of all the 'superstructure', political, legal, philosophical, and religious. And it goes beyond this to suggest that just as capitalism replaced feudalism, so socialism, and with it the social superstructure of socialism, must replace capitalism. It gives a theoretical basis for the class struggle which it places at the very heart of history. As the foundation of a revolutionary political theory, this has much to commend it, and not least, it gives a question-begging means of cutting away the ground from underneath any opposite argument by reference to an impersonal economic force. It is not hard to demolish the theory of historical materialism, or to show how subsequent developments of Marxist political theory are incompatible with it. Nor is it hard to appreciate the force of this theory as the foundation of a revolutionary view of politics. The quotation from the *History of the Communist Party of the Soviet Union* gives the current application of the theory.

Historical materialism is the starting point, taking all human history into its critical span. Marxist economics, on the other hand, concentrated on the capitalism of the mid-nineteenth century, and criticised it mainly by its own arguments. Many of the theories advanced in *Capital* fall to the ground because they are based on the assumptions of that same Ricardian economics which they were intended to confute. Marx's labour theory of value had honourable antecedents and an elementary popular appeal, but more important by far was his general assault on capitalism, based on the view that capital would steadily accumulate in the hands of larger and larger concerns which in turn would lead to the increasing poverty of the working class and the inevitable approach of the day when the expropriators would be expropriated. By the end of the nineteenth century it had become clear that this picture did not correspond with the facts of life in the most advanced industrial nations. Marxist writers explained this by reference to the export of capital and industrial misery to the colonies. Lenin's writings on imperialism followed J. A. Hobson and others in linking the colonial expansion of the late nineteenth and early twentieth century with economic conditions at home, and gave new life to the Marxist analysis of capitalism.

The theory of the state inherent in the theory of historical materialism is that the state, like every other aspect of social and political life, is the product of economic relationships, and therefore of class conflicts. The state is the instrument by which the capitalist class keeps the workers in subjection. Thus, Engels describes the modern state as 'only the organisation that bourgeois society takes on in order to support the general external condition of the capitalist mode of production against the encroachments as well of the workers as of individual capitalists. The modern state, no matter what its form, is essentially a capitalist machine, the state of the capitalist, the ideal personification of the total national capital' (*Anti-Dühring*, Part III, ch. II). Marx at one point develops a different theory. He described the French state under Louis Napoleon which seemed 'to have made itself completely independent'—a parasite living off the backs of the different classes, while the class struggle was in stalemate. The first view of the state coincides with the Marxist projection of what the socialist state should be. In the first place, the revolutionary working class should capture the state and use it for their own class interests, as ruthlessly as the capitalists, to crush their class enemies. This would form the period of the dictatorship of the proletariat of which Marx and Engels talked with a frustrating vagueness, and which Lenin discusses in part of *The State and the Revolution*. But in the second place, the Marxist doctrine of the state looks beyond the immediate period after the revolution to the day when the classless society has been achieved. Then in the absence of any ruling class who might care to use state power against anybody else, the state withers away, and 'the government of persons is replaced by the administration of things'.

Both these aspects of this theory of the state are inherent in Marxist writing from the Communist Manifesto onwards, but by the time the Russian revolution enabled Communists to translate theory into practice, the theoretical nature of the dictatorship of the proletariat had become one of a number of more practical questions governing the relations between the workers and the peasants, and the improvisation needed to defend the revolution from external and internal enemies. Inevitably at this point, great as remained the devotion of the leaders of the Russian revolution to theory, the temptation to develop the arguments after the actions became insuperable. The extract from Stalin's address to the 18th Congress of the Party in 1939, explains why the state cannot wither away so long as 'capitalist encirclement' remains.

In the extracts which follow there are three devoted to political action. The first is from *Two Tactics of Social Democracy* which Lenin wrote as an argument against those who, foreseeing the advent of a bourgeois revolution in Russia, argued against the Marxists taking part in it. Lenin accepted that the revolution would be bourgeois (there was no doubt that Russia had yet to develop capitalism to the full, as prescribed by the theory of historical materialism) but suggested that the bourgeois revolution could be captured by the workers, on the principle of a 'continuous revolution'.

The second extract is from Stalin's *Foundations of Leninism* and gives an official attempt to square Lenin's brilliant revolutionary method with Marxist theory. It is written well after the events and is valuable in that it shows how a theory of political action which remained vague before the revolution has been crystallised by events.

The third is different in time and in temper. It is from Engels's famous preface to the 1895 edition of Marx's *Class Struggles in France*. Writing in the hey-day of German-Social Democracy, when Marxist politicians seemed to be gaining all they wanted by legitimate means, Engels speculated on the successful use of universal suffrage, and the introduction of socialism by orthodox political means.

The last extract is from the report of the Central Committee rendered by Mr Khrushchev to the twentieth congress of the Soviet Communist Party in February 1956. In view of the great political importance of the changes in Russia since the death of Stalin, and the somersaults which have been performed by Communists inside and outside Russia over certain aspects of Stalin's regime, the speeches at this congress have received very careful attention everywhere.

There is nothing in them, however, to indicate any major contribution to the development of the political philosophy of Communism. On two points only does Mr Khrushchev add to or modify the general Marx-Lenin-Stalinist line. He argues that, in present day terms, both the Leninist theory of the peaceful coexistence of states with different social systems, and the Marxist thesis that Communism and Capitalism are fighting a battle which Communism must win in the end, are fully compatible. And he goes on to reconcile the Marxist-Leninist precept that war is inevitable, with the new theory that, in the changed circumstances of the modern age with 'a large group of countries with a population running into many hundreds of millions which are actively working to avert war', and labour movements and peace supporters everywhere, 'war is not fatalistically inevitable'. He goes on to consider the possibility of countries travelling to Socialism by other routes than that taken by Russia. 'Forms of social revolution vary', says Mr Khrushchev.

Mr Khrushchev has done no more than emphasise those aspects of what his predecessors have taught which must suit the ideological needs of the present time. It is too soon to attribute to him any major philosophical additions to Communist political science.

It should be observed in conclusion that to make a selection from the profusion of Communist literature, and to collect extracts of a manageable size, is an exercise in ruthless exclusion and cutting. Some of the extracts have inevitably suffered in the process, and it has been necessary to leave out much that might profitably have been included. The full texts of all the passages quoted are easily obtainable in English editions.

SECTION A

GENERAL

Marx and Engels, *The Communist Manifesto*

I. BOURGEOIS AND PROLETARIANS

The history of all hitherto existing society is the history of class struggles.

Freeman and patrician and slave, plebeian, lord and serf, guild-master and journeyman, in a word, oppressor and oppressed, stood in constant opposition to one another, carried on an uninterrupted now hidden, now open fight, a fight that each time ended, either in a revolutionary reconstitution of society at large, or in the common ruin of the contending classes.

In the earlier epochs of history, we find almost everywhere a complicated arrangement of society into various orders, a manifold gradation of social rank. In ancient Rome we have patricians, knights, plebeians, slaves; in the Middle Ages, feudal lords, vassals, guildmasters, journeymen, apprentices, serfs; in almost all of these classes, again, subordinate gradations.

The modern bourgeois society that has sprouted from the ruins of feudal society, has not done away with class antagonisms. It has but established new classes, new conditions of oppression, new forms of struggle in place of the old ones.

Our epoch, the epoch of the bourgeoisie, possesses, however, this distinctive feature: it has simplified the class antagonisms. Society as a whole is more and more splitting up into two great hostile camps, into two great classes directly facing each other—bourgeoisie and proletariat.

From the serfs of the Middle Ages sprang the chartered burghers of the earliest towns. From these burgesses the first elements of the bourgeoisie were developed.

The discovery of America, the rounding of the Cape, opened up fresh ground for the rising bourgeoisie. The East Indian and Chinese markets, the colonisation of America, trade with the colonies, the increase in the means of exchange and in commodities generally, gave to commerce, to navigation, to industry, an impulse never before known, and thereby, to the revolutionary element in the tottering feudal society, a rapid development.

The feudal system of industry, in which industrial production was monopolised by closed guilds, now no longer sufficed for the growing wants of the new markets. The manufacturing system took its place. The guildmasters were pushed aside by the manufacturing middle class; division of labour between the different corporate guilds vanished in the face of division of labour in each single workshop.

Meantime the markets kept ever growing, the demand ever rising. Even manufacture no longer sufficed. Thereupon, steam and machinery revolutionised industrial production. The place of manufacture was taken by the giant, modern industry, the place of the industrial middle class, by industrial millionaires, the leaders of whole industrial armies, the modern bourgeois.

Modern industry has established the world market, for which the discovery of America paved the way. This market has given an immense development to commerce, to navigation, to communication by land. This development has, in its turn, reacted on the extension of industry; and in proportion as industry, commerce, navigation, railways extended, in the same proportion the bourgeoisie developed, increased its capital, and pushed into the background every class handed down from the Middle Ages.

We see, therefore, how the modern bourgeoisie is itself the product of a long course of development, of a series of revolutions in the modes of production and exchange.

Each step in the development of the bourgeoisie was accompanied by a corresponding political advance of that class. An oppressed class under the sway of the feudal nobility, an armed and self-governing association in the medieval commune; here independent urban republic (as in Italy and Germany), there taxable 'third estate' of the monarchy (as in France); afterwards, in the period of manufacture proper, serving either the semi-feudal or the absolute monarchy as a counterpoise against the nobility, and, in fact, corner-stone of the great monarchies in general, the bourgeoisie has at last, since the establishment of Modern Industry and of the world market, conquered for itself, in the modern representative state, exclusive political sway. The executive of the modern state is but a committee for managing the common affairs of the whole bourgeoisie.

The bourgeoisie, historically, has played a most revolutionary part.

The bourgeoisie, wherever it has got the upper hand, has put an end to all feudal, patriarchal, idyllic relations. It has pitilessly torn asunder the motley feudal ties that bound man to his 'natural superiors', and has left no other nexus between man and man than naked self-interest, than callous 'cash payment'. It has drowned the most heavenly ecstacies of religious fervour, of chivalrous enthusiasm, of philistine sentimentalism, in the icy water of egotistical calculation. It has resolved personal worth into exchange value, and in place of the numberless indefeasible chartered freedoms, has set up that single, unconscionable freedom—Free Trade. In one word, for exploitation, veiled by religious and political illusions, it has substituted naked, shameless, direct, brutal exploitation.

The bourgeoisie has stripped of its halo every occupation hitherto honoured and looked up to with reverent awe. It has converted the physician, the lawyer, the priest, the poet, the man of science, into its paid wage-labourers.

The bourgeoisie has torn away from the family its sentimental veil, and has reduced the family relation to a mere money relation.

The bourgeoisie has disclosed how it came to pass that the brutal display of vigour in the Middle Ages, which reactionaries so much admire, found its fitting complement in the most slothful indolence. It has been the first to show what man's activity can bring about. It has accomplished wonders far surpassing the Egyptian pyramids, Roman aqueducts, and Gothic cathedrals; it has conducted expeditions that put in the shade all the former Exoduses of nations and crusades.

The bourgeoisie cannot exist without constantly revolutionising the instruments of production, and thereby the relations of production, and with them the whole relations of society. Conservation of the old modes of production in unaltered form, was, on the contrary, the first condition of existence for all earlier industrial classes. Constant revolutionising of production, uninterrupted disturbance of all social conditions, everlasting uncertainty and agitation distinguish the bourgeois epoch from all earlier ones. All fixed, fast-frozen relations, with their train of ancient and venerable prejudices and opinions, are swept away, all new-formed ones become antiquated before they can ossify.

All that is solid melts into air, all that is holy is profaned, and man is at last compelled to face with sober senses his real conditions of life and his relations with his kind.

The need of a constantly expanding market for its product chases the bourgeoisie over the whole surface of the globe. It must nestle everywhere, settle everywhere, establish connections everywhere.

The bourgeoisie has through its exploitation of the world market given a cosmopolitan character to production and consumption in every country. To the great chagrin of reactionaries, it has drawn from under the feet of industry the national ground on which it stood. All old-established national industries have been destroyed or are daily being destroyed. They are dislodged by new industries, whose introduction becomes a life and death question for all civilised nations, by industries that no longer work up indigenous raw material, but raw material drawn from the remotest zones; industries whose products are consumed, not only at home, but in every quarter of the globe. In place of the old wants, satisfied by the production of the country, we find new wants, requiring for their satisfaction the products of distant lands and climes. In place of the old local and national seclusion and self-sufficiency, we have intercourse in every direction, universal inter-dependence of nations. And as in material, so also in intellectual productions. The intellectual creations of individual nations become common property. National one-sidedness and narrow-mindedness become more and more impossible, and from the numerous national and local literatures there arises a world literature.

The bourgeoisie, by the rapid improvement of all instruments of production, by the immensely facilitated means of communication, draws all, even the most barbarian, nations into civilisation. The cheap prices of its commodities are the heavy artillery with which it batters down all Chinese walls, with which it forces the barbarians' intensely obstinate hatred of foreigners to capitulate. It compels all nations, on pain of extinction, to adopt the bourgeois mode of production; it compels them to introduce what it calls civilisation into their midst, i.e. to become bourgeois themselves. In one word, it creates a world after its own image.

The bourgeoisie has subjected the country to the rule of the towns. It has created enormous cities, has greatly increased the urban population as compared to the rural, and has thus rescued a considerable part of the population from the idiocy of rural life. Just as it has made the country dependent on the towns, so it has made barbarian and semi-barbarian countries dependent on the civilised ones, nations of peasants on nations of bourgeois, the East on the West.

The bourgeoisie keeps more and more doing away with the scattered state of the population, of the means of production, and of property. It has agglomerated population, centralised means of production, and has concentrated property in a few hands. The necessary consequence of this was political centralisation. Independent, or but loosely connected provinces, with separate interests, laws, governments and systems of taxation, became lumped together into one nation, with one government, one code of laws, one national class interest, one frontier, and one customs tariff.

The bourgeoisie, during its rule of scarce one hundred years, has created more massive and more colossal productive forces, than have all preceding generations together. Subjection of nature's forces to man, machinery, application of chemistry to industry and agriculture, steam-navigation, railways, electric telegraphs, clearing of whole continents for cultivation, canalisation of rivers, whole populations conjured out of the ground—what earlier century had even a presentiment that such productive forces slumbered in the lap of social labour?

We see then; the means of production and exchange, on whose foundation the bourgeoisie built itself up, were generated in feudal society. At a certain stage in the development of these means of production and of exchange, the conditions under which feudal society produced and exchanged, the feudal organisation of agriculture and manufacturing industry, in one word, the feudal relations of property became no longer compatible with the already developed productive forces; they became so many fetters. They had to be burst asunder; they were burst asunder.

Into their place stepped free competition, accompanied by a social and political constitution adapted to it, and by the economical and political sway of the bourgeois class.

A similar movement is going on before our own eyes. Modern bourgeois society with its relations of production, of exchange and of property, a society that has conjured up such gigantic means of production and exchange, is like the sorcerer who is no longer able to control the powers of the nether world whom he has called up by his spells. For many a decade past the history of industry and commerce is but the history of the revolt of modern productive forces against modern conditions of production, against the property relations that are the conditions for the existence of the bourgeoisie and of its rule. It is enough to mention the commercial crises that by their periodical return put the existence of the entire bourgeois society on its trial, each time more threateningly. In these crises a great part not only of the existing products, but also of the previously created productive forces, are periodically destroyed. In these crises there breaks out an epidemic that, in all earlier epochs, would have seemed an absurdity—the epidemic of over-production. Society suddenly finds itself put back into a state of momentary barbarism; it appears as if famine, a universal war or devastation had cut off the supply of every means of subsistence; industry and commerce seem to be destroyed. And why? Because there is too much civilisation, too much means of subsistence, too much industry, too much commerce. The productive forces at the disposal of society no longer tend to further the development of the conditions of bourgeois property; on the contrary, they have become too powerful for these conditions, by which they are fettered, and so soon as they overcome these fetters, they bring disorder into the whole of bourgeois society, endanger the existence of bourgeois property. The conditions of bourgeois society are too narrow to comprise the wealth created by them. And how does the bourgeoisie get over these crises? On the one hand, by enforced destruction of a mass of productive forces; on the other, by the conquest of new markets, and by the more thorough exploitation of the old ones. That is to say, by paving the way for more extensive and more destructive crises, and by diminishing the means whereby crises are prevented.

The weapons with which the bourgeosie felled fuedalism to the ground are now turned against the bourgeoisie itself.

But not only has the bourgeoisie forged the weapons that bring death to itself; it has also called into existence the men who are to wield those weapons—the modern working class—the proletarians.

In proportion as the bourgeoisie, i.e. capital, is developed, in the same proportion is the proletariat, the modern working class, developed—a class of labourers, who live only so long as they find work, and who find work only so long as their labour increases capital. These labourers, who must sell themselves piecemeal, are a commodity, like every other article of commerce, and are consequently exposed to all the vicissitudes of competition, to all the fluctuations of the market.

Owing to the extensive use of machinery and to division of labour, the work of the proletarians has lost all individual character, and, consequently, all charm for the workman. He becomes an appendage of the machine, and it is only the most simple, the most monotonous, and most easily acquired knack, that is required of him. Hence, the cost of production of a workman is restricted, almost entirely, to the means of subsistence that he requires for his maintenance, and for the propagation of his race. But the price of a commodity, and therefore, also of labour, is equal to its cost of production. In proportion, therefore, as the repulsiveness of the work increases, the wage decreases. Nay more, in proportion as the use of machinery and division of labour increases, in the same proportion the burden of toil also increases, whether by prolongation of the working hours, by increase of the work exacted in a given time, or by increased speed of the machinery.

Modern industry has converted the little workshop of the patriarchal master into the great factory of the industrial capitalist. Masses of labourers, crowded into the factory, are organised like soldiers. As privates of the industrial army, they are placed under the command of a positive hierarchy of officers and sergeants. Not only are they slaves of the bourgeois class, and of the bourgeois state; they are daily and hourly enslaved by the machine, by the overseer, and, above all, by the individual bourgeois manufacturer himself. The more openly this despotism proclaims gain to be its end and aim, the more petty, the more hateful and the more embittering it is.

The less the skill and exertion of strength implied in manual labour, in other words, the more modern industry becomes developed, the more is the labour of men superseded by that of women. Differences of age and sex have no longer any distinctive social validity for the working class. All are instruments of labour, more or less expensive to use, according to their age and sex.

No sooner is the exploitation of the labourer by the manufacturer, so far at an end, that he receives his wages in cash, than he is set upon by the other portions of the bourgeoisie, the landlord, the shopkeeper, the pawnbroker, etc.

The lower strata of the middle class—the small tradespeople, shopkeepers, and retired tradesmen generally, the handicraftsmen and the peasants—all these sink gradually into the proletariat, partly because their diminutive capital does not suffice for the scale on which modern industry is carried on, and is swamped in the competition with the large capitalists, partly because their specialised skill is rendered worthless by new methods of production. Thus the proletariat is recruited from all classes of the population.

The proletariat goes through various stages of development. With its birth begins its struggle with the bourgeoisie. At first the contest is carried on by individual labourers, then by the work people of a factory, then by the operatives of one trade, in one locality, against the individual bourgeois who directly exploits them. They direct their attacks not against the bourgeois conditions of production, but against the instruments of production themselves; they destroy imported wares that compete with their labour, they smash to pieces machinery, they set factories ablaze, they seek to restore by force the vanished status of the workman of the Middle Ages.

At this stage the labourers still form an incoherent mass scattered over the whole country, and broken up by their mutual competition. If anywhere they unite to form more compact bodies, this is not yet the consequence of their own active union, but of the union of the bourgeoisie, which class, in order to attain its own political ends, is compelled to set the whole proletariat in motion, and is moreover yet, for a time, able to do so. At this stage, therefore, the proletarians do not fight their enemies, but the enemies of their enemies, the remnants of absolute monarchy, the landowners, the non-industrial bourgeois, the petty bourgeoisie; every victory so obtained is a victory for the bourgeoisie.

But with the development of industry the proletariat not only increases in number; it becomes concentrated in greater masses, its strength grows, and it feels that strength more. The various interests and conditions of life within the ranks of the proletariat are more and more equalised, in proportion as machinery obliterates all distinctions of labour, and nearly everywhere reduces wages to the same low level. The growing competition among the bourgeois, and the resulting commercial crises, make the wages of the workers ever more fluctuating. The unceasing improvement of machinery, ever more rapidly developing, makes their livelihood ever more precarious; the collisions between individual workmen and individual bourgeois take more and more the character of collisions between two classes. Thereupon the workers begin to form combinations (trades' unions) against the bourgeois; they club together in order to keep up the rate of wages; they found permanent associations in order to make provision beforehand for these occasional revolts. Here and there the contests break out into riots.

Now and then the workers are victorious, but only for a time. The real fruit of their battle lies, not in the immediate result, but in the ever expanding union of the workers. This union is helped on by the improved means of communication that are created by modern industry, and that place the workers of different localities in contact one with another. It was just this contact that was needed to centralise the numerous local struggles, all of the same character, into one national struggle between classes. But every class struggle is a political struggle. And that union, to attain which the burghers of the Middle Ages, with their miserable highways, required centuries, the modern proletarians, thanks to railways, achieve in a few years.

This organisation of the proletarians into a class, and consequently into a political party, is continually being upset again by the competition between the workers themselves. But it ever rises up again, stronger, firmer, mightier. It compels legislative recognition of particular interests of the workers, by taking advantage of the divisions among the bourgeoisie itself. Thus the ten-hours' bill in England was carried.

Altogether, collisions between the classes of the old society further in many ways the course of development of the proletariat. The bourgeoisie finds itself involved in a constant battle. At first with the aristocracy; later on, with those portions of the bourgeoisie itself, whose interests have become antagonistic to the progress of industry; at all times with the bourgeoisie of foreign countries. In all these battles it sees itself compelled to appeal to the proletariat, to ask for its help, and thus, to drag it into the political arena. The bourgeoisie itself, therefore, supplies the proletariat with its own elements of political and general education, in other words, it furnishes the proletariat with weapons for fighting the bourgeoisie.

Further, as we have already seen, entire sections of the ruling classes are, by the advance of industry, precipitated into the proletariat, or are at least threatened in their conditions of existence. These also supply the proletariat with fresh elements of enlightenment and progress.

Finally, in time when the class struggle nears the decisive hour, the process of dissolution going on within the ruling class, in fact within the whole range of old society, assumes such a violent, glaring character, that a small section of the ruling class cuts itself adrift, and joins the revolutionary class, the class that holds the future in its hands. Just as, therefore, at an earlier period, a section of the nobility went over to the bourgeoisie, so now a portion of the bourgeoisie goes over to the proletariat, and in particular, a portion of the bourgeois ideologists, who have raised themselves to the level of comprehending theoretically the historical movement as a whole.

Of all the classes that stand face to face with the bourgeoisie today, the proletariat alone is a really revolutionary class. The other classes decay and finally disappear in the face of modern industry; the proletariat is its special and essential product.

The lower middle class, the small manufacturer, the shopkeeper, the artisan, the peasant, all these fight against the bourgeoisie, to save from extinction their existence as fractions of the middle class. They are therefore not revolutionary, but conservative. Nay more, they are reactionary, for they try to roll back the wheel of history. If by chance they are revolutionary, they are so only in view of their impending transfer into the proletariat; they thus defend not their present, but their future interests; they desert their own standpoint to place themselves at that of the proletariat.

The 'dangerous class', the social scum, that passively rotting mass thrown off by the lowest layers of old society, may, here and there, be swept into the movement by a proletarian revolution; its conditions of life, however, prepare it far more for a bribed tool of reactionary intrigue.

In the conditions of the proletariat, those of old society at large are already virtually swamped. The proletarian is without property; his relation to his wife and children has no longer anything in common with the bourgeois family relations; modern industrial labour, modern subjection to capital, the same in England as in France, in America as in Germany, has stripped him of every trace of national character. Law, morality, religion, are to him so many bourgeois prejudices, behind which lurk in ambush just as many bourgeois interests.

All the preceding classes that got the upper hand, sought to fortify their already acquired status by subjecting society at large to their conditions of appropriation. The proletarians cannot become masters of the productive forces of society, except by abolishing their own previous mode of appropriation, and thereby also every other previous mode of appropriation. They have nothing of their own to secure and to fortify; their mission is to destroy all previous securities for, and insurances of, individual property.

All previous historical movements were movements of minorities, or in the interests of minorities. The proletarian movement is the self-conscious, independent movement of the immense majority, in the interest of the immense majority. The proletariat, the lowest stratum of our present society, cannot stir, cannot raise itself up, without the whole superincumbent strata of official society being sprung into the air.

Though not in substance, yet in form, the struggle of the proletariat with the bourgeoisie is at first a national struggle. The proletariat of each country must, of course, first of all settle matters with its own bourgeoisie.

In depicting the most general phases of the development of the proletariat, we traced the more or less veiled civil war, raging within existing society, up to the point where that war breaks out into open revolution, and where the violent overthrow of the bourgeoisie lays the foundation for the sway of the the proletariat.

Hitherto, every form of society has been based, as we have already seen, on the antagonism of oppressing and oppressed classes. But in order to oppress a class, certain conditions must be assured to it under which it can, at least, continue its slavish existence. The serf, in the period of serfdom, raised himself to membership in the commune, just as the petty bourgeois, under the yoke of feudal absolutism, managed to develop into a bourgeois. The modern labourer, on the contrary, instead of rising with the progress of industry, sinks deeper and deeper beneath the conditions of existence of his own class. He becomes a pauper, and pauperism develops more rapidly than population and wealth. And here it becomes evident, that the bourgeoisie is unfit any longer to be the ruling class in society, and to impose its conditions of existence upon society as an overriding law. It is unfit to rule because it is incompetent to assure an existence to its slave within his slavery, because it cannot help letting him sink into such a state, that it has to feed him, instead of being fed by him. Society can no longer live under this bourgeoisie, in other words, its existence is no longer compatible with society.

The essential condition for the existence and the sway of the bourgeois class, is the formation and augmentation of capital; the condition for capital is wage-labour. Wage-labour rests exclusively on competition between the labourers. The advance of industry, whose involuntary promoter is the bourgeoisie, replaces the isolation of the labourers, due to competition, by their revolutionary competition, due to association. The development of modern industry, therefore, cuts from under its feet the very foundation on which the bourgeoisie produces and appropriates products. What the bourgeoisie therefore produces, above all, are its own grave-diggers. Its fall and the victory of the proletariat are equally inevitable.

II. PROLETARIANS AND COMMUNISTS

In what relation do the Communists stand to the proletarians as a whole?

The Communists do not form a separate party opposed to other working class parties.

They have no interests separate and apart from those of the proletariat as a whole.

They do not set up any sectarian principles of their own, by which to shape and mould the proletarian movement.

The Communists are distinguished from the other working class parties by this only: (1) In the national struggles of the proletarians of the different countries, they point out and bring to the front the common interests of the entire proletariat, independently of all nationality. (2) In the various stages of development which the struggle of the working class against the bourgeoisie has to pass through, they always and everywhere represent the interests of the movement as a whole.

The Communists, therefore, are on the one hand, practically, the most advanced and resolute section of the working class parties of every country, that section which pushes forward all others; on the other hand, theoretically, they have over the great mass of the proletariat the advantage of clearly understanding the line of march, the conditions, and the ultimate general results of the proletarian movement.

The immediate aim of the Communists is the same as that of all the other proletarian parties; formation of the proletariat into a class, overthrow of the bourgeois supremacy, conquest of political power by the proletariat.

The theoretical conclusions of the Communists are in no way based on ideas or principles that have been invented, or discovered, by this or that would-be universal reformer.

They merely express, in general terms, actual relations springing from an existing class struggle, from a historical movement going on under our very eyes. The abolition of existing property relations is not at all a distinctive feature of Communism.

All property relations in the past have continually been subject to historical change consequent upon the change in historical conditions.

The French Revolution, for example, abolished feudal property in favour of bourgeois property.

The distinguishing feature of Communism is not the abolition of property generally, but the abolition of bourgeois property. But modern bourgeois private property is the final and most complete expression of the system of producing and appropriating products that is based on class antagonisms, on the exploitation of the many by the few.

In this sense, the theory of the Communists may be summed up in the single sentence: Abolition of private property.

We Communists have been reproached with the desire of abolishing the right of personally acquiring property as the fruit of a man's own labour, which property is alleged to be the groundwork of all personal freedom, activity and independence.

Hard-won, self-acquired, self-earned property! Do you mean the property of the petty artisan and of the small peasant, a form of property that preceded the bourgeois form? There is no need to abolish that; the development of industry has to a great extent already destroyed it, and is still destroying it daily.

Or do you mean modern bourgeois private property?

But does wage-labour create any property for the labourer? Not a bit. It creates capital, i.e. that kind of property which exploits wage-labour, and which cannot increase except upon condition of begetting a new supply of wage-labour for fresh exploitation. Property, in its present form, is based on the antagonism of capital and wage-labour. Let us examine both sides of this antagonism.

To be a capitalist, is to have not only a purely personal, but a social, *status* in production. Capital is a collective product, and only by the united action of many members, nay, in the last resort, only by the united action of all members of society, can it be set in motion.

Capital is therefore not a personal, it is a social power.

When, therefore, capital is converted into common property, into the property of all members of society, personal property is not thereby transformed into social property. It is only the social character of the property that is changed. It loses its class character.

Let us now take wage-labour.

The average price of wage-labour is the minimum wage, i.e. that quantum of the means of subsistence which is absolutely requisite to keep the labourer in bare existence as a labourer. What, therefore, the wage-labourer appropriates by means of his labour, merely suffices to prolong and reproduce a bare existence. We by no means intend to abolish this personal appropriation of the products of labour, an appropriation that is made for the maintenance and reproduction of human life, and that leaves no surplus with which to command the labour of others. All that we want to do away with is the miserable character of this appropriation under which the labourer lives merely to increase capital, and is allowed to live only in so far as the interest of the ruling class requires it.

In bourgeois society, living labour is but a means to increase accumulated labour. In Communist society, accumulated labour is but a means to widen, to enrich, to promote the existence of the labourer.

In bourgeois society, therefore, the past dominates the present; in Communist society, the present dominates the past. In bourgeois society capital is independent and has individuality, while the living person is dependent and has no individuality.

And the abolition of this state of things is called by the bourgeois, abolition of individuality and freedom! And rightly so.

The abolition of bourgeois individuality, bourgeois independence, and bourgeois freedom is undoubtedly aimed at.

By freedom is meant, under the present bourgeois conditions of production, free trade, free selling and buying.

But if selling and buying disappears, free selling and buying disappears also. This talk about free selling and buying, and all the other 'brave words' of our bourgeoisie about freedom in general have a meaning, if any, only in contrast with restricted selling and buying, with the fettered traders of the Middle Ages, but have no meaning when opposed to the Communist abolition of buying and selling, of the bourgeois conditions of production, and of the bourgeoisie itself.

You are horrified at our intending to do away with private property. But in your existing society, private property is already done away with for nine-tenths of the population; its existence for the few is solely due to its non-existence in the hands of those nine-tenths. You reproach us, therefore, with intending to do away with a form of property, the necessary condition for whose existence is the non-existence of any property for the immense majority of society.

In one word, you reproach us with intending to do away with your property. Precisely so; that is just what we intend.

From the moment when labour can no longer be converted into capital, money, or rent, into a social power capable of being monopolised, i.e. from the moment when individual property can no longer be transformed into bourgeois property, into capital, from that moment, you say, individuality vanishes.

You must, therefore, confess that by 'individual' you mean no other person than the bourgeois, than the middle class owner of property. This person must, indeed, be swept out of the way, and made impossible.

Communism deprives no man of the power to appropriate the products of society; all that it does is to deprive him of the power to subjugate the labour of others by means of such appropriation.

It has been objected, that upon the abolition of private property all work will cease, and universal laziness will overtake us.

According to this, bourgeois society ought long ago to have gone to the dogs through sheer idleness; for those of its members who work, acquire nothing, and those who acquire anything, do not work. The whole of this objection is but another expression of the tautology: there can no longer be any wage-labour when there is no longer any capital.

All objections urged against the Communistic mode of producing and appropriating material products, have, in the same way, been urged against the Communistic modes of producing and appropriating intellectual products. Just as to the bourgeois, the disappearance of class property is the disappearance of production itself, so the disappearance of class culture is to him identical with the disappearance of all culture.

That culture, the loss of which he laments, is, for the enormous majority, a mere training to act as a machine.

But don't wrangle with us so long as you apply, to our intended abolition of bourgeois property, the standard of your bourgeois notions of freedom, culture, law, etc. Your very ideas are but the very outgrowth of the conditions of your bourgeois production and bourgeois property, just as your jurisprudence is but the will of your class made into a law for all, a will, whose essential character and direction are determined by the economical conditions of existence of your class.

The selfish misconception that induces you to transform into eternal laws of nature and of reason, the social forms springing from your present mode of production and form of property—historical relations that rise and disappear in the progress of production—this misconception you share with every ruling class that has preceded you. What you see clearly in the case of ancient property, what you admit in the case of feudal property, you are of course forbidden to admit in the case of your own bourgeois form of property.

Abolition of the family! Even the most radical flare up at this infamous proposal of the Communists.

On what foundation is the present family, the bourgeois family, based? On capital, on private gain. In its completely developed form this family exists only among the bourgeoisie. But this state of things finds its complement in the practical absence of the family among the proletarians, and in public prostitution.

The bourgeois family will vanish as a matter of course when its complement vanishes, and both will vanish with the vanishing of capital.

Do you charge us with wanting to stop the exploitation of children by their parents? To this crime we plead guilty.

But, you will say, we destroy the most hallowed of relations, when we replace home education by social.

And your education! Is not that also social, and determined by the social conditions under which you educate, by the intervention, direct or indirect, of society, by means of schools, etc? The Communists have not invented the intervention of society in education; they do but seek to alter the character of that intervention, and to rescue education from the influence of the ruling class.

The bourgeois claptrap about the family and education, about the hallowed correlation of parent and child, becomes all the more disgusting, the more, by the action of modern industry, all family ties among the proletarians are torn asunder, and their children transformed into simple articles of commerce and instruments of labour.

But you Communists would introduce community of women, screams the whole bourgeoisie in chorus.

The bourgeois sees in his wife a mere instrument of production. He hears that the instruments of production are to be exploited in common, and, naturally, can come to no other conclusion than that the lot of being common to all will likewise fall to the women.

He has not even a suspicion that the real point aimed at is to do away with the status of women as mere instruments of production.

For the rest, nothing is more ridiculous than the virtuous indignation of our bourgeois at the community of women which, they pretend, is to be openly and officially established by the Communists. The Communists have no need to introduce community of women; it has existed almost from time immemorial.

Our bourgeois, not content with having the wives and daughters of their proletarians at their disposal, not to speak of common prostitutes, take the greatest pleasure in seducing each other's wives.

Bourgeois marriage is in reality a system of wives in common and thus, at the most, what the Communists might possibly be reproached with is that they desire to introduce, in substitution for a hypocritically concealed, an openly legalised community of women. For the rest, it is self-evident, that the abolition of the present system of production must bring with it the abolition of the community of women springing from that system, i.e. of prostitution both public and private.

The Communists are further reproached with desiring to abolish countries and nationality.

The working men have no country. We cannot take from them what they have not got. Since the proletariat must first acquire political supremacy, must rise to be the leading class of the nation, must constitute itself *the* nation, it is, so far, itself national, though not in the bourgeois sense of the word.

National differences and antagonisms between peoples are daily more and more vanishing, owing to the development of the bourgeoisie to freedom of commerce, to the world market, to uniformity in the mode of production and in the conditions of life corresponding thereto.

The supremacy of the proletariat will cause them to vanish still faster. United action of the leading civilised countries at least, is one of the first conditions for the emancipation of the proletariat.

In proportion as the exploitation of one individual by another is put an end to, the exploitation of one nation by another will also be put an end to. In proportion as the antagonism between classes within the nation vanishes, the hostility of one nation to another will come to an end.

The charges against Communism made from a religious, a philosophical and, generally, from an ideological standpoint, are not deserving of serious examination.

Does it require deep intuition to comprehend that man's ideas, views, and conceptions, in one word, man's consciousness, changes with every change in the conditions of his material existence, in his social relations and in his social life?

What else does the history of ideas prove, than that intellectual production changes its character in proportion as material production is changed? The ruling ideas of each age have ever been the ideas of its ruling class.

When people speak of ideas that revolutionise society, they do but express the fact, that within the old society, the elements of a new one have been created, and that the dissolution of the old ideas keeps even pace with the dissolution of the old conditions of existence.

When the ancient world was in its last throes, the ancient religions were overcome by Christianity. When Christian ideas succumbed in the eighteenth century to rationalist ideas, feudal society fought its death-battle with the then revolutionary bourgeoisie. The ideas of religious liberty and freedom of conscience, merely gave expression to the sway of free competition within the domain of knowledge.

'Undoubtedly,' it will be said, 'religious, moral, philosophical and juridical ideas have been modified in the course of historical development. But religion, morality, philosophy, political science, and law, constantly survived this change'.

'There are, besides, eternal truths, such as Freedom, Justice, etc., that are common to all states of society. But Communism abolishes eternal truths, it abolishes all religion, and all morality, instead of constituting them on a new basis; it therefore acts in contradiction to all past historical experience'.

What does this accusation reduce itself to? The history of all past society has consisted in the development of class antagonisms, antagonisms that assumed different forms at different epochs.

But whatever form they may have taken, one fact is common to all past ages, viz. the exploitation of one part of society by the other. No wonder, then, that the social consciousness of past ages, despite all the multiplicity and variety it displays, moves within certain common forms, or general ideas, which cannot completely vanish except with the total disappearance of class antagonisms.

The Communist revolution is the most radical rupture with traditional property relations; no wonder that its development involves the most radical rupture with traditional ideas.

But let us have done with the bourgeois objections to Communism.

We have seen above, that the first step in the revolution by the working class, is to raise the proletariat to the position of ruling class, to win the battle of democracy.

The proletariat will use its political supremacy, to wrest, by degrees, all capital from the bourgeoisie, to centralise all instruments of production in the hands of the state, i.e. of the proletariat organised as the ruling class; and to increase the total of productive forces as rapidly as possible.

Of course, in the beginning, this cannot be effected except by means of despotic inroads on the rights of property, and on the conditions of bourgeois production; by means of measures, therefore, which appear economically insufficient and untenable, but which, in the course of the movement, outstrip themselves, necessitate further inroads upon the old social order, and are unavoidable as a means of entirely revolutionising the mode of production.

These measures will of course be different in different countries.

Nevertheless, in the most advanced countries, the following will be pretty generally applicable:

1. Abolition of property in land and application of all rents of land to public purposes.

2. A heavy progressive or graduated income tax.

3. Abolition of all right of inheritance.

4. Confiscation of the property of all emigrants and rebels.

5. Centralisation of credit in the hands of the state, by means of a national bank with state capital and an exclusive monopoly.

6. Centralisation of the means of communication and transport in the hands of the state.

7. Extension of factories and instruments of production owned by the state; the bringing into cultivation of waste lands, and the improvement of the soil generally in accordance with a common plan.

8. Equal obligation of all to work. Establishment of industrial armies, especially for agriculture.

9. Combination of agriculture with manufacturing industries; gradual abolition of the distinction between town and country, by a more equitable distribution of the population over the country.

10. Free education for all children in public schools. Abolition of children's factory labour in its present form. Combination of education with industrial production, etc.

When, in the course of development, class distinctions have disappeared, and all production has been concentrated in the hands of a vast association of the whole nation, the public power will lose its political character. Political power, properly so called, is merely the organised power of one class for oppressing another. If the proletariat during its contest with the bourgeoisie is compelled, by the force of circumstances, to organise itself as a class; if, by means of a revolution, it makes itself the ruling class, and, as such, sweeps away by force the old conditions of production, then it will, along with these conditions, have swept away the conditions for the existence of class antagonisms and of classes generally, and will thereby have abolished its own supremacy as a class.

In place of the old bourgeois society, with its classes and class antagonisms, we shall have an association, in which the free development of each is the condition for the free development of all.

From *Manifesto of the Communist Party* (1848).

SECTION B

DIALECTICAL MATERIALISM

MARX, *Preface to 'Critique of Political Economy'*

In the social production which men carry on they enter into definite relations that are indispensable and independent of their will; these relations of production correspond to a definite stage of development of their material forces of production. The sum total of these relations of production constitutes the economic structure of society—the real foundation, on which rises a legal and political superstructure and to which correspond definite forms of social consciousness. The mode of production in material life determines the social, political and intellectual life process in general. It is not the consciousness of men that determines their being, but on the contrary, their social being that determines their consciousness. At a certain stage of their development, the material forces of production in society come in conflict with the existing relations of production, or—what is but a legal expression for the same thing—with the property relations within which they have been at work before. From forms of development of the forces of production these relations turn into their fetters. Then begins an epoch of social revolution. With the change of the economic foundation the entire immense superstructure is more or less rapidly transformed. In considering such transformations a distinction should always be made between the material transformation of the economic conditions of production, which can be determined with the precision of natural science, and legal, political, religious, aesthetic or philosophic—in short, ideological forms in which men become conscious of this conflict and fight it out. Just as our opinion of an individual is not based on what he thinks of himself, so can we not judge of such a period of transformation by its own consciousness; on the contrary, this consciousness must be explained rather from the contradictions of material life, from the existing conflict between the social forces of production and the relations of production. No social order ever disappears before all the productive forces for which there is room in it have been developed: and new higher relations of production never appear before the material conditions of their existence have matured in the womb of the old society itself. Therefore, mankind always sets itself only such tasks as it can solve; since, looking at the matter more closely, we will always find that the task itself arises only when the material conditions necessary for its solution already exist or are at least in the process of formation.

(1859)

ENGELS, *Anti-Dühring*

The materialist conception of history starts from the proposition that the production (of the means to support human life) and, next to production, the exchange of things produced, is the basis of all social structure; that in every society that has appeared in history, the manner in which wealth is distributed and society divided into classes or orders is dependent upon what is produced, how it is produced, and how the products are exchanged. From this point of view the final causes of all social changes and political revolutions are to be sought, not in men's brains, not in man's better insight into eternal truth and justice, but in changes in the modes of production and exchange. They are to be sought, not in the *philosophy*, but in the *economics* of each particular epoch. The growing perception that existing social institutions are unreasonable and unjust, that reason has become unreason, and right wrong, is only proof that in the modes of production and exchange changes have silently taken place with which the social order, adapted to earlier economic conditions, is no longer in keeping. From this it also follows that the means of getting rid of the incongruities that have been brought to light must also be present, in a more or less developed condition, within the changed modes of production themselves. These means are not to be *invented*, spun out of the head, but *discovered* with the aid of the head in the existing material facts of production.

What is, then, the position of modern socialism in this connection?

The present structure of society—this is now pretty generally conceded—is the creation of the ruling class of today, of the bourgeoisie. The mode of production peculiar to the bourgeoisie, known, since Marx, as the capitalist mode of production, was incompatible with the local privileges and the privileges of estate as well as with the reciprocal personal ties of the feudal system. The bourgeoisie broke up the feudal system and built upon its ruins the capitalist order of society, the kingdom of free competition, of personal liberty, of the equality, before the law, of all commodity owners, of all the rest of the capitalist blessings. Thenceforward the capitalist mode of production could develop in freedom. Since steam, machinery, and the making of machines by machinery transformed the older manufacture into modern industry, the productive forces evolved under the guidance of the bourgeoisie developed with a rapidity and in a degree unheard of before. But just as the older manufacture, in its time, and handicraft, becoming more developed under its influence, had come into collision with the feudal trammels of the guilds, so now modern industry, in its more complete development, comes into collision with the bounds within which the capitalistic mode of production holds it confined. The new productive forces have already outgrown the capitalistic mode of using them. And this conflict between productive forces and modes of production is not a conflict engendered in the mind of man, like that between original sin and divine justice. It exists, in fact, objectively, outside us, independently of the will and actions even of the men that have brought it on. Modern socialism is nothing but the reflex, in thought, of this conflict in fact; its ideal reflection in the minds, first, of the class directly suffering under it, the working class.

From *Anti-Dühring* (1877), pt. III, ch. II
(Foreign Languages Publishing House, Moscow, 1954),
pp. 369-71.

STALIN, *History of the Communist Party of the Soviet Union*

What, then, is the chief force in the complex of conditions of material life of society which determines the physiognomy of society, the character of the social system, the development of society from one system to another?

This force, historical materialism holds, is the *method of procuring the means of life* necesssary for human existence, the *mode of production of material values*—food, clothing, footwear, houses, fuel, instruments of production, etc.—which are indispensable for the life and development of society.

In order to live, people must have food, clothing, footwear, shelter, fuel, etc.; in order to have these material values, people must produce them; and in order to produce them, people must have the instruments of production with which food, clothing, footwear, shelter, fuel, etc., are produced; they must be able to produce these instruments and to use them.

The *instruments of production* wherewith material values are produced, the *people* who operate the instruments of production and carry on the production of material values thanks to a certain *production experience* and *labour skill*—all these elements jointly constitute the *productive forces* of society.

But the productive forces are only one aspect of production, only one aspect of the mode of production, an aspect that expresses the relation of men to the objects and forces of nature which they make use of for the production of material values. Another aspect of production, another aspect of the mode of production, is the relation of men to each other in the process of production, men's *relations of production.* Men carry on a struggle against nature and utilise nature for the production of material values not in isolation from each other, not as separate individuals, but in common, in groups, in societies. Production, therefore, is at all times and under all conditions *social* production. In the production of material values men enter into mutual relations of one kind or another within production, into relations of production of one kind or another. These may be relations of co-operation and mutual help between people who are free from exploitation; they may be relations of domination and subordination; and, lastly, they may be transitional from one form of relations of production to another. But whatever the character of the relations or production may be always and in every system, they constitute just as essential an element of production as the productive forces of society.

In production, [Marx says] men not only act on nature but also on one another. They produce only by co-operating in a certain way and mutually exchanging their activities. In order to produce, they enter into definite connections and relations with one another and only within these social connections does their action on nature, does production, take place.

Consequently, production, the mode of production, embraces both the productive forces of society and men's relations of production, and is thus the embodiment of their unity in the process of production of material values.

One of the features of production is that it never stays at one point for a long time and is always in a state of change and development, and that, furthermore, changes in the mode of production inevitably call forth changes in the whole social system, social ideas, political views and political institutions—they call forth a reconstruction of the whole social and political order. At different stages of development people make use of different modes of production, or, to put it more crudely, lead different manners of life. In the primitive commune there is one mode of production, under slavery there is another mode of production, under feudalism a third mode of production, and so on. And, correspondingly, men's social system, the spiritual life of men, their views and political institutions also vary.

Whatever is the mode of production of a society, such in the main is the society itself, its ideas and theories, its political views and institutions.

Or, to put it more crudely, whatever is man's manner of life, such is his manner of thought....

... *A second feature* of production is that its changes and development always begin with changes and development of the productive forces, and in the first place, with changes and development of the instruments of production. Productive forces are therefore the most mobile and revolutionary element of production. First, the productive forces of society change and develop, and then, *depending* on these changes and *in conformity with them*, men's relations of production, their economic relations, change. This, however, does not mean that the relations of production do not influence the development of the productive forces and that the latter are not dependent on the former....

Whatever are the productive forces such must be the relations of production ...

... Five *main* types of relations of production are known to history: primitive communal, slave, feudal, capitalist and socialist.

The basis of the relations of production under the primitive communal system is that the means of production are socially owned. This in the main corresponds to the character of the productive forces of that period. Stone tools, and later, the bow and arrow, precluded the possibility of men individually combating the forces of nature and beasts of prey. In order to gather the fruits of the forest, to catch fish, to build some sort of habitation, men were obliged to work in common if they did not want to die of starvation, or fall victim to beasts of prey or to neighbouring societies. Labour in common led to the common ownership of the means of production, as well as of the fruits of production. Here the conception of private ownership of the means of production did not yet exist, except for the personal ownership of certain implements of production which were at the same time means of defence against beasts of prey. Here there was no exploitation, no classes.

The basis of the relations of production under the slave system is that the slave owner owns the means of production; he also owns the worker in production—the slave, whom he can sell, purchase, or kill as though he were an animal. Such relations of production in the main correspond to the state of the productive forces of that period. Instead of stone tools, men now have metal tools at their command; instead of the wretched and primitive husbandry of the hunter, who knew neither pasturage nor tillage, there now appear pasturage, tillage, handicrafts, and a division of labour between the branches of production. There appears the possibility of the exchange of products between individuals and between societies, of the accumulation of wealth in the hands of a few, the actual accumulation of the means of production in the hands of a minority, and the possibility of subjugation of the majority by a minority and their conversion into slaves. Here we no longer find the common and free labour of all members of society in the production process—here there prevails the forced labour of slaves, who are exploited by the non-labouring slave owners. Here, therefore, there is no common ownership of the means of production or of the fruits of production. It is replaced by private ownership. Here the slave owner appears as the prime and principal property owner in the full sense of the term.

Rich and poor, exploiters and exploited, people with full rights and people with no rights, and a fierce class struggle between them—such is the picture of the slave system. The basis of the relations of production under the feudal system is that the feudal lord owns the means of production and does not fully own the worker in production—the serf, whom the feudal lord can no longer kill, but whom he can buy and sell. Alongside of feudal ownership there exists individual ownership by the peasant and the handicraftsman of his implements of production and his private enterprise based on his personal labour. Such relations of production in the main correspond to the state of the productive forces of that period. Further improvements in the smelting and working of iron; the spread of the iron plough and the loom; the further development of agriculture, horticulture, viniculture, and dairying; the appearance of manufactories alongside of the handicraft workshops—such are the characteristic features of the state of the productive forces.

The new productive forces demand that the labourer shall display some kind of initiative in production and an inclination for work, and interest in work. The feudal lord therefore discards the slave as a labourer who has no interest in work and is entirely without initiative, and prefers to deal with the serf who has his own husbandry, implements of production, and a certain interest in work essential for the cultivation of the land and for the payment in kind of a part of his harvest to the feudal lord.

Here private ownership is further developed. Exploitation is nearly as severe as it was under slavery—it is only slightly mitigated. A class struggle between exploiters and exploited is the principal feature of the feudal system.

The basis of the relations of production under the capitalist system is that the capitalist owns the means of production, but not the workers in production—the wage labourers, whom the capitalist can neither kill nor sell because they are personally free, but who are deprived of means of production and, in order not to die of hunger, are obliged to sell their labour power to the capitalist and to bear the yoke of exploitation. Alongside of capitalist property in the means of production, we find, at first on a wide scale, private property of the peasants and handicraftsmen in the means of production, these peasants and handicraftsmen no longer being serfs, and their private property being based on personal labour. In place of the handicraft workshops and manufactories there appear huge mills and factories equipped with machinery. In place of the manorial estates tilled by the primitive implements of production of the peasant, there now appear large capitalist farms run on scientific lines and supplied with agricultural machinery.

The new productive forces require that the workers in production shall be better educated and more intelligent than the downtrodden and ignorant serfs, that they are able to understand machinery and operate it properly. Therefore, the capitalists prefer to deal with wage workers who are free from the bonds of serfdom and who are educated enough to be able properly to operate machinery.

But having developed productive forces to a tremendous extent capitalism has become enmeshed in contradictions which it is unable to solve. By producing larger and larger quantities of commodities, and reducing their prices, capitalism intensifies competition, ruins the mass of small and medium private owners, converts them into proletarians and reduces their purchasing power, with the result that it becomes impossible to dispose of the commodities produced. On the other hand, by expanding production and concentrating millions of workers in huge mills and factories, capitalism lends the process of production a social character and thus undermines its own foundation, inasmuch as the social character of the process of production demands the social ownership of the means of production; yet the means of production remain private capitalist property, which is incompatible with the social character of the process of production.

These irreconcilable contradictions between the character of the productive forces and the relations of production make themselves felt in periodical crises of overproduction, when the capitalists, finding no effective demand for their goods owing to the ruin of the mass of the population which they themselves have brought about, are compelled to burn products, destroy manufactured goods, suspend production, and destroy productive forces at a time when millions of people are forced to suffer unemployment and starvation, not because there are not enough goods, but because there is an overproduction of goods.

This means that the capitalist relations of production have ceased to correspond to the state of productive forces of society and have come into irreconcilable contradiction with them.

This means that capitalism is pregnant with revolution, whose mission it is to replace the existing capitalist ownership of the means of production by socialist ownership.

This means that the main feature of the capitalist system is a most acute class struggle between the exploiters and the exploited.

The basis of the relations of production under the socialist system, which has so far been established only in the U.S.S.R., is the social ownership of the means of production. Here there are no longer exploiters and exploited. The goods produced are distributed according to labour performed on the principle: 'He who does not work neither shall he eat'. Here the mutual relations of people in the process of production are marked by comradely co-operation and the socialist mutual assistance of workers who are free from exploitation. Here the relations of production fully correspond to the state of productive forces, for the social character of the process of production is reinforced by the social ownership of the means of production.

From *History of the Communist Party of the Soviet Union* (1938), ch. IV, pt. II
(Foreign Languages Publishing House, Moscow, 1941).

SECTION C

ECONOMIC ANALYSIS

MARX, *Production of Surplus Value*

When he came to explain how the capitalist system works, and in particular how capital is accumulated and surplus-value created, Marx put forward a hypothetic manufacturing example—the process by which 10 lb. of cotton are turned into 10 lb. of yarn, assuming that labour costs three shillings a day.

... Let us now examine production as a creation of value.

We know that the value of each commodity is determined by the quantity of labour expended on and materialised in it, by the working-time necessary, under given social conditions, for its production. This rule also holds good in the case of the product that accrued to our capitalist, as the result of the labour-process carried on for him. Assuming this product to be 10 lb. of yarn, our first step is to calculate the quantity of labour realised in it.

For spinning the yarn, raw material is required; suppose in this case 10 lb. of cotton. We have no need at present to investigate the value of this cotton, for our capitalist has, we will assume, bought it at its full value, say of ten shillings. In this price the labour required for the production of the cotton is already expressed in terms of the average labour of society. We will further assume that the wear and tear of the spindle, which, for our present purpose, may represent all other instruments of labour employed, amounts to the value of two shillings. If, then, twenty-four hours' labour, or two working-days, are required to produce the quantity of gold represented by twelve shillings, we have here, to begin with, two days' labour already incorporated in the yarn....

The labour required for the production of the cotton, the raw material of the yarn, is part of the labour necessary to produce the yarn, and is therefore contained in the yarn. The same applies to the labour embodied in the spindle, without whose wear and tear the cotton could not be spun.

Hence, in determining the value of the yarn, or the labour-time required for its production, all the special processes carried on at various times and in different places, which were necessary, first to produce the cotton and the wasted portion of the spindle, and then with the cotton and spindle to spin the yarn, may together be looked on as different and successive phases of one and the same process. The whole of the labour in the yarn is past labour; and it is a matter of no importance that the operations necessary for the production of its constituent elements were carried on at times which, referred to the present, are more remote than the final operation of spinning . . . .

The raw material serves . . . merely as an absorbent of a definite quantity of labour. By this absorption it is in fact changed into yarn, because it is spun, because labour-power in the form of spinning is added to it; but the product, the yarn, is now nothing more than a measure of the labour absorbed by the cotton. If in one hour $1\frac{2}{3}$ lb. of cotton can be spun into $1\frac{2}{3}$ lb. of yarn, then 10 lb. of yarn indicate the absorption of six hours' labour. Definite quantities of product, these quantities being determined by experience, now represent nothing but definite quantities of labour, definite masses of crystallised labour time. They are nothing more than the materialisation of so many hours or so many days of social labour . . . .

We assumed, on the occasion of its sale, that the value of a day's labour-power is three shillings, and that six hours' labour is incorporated in that sum; and consequently that this amount of labour is requisite to produce the necessaries of life daily required on an average by the labourer. If now our spinner by working for one hour, can convert $1\frac{2}{3}$ lb. of cotton into $1\frac{2}{3}$ lb. of yarn,[1] it follows that in six hours he will convert 10 lb. of cotton into 10 lb. of yarn. Hence, during the spinning process, the cotton absorbs six hours' labour. The same quantity of labour is also embodied in a piece of gold of the value of three shillings. Consequently by the mere labour of spinning, a value of three shillings is added to the cotton.

Let us now consider the total value of the product, the 10 lb. of yarn. Two and a half days' labour has been embodied in it, of which two days were contained in the cotton and in the substance of the spindle worn away, and half a day was absorbed during the process of spinning. This two and a half days' labour is also represented by a piece of gold of the value of fifteen shillings. Hence, fifteen shillings is an adequate price for the

[1] These figures are quite arbitrary.

10 lb. of yarn, or the price of one pound is eighteen pence.

Our capitalist stares in astonishment. The value of the product is exactly equal to the value of the capital advanced. The value so advanced has not expanded, no surplus-value has been created, and consequently money has not been converted into capital. The price of the yarn is fifteen shillings, and fifteen shillings were spent in the open market upon the constituent elements of the product, or, what amounts to the same thing, upon the factors of the labour-process; ten shillings were paid for the cotton, two shillings for the substance of the spindle worn away, and three shillings for the labour-power. The swollen value of the yarn is of no avail, for it is merely the sum of the values formerly existing in the cotton, the spindle, and the labour-power: out of such a simple addition of existing values, no surplus-value can possibly arise. These separate values are now all concentrated in one thing; but so they were also in the sum of fifteen shillings, before it was split up into three parts, by the purchase of the commodities.

There is in reality nothing very strange in this result. The value of one pound of yarn being eighteen pence, if our capitalist buys 10 lb. of yarn in the market, he must pay fifteen shillings for them. It is clear that, whether a man buys his house ready built, or gets it built for him, in neither case will the mode of acquisition increase the amount of money laid out on the house.

Our capitalist, who is at home in his vulgar economy, exclaims: 'Oh! but I advanced my money for the express purpose of making more money'. The way to Hell is paved with good intentions, and he might just as easily have intended to make money, without producing at all. He threatens all sorts of things. He won't be caught napping again. In future he will buy the commodities in the market, instead of manufacturing them himself. But if all his brother capitalists were to do the same, where would he find his commodities in the market? And his money he cannot eat. He tries persuasion. 'Consider my abstinence; I might have played ducks and drakes with the fifteen shillings; but instead of that I consumed it productively, and made yarn with it'. Very well, and by way of reward he is now in possession of good yarn instead of a bad conscience; and as for playing the part of a miser, it would never do for him to relapse into such bad ways as that; we have seen before to what results such asceticism leads. Besides, where nothing is, the king has lost his rights; whatever may be the merit of his abstinence, there is nothing wherewith specially to remunerate it, because the value of the product is merely the sum of the values of the commodities that were thrown into the process of production. Let him therefore console himself with the reflection that virtue is its own reward. But no, he becomes importunate. He says: 'The yarn is of no use to me: I produced it for sale'. In that case let him sell it, or, still better, let him for the future produce only things for satisfying his personal wants, a remedy that his physician MacCulloch has already prescribed as infallible against an epidemic of overproduction. He now gets obstinate. 'Can the labourer', he asks, 'merely with his arms and legs, produce commodities out of nothing? Did I not supply him with the materials, by means of which, and in which alone, his labour could be embodied? And as the greater part of society consists of such ne'er-do-wells, have I not rendered society incalculable service by my instruments of production, my cotton and my spindle, and not only society, but the labourer also, whom in addition I have provided with the necessaries of life? And am I to be allowed nothing in return for all this service?' Well, but has not the labourer rendered him the equivalent service of changing his cotton and spindle into yarn? Moreover, there is here no question of service. A service is nothing more than the useful effect of a use-value, be it of a commodity, or be it of labour. But here we are dealing with the exchange-value. The capitalist paid to the labourer a value of three shillings, and the labourer gave him back an exact equivalent in the value of three shillings, added by him to the cotton: he gave him value for value. Our friend, up to this time so purse-proud, suddenly assumes the modest demeanour of his own workman, and exclaims: 'Have I myself not worked? Have I not performed the labour of superintendence and of overlooking the spinner? And does not this labour, too, create value?' His overlooker and his manager try to hide their smiles. Meanwhile, after a hearty laugh, he reassumes his usual mien. Though he chanted to us the whole creed of the economists, in reality, he says, he would not give a brass farthing for it. He leaves this and all such like subterfuges and juggling tricks to the professors of Political Economy, who are paid for it. He himself is a practical man; and though he does not always consider what he says outside his business, yet in his business he knows what he is about.

Let us examine the matter more closely. The value of a day's labour-power amounts to three shillings, because on our assumption half a day's labour is embodied in that quantity of labour-power, i.e. because the means of subsistence that are daily required for the production of labour-power, cost half a day's labour. But the past labour that is embodied in the labour-power, and the living labour that it can call into action; the daily cost of maintaining it, and its daily expenditure in work, are two totally different things. The former determines the exchange-value of the labour-power, the latter is its use-value. The fact that half a day's labour is necessary to keep the labourer alive during twenty-four hours, does not in any way prevent him from working a whole day. Therefore, the value of labour-power, and the value which that labour-power creates in the labour-process, are two entirely different magnitudes: and this difference of the two values was what the capitalist had in view, when he was purchasing the labour-power. The useful qualities that labour-power possesses, and by virtue of which it makes yarn or boots, were to him nothing more than a *conditio sine qua non;* for in order to create value, labour must be expended in a useful manner. What really influenced him was the specific use-value which this commodity possesses of being *a source not only of value, but of more value than it has itself.* This is the special service that the capitalist expects from labour-power, and in this transaction he acts in accordance with the 'eternal laws' of the exchange of commodities. The seller of labour-power, like the seller of any other commodity, realises its exchange-value, and parts with its use-value. He cannot take the one without giving the other. The use-value of labour-power, or in other words, labour, belongs just as little to its seller, as the use-value of oil after it has been sold belongs to the dealer who has sold it. The owner of the money has paid the value of a day's labour-power; his, therefore, is the use of it for a day's labour belongs to him. The circumstance, that on the one hand the daily sustenance of labour-power costs only half a day's labour, while on the other hand the very same labour-power can work during a whole day, that consequently the value which its use during one day creates, is double what he pays for that use, this circumstance is, without doubt, a piece of good luck for the buyer, but by no means an injury to the seller.

Our capitalist foresaw this state of things, and that was the cause of his laughter. The labourer therefore finds, in the workshop, the means of production necessary for working, not only during six, but during twelve hours. Just as during the six hours' process our 10 lb. of cotton absorbed six hours' labour, and became 10 lb. of yarn, so now, 20 lb. of cotton will absorb twelve hours' labour and be changed into 20 lb. of yarn. Let us now examine the product of this prolonged process. There is now materialised in this 20 lb. of yarn the labour of five days, of which four days are due to the cotton and the lost steel of the spindle, the remaining day having been absorbed by the cotton during the spinning process. Expressed in gold, the labour of five days is thirty shillings. This is therefore the price of the 20 lb. of yarn, giving, as before, eighteen pence as the price of a pound. But the sum of the values of the commodities that entered into the process amounts to twenty-seven shillings. The value of the yarn is thirty shillings. Therefore the value of the product is $\frac{1}{9}$ greater than the value advanced for its production; twenty-seven shillings have been transformed into thirty shillings; a surplus-value of three shillings has been created. The trick has at last succeeded; money has been converted into capital.

From *Capital* (1867), vol. I, pt. III, ch. VII, sect. 2. (Foreign Languages Publishing House, Moscow, 1954), pp. 186-194. (Published in Great Britain by Lawrence and Wishart.)

MARX, *Effect of Capitalist Accumulation on the Working Class*

In his analysis of capitalism Marx attempts to show how the capitalist system creates an army of unemployed which can be pressed into service at times of boom and left to pauperism when trade is slack.

The lowest sediment of the relative surplus-population finally dwells in the sphere of pauperism. Exclusive of vagabonds, criminals, prostitutes, in a word, the 'dangerous' classes, this layer of society consists of three categories. First, those able to work. One need only glance superficially at the statistics of English pauperism to find that the quantity of paupers increases with every crisis, and diminishes with every revival of trade. Second, orphans and pauper children. These are candidates for the industrial reserve army, and are, in times of great prosperity, as 1860, e.g. speedily and in large numbers enrolled in the active army of labourers. Third, the demoralised and ragged, and those unable to work, chiefly people who succumb to their incapacity for adaptation, due to the division of labour; people who have passed the normal age of the labourer; the victims of industry, whose number increases with the increase of dangerous machinery, of mines, chemical works, etc., the mutilated, the sickly, the widows, etc. Pauperism is the hospital of the active labour-army and the dead weight of the industrial reserve army. Its production is included in that of the relative surplus-population, its necessity in theirs; along with the surplus-population, pauperism forms a condition of capitalist production, and of the capitalist development of wealth. It enters into the *faux frais* of capitalist production; but capital knows how to throw these, for the most part, from its own shoulders on to those of the working class and the lower middle class.

The greater the social wealth, the functioning capital, the extent and energy of its growth, and, therefore, also the absolute mass of the proletariat and the productiveness of its labour, the greater is the industrial reserve army. The same causes which develop the expansive power of capital, develop also the labour-power at its disposal. The relative mass of the industrial reserve army increases therefore with the potential energy of wealth. But the greater this reserve army in proportion to the active labour-army, the greater is the mass of a consolidated surplus-population, whose misery is in inverse ratio to its torment of labour. The more extensive, finally, the Lazarus-layers of the working class, and the industrial reserve army, the greater is official pauperism. *This is the absolute general law of capitalist accumulation.* Like all other laws it is modified in its working by many circumstances, the analysis of which does not concern us here.

The folly is now patent of the economic wisdom that preaches to the labourers the accommodation of their number to the requirements of capital. The mechanism of capitalist production and accumulation constantly effects this adjustment. The first word of this adaptation is the creation of a relative surplus-population, or industrial reserve army. Its last word is the misery of constantly extending strata of the active army of labour, and the dead weight of pauperism.

The law by which a constantly increasing quantity of means of production, thanks to the advance in the productiveness of social labour, may be set in movement by a progressively diminishing expenditure of human power, this law, in a capitalist society—where the labourer does not employ the means of production, but the means of production employ the labourer—undergoes a complete inversion and is expressed thus: the higher the productiveness of labour, the greater is the pressure of the labourers on the means of employment, the more precarious, therefore, becomes their condition of existence, viz., the sale of their own labour-power for the increasing of another's wealth, or for the self-expansion of capital. The fact that the means of production, and the productiveness of labour, increase more rapidly than the productive population, expresses itself, therefore, capitalistically in the inverse form that the labouring population always increases more rapidly than the conditions under which capital can employ this increase for its own self-expansion.

From *Capital* (1867), vol. I, pt. VII, ch. XXV, sect. 4 (Foreign Languages Publishing House, Moscow, 1954), pp. 643-5. (Published in Great Britain by Lawrence and Wishart.)

MARX, *Effect of Capitalist Accumulation on the Concentration of Wealth and Poverty*

The historical tendency of Capitalist accumulation: the concentration of industrial activity . . . 'the rich get richer and the poor get poorer . . .'.

The private property of the labourer in his means of production is the foundation of petty industry, whether agricultural, manufacturing, or both; petty industry, again, is an essential condition for the development of social production and of the free individuality of the labourer himself. Of course, this petty mode of production exists also under slavery, serfdom, and other states of dependence. But it flourishes, it lets loose its whole energy, it attains its adequate classical form, only where the labourer is the private owner of his own means of labour set in action by himself: the peasant of the land which he cultivates, the artisan of the tool which he handles as a virtuoso. This mode of production presupposes parcelling of the soil, and scattering of the other means of production. As it excludes the concentration of these means of production, so also it excludes co-operation, division of labour within each separate process of production, the control over, and the productive application of the forces of Nature by society, and the free development of the social productive powers. It is compatible only with a system of production, and a society, moving within narrow and more or less primitive bounds. To perpetuate it would be, as Pecqueur rightly says, 'to decree universal mediocrity'. At a certain stage of development it brings forth the material agencies for its own dissolution. From that moment new forces and new passions spring up in the bosom of society; but the old social organisation fetters them and keeps them down. It must be annihilated; it is annihilated. Its annihilation, the transformation of the individualised and scattered means of production into socially concentrated ones, of the pigmy property of the many into the huge property of the few, the expropriation of the great mass of the people from the soil, from the means of subsistence, and from the means of labour, this fearful and painful expropriation of the mass of the people forms the prelude to the history of capital. It comprises a series of forcible methods, of which we have passed in review only those that have been epoch-making as methods of the primitive accumulation of capital. The expropriation of the immediate producers was accomplished with merciless Vandalism, and under the stimulus of passions the most infamous, the most sordid, the pettiest, the most meanly odious. Self-earned private property, that is based, so to say, on the fusing together of the isolated, independent labouring-individual with the conditions of his labour, is supplanted by capitalistic private property, which rests on exploitation of the nominally free labour of others, i.e. on wages-labour.

As soon as this process of transformation has sufficiently decomposed the old society from top to bottom, as soon as the labourers are turned into proletarians, their means of labour into capital, as soon as the capitalist mode of production stands on its own feet, then the further socialisation of labour and further transformation of the land and other means of production into socially exploited and, therefore, common means of production, as well as the further expropriation of private proprietors, takes a new form. That which is now to be expropriated is no longer the labourer working for himself, but the capitalist exploiting many labourers. This expropriation is accomplished by the action of the immanent laws of capitalistic production itself, by the centralisation of capital. One capitalist always kills many. Hand in hand with this centralisation, or this expropriation of many capitalists by few, develop, on an ever-extending scale, the co-operative form of the labour-process, the conscious technical application of science, the methodical cultivation of the soil, the transformation of the instruments of labour into instruments of labour only usable in common, the economising of all means of production by their use as the means of production of combined, socialised labour, the entanglement of all peoples in the net of the world-market, and with this, the international character of the capitalistic regime. Along with the constantly diminishing number of the magnates of capital, who usurp and monopolise all advantages of this process of transformation, grows the mass of misery, oppression, slavery, degradation, exploitation; but with this too grows the revolt of the working-class, a class always increasing in numbers, and disciplined, united, organised by the very mechanism of the process of capitalist production itself. The monopoly of capital becomes a fetter upon the mode of production, which has sprung up and flourished along with, and under it. Centralisation of the means of production and socialisation of labour at last reach a point where they become incompatible with their capitalist integument. This integument is burst asunder. The knell of capitalist private property sounds. The expropriators are expropriated.

From *Capital* (1867), vol. III, pt. VIII, ch. XXXII, (Foreign Languages Publishing House, Moscow, 1954) pp. 761-3. (Published in Great Britain by Lawrence and Wishart.)

LENIN, *Imperialism*

By its economic essence imperialism is monopolist capitalism. This fact alone determines the place of imperialism in history, for monopoly growing up on the basis of free competition, and precisely out of free competition, is the transition from the capitalist to a higher social economic order. We must take special note of four main aspects of monopolies, or principal manifestations of monopoly capitalism, which are characteristic of the period under discussion.

First, monopoly arose out of the concentration of production at a very high stage of development. This refers to the monopolist capitalist combines: cartels, syndicates and trusts. We have seen the important part they play in modern economic life. Towards the beginning of the twentieth century, they acquired complete supremacy in the advanced countries, and although the initial steps towards the formation of combines were first taken by countries with high protective tariffs (Germany, America), Great Britain, with her system of free trade, was not far behind in revealing the same fundamental fact, namely, the birth of monopolies out of the concentration of production.

Second, monopolies have accelerated seizure of the most important sources of raw materials, especially for the coal and iron industry, which is the basic and most highly trustified industry in capitalist society. The monopolistic control of the most important sources of raw materials has enormously increased the power of big capital, and has sharpened the antagonism between trustified and non-trustified industry.

Third, monopoly arose out of the banks. The banks changed from modest intermediary enterprises into the monopolists of finance capital. Some three or five of the biggest banks in any of the most advanced capitalist countries have achieved a 'personal union' of industrial and banking capital, and have concentrated in their hands the control of billions upon billions, which form the greatest part of the capital and revenue of an entire country. A financial oligarchy, creating a close network of ties of dependence upon all the economic and political institutions of contemporary bourgeois society without exception—this is the most striking manifestation of this monopoly.

Fourth, monopoly arose out of colonial policy. To the numerous 'old' motives of colonial policy finance capital has added the struggle for sources of raw materials, for the export of capital, for 'spheres of influence', i.e. spheres of good business, concessions, monopolist profits, and so on; in fine, for economic territory in general. When the colonies of the European powers in Africa comprised only one-tenth of that territory, as was still the case in 1876, colonial policy was able to develop in a non-monopolist manner, like 'freebooters' taking land, so to speak. But when nine-tenths of Africa had been seized (by 1900); when the whole world had been divided up, there was inevitably ushered in a period of monopolist possession of colonies, and, consequently, of particularly intense struggle for the partition and for the re-partition of the world.

The extent to which monopolist capital has intensified all the contradictions of capitalism is generally known. It is sufficient to mention the high cost of living and the heavy hand of the cartels. This intensification of contradictions constitutes the most powerful driving force in the transitional period of history, which began at the time of the final victory of world finance capital.

Monopolies, oligarchy, striving for domination instead of striving for liberty, exploitation of an increasing number of small or weak nations by an extremely small group of the richest or most powerful nations—all these have given birth to those distinctive characteristics of imperialism which compel us to define it as parasitic or decaying capitalism. More and more prominently there appears, as one of the tendencies of imperialism, the creation of the 'rentier-state,' the usurer state, whose bourgeoisie lives more and more on capital exports and by 'clipping coupons'. It would be a mistake to believe that this tendency to decay precludes a rapid growth of capitalism. It does not; in the epoch of imperialism, now one, now another of these tendencies is displayed, to greater or less degree by certain branches of industry, by certain strata of the bourgeoisie, and by individual countries. As a whole, capitalism is growing far more rapidly than before, but not only is this growth becoming more and more uneven, but also this unevenness is showing itself in particular in the decay of the countries which are richest in capital (such as England).

From *Imperialism: the Highest Stage of Capitalism* (1917), ch. x, 'The Place of Imperialism in History'.

Three years after *Imperialism, the Highest Stage of Capitalism* first appeared in 1917, Lenin wrote a preface to the French and German editions. This provided a footnote to the general analysis of imperialism, to explain the behaviour of Socialist parties outside Russia.

The international split of the whole labour movement is now quite evident (Second and Third Internationals). Armed struggle and civil war between the two tendencies is now an established fact: the support given to Kolchak and Denikin by the Mensheviks and 'Socialist-Revolutionaries' against the Bolsheviks in Russia; the Scheidemanns, Noskes and Co., in conjunction with the bourgeoisie against the Spartacists in Germany; the same thing in Finland, Poland, Hungary, etc. What then, is the economic basis of this world-historic phenomenon?

Precisely the parasitism and decay of capitalism which are the characteristic features of its highest historic stage, i.e., imperialism. As has been proven in this book, capitalism has brought to the fore a handful (less than a tenth of the inhabitants of the globe; less than one-fifth, if most 'generously' and liberally calculated) of particularly rich and powerful states which plunder the whole world by simply 'clipping coupons'. Capital exports yield a return of 8 to 10 billion francs per year at pre-war prices, according to pre-war bourgeois statistics. Now, of course, it is much more.

Obviously, out of such enormous *super-profits* (since they are obtained over and above the profits which capitalists squeeze out of the workers of their 'own' country) *it is possible to bribe* the labour leaders and an upper stratum of the labour aristocracy. And the capitalists of the 'advanced' countries do bribe them; they bribe them in a thousand different ways, direct and indirect, overt and covert.

This stratum of bourgeoisified workers or 'labour aristocracy', who have become completely petty-bourgeois in their mode of life, in the amount of their earnings, and their point of view, serve as the main support of the Second International, and, in our day, the principal *social* (not military) *support of the bourgeoisie.* They are the real *agents of the bourgeoisie in the labour movement,* the labour lieutenants of the capitalist class, the real carriers of reformism and chauvinism . . . .

From *Imperialism: The Highest Stage of Capitalism,* (1920),
Preface to the French and German editions.

SECTION D

THE STATE

ENGELS, *Barbarism and Civilisation*

... The state is, therefore, by no means a power forced on society from without; just as little is it 'the reality of the ethical idea', 'the image and reality of reason', as Hegel maintains. Rather, it is a product of society at a certain stage of development; it is the admission that this society has become entangled in an insoluble contradiction with itself, that it is cleft into irreconcilable antagonisms which it is powerless to dispel. But in order that these antagonisms, classes with conflicting economic interests, might not consume themselves and society in sterile struggle, a power seemingly standing above society became necessary for the purpose of moderating the conflict, of keeping it within the bounds of 'order'; and this power, arisen out of society, but placing itself above it, and increasingly alienating itself from it, is the state ...

... As the state arose from the need to hold class antagonisms in check, but as it arose, at the same time, in the midst of the conflict of these classes, it is, as a rule, the state of the most powerful, economically dominant class, which, through the medium of the state, becomes also the politically dominant class, and thus acquires new means of holding down and exploiting the oppressed class. Thus, the state of antiquity was above all the state of the slave owners for the purpose of holding down the slaves, as the feudal state was the organ of the nobility for holding down the peasant serfs and bondsmen, and the modern representative state is an instrument of exploitation of wage labour by capital. By way of exception, however, periods occur in which the warring classes balance each other so nearly that the state power, as ostensible mediator, acquires, for the moment, a certain degree of independence of both. Such was the absolute monarchy of the seventeenth and eighteenth centuries, which held the balance between the nobility and the class of burghers; such was the Bonapartism[1] of the First, and

[1] See over.

still more of the Second French Empire, which played off the proletariat against the bourgeoisie and the bourgeoisie against the proletariat. The latest performance of this kind, in which ruler and ruled appear equally ridiculous, is the new German Empire of the Bismarck nation: here capitalists and workers are balanced against each other and equally cheated for the benefit of the impoverished Prussian cabbage junkers.

... Only under the second Bonaparte does the state seem to have made itself completely independent. As against civil society, the state machine has consolidated its position so thoroughly that the chief of the Society of December 10 suffices for its head, an adventurer blown in from abroad, raised on the shield by a drunken soldiery, which he has bought with liquor and sausages, and which he must continually ply with sausage anew. Hence the downcast despair, the feeling of most dreadful humiliation and degradation that oppresses the breast of France and makes her catch her breath. She feels dishonoured.

And yet the state power is not suspended in mid air. Bonaparte represents a class, and the most numerous class of French society at that, the *small-holding peasants*.

From *The Origin of the Family, Private Property and the State* (1884), ch. IX, 'Barbarism and Civilisation', pp. 277-8 (Foreign Languages Publishing House, Moscow, 1954). (Library of Marxist Leninist Classics.)

ENGELS, *Anti-Dühring*

... The modern state, ... is only the organisation that bourgeois society takes on in order to support the general external conditions of the capitalist mode of production against the encroachments as well of the workers as of individual capitalists. The modern state, no matter what its form, is essentially a capitalist machine, the state of the capitalists, the ideal personification of the total national capital. The more it proceeds to the taking over the productive forces, the more does it actually become the national capitalist, the more citizens does it exploit.

[1] For a detailed examination of Bonapartism and the failure of the French revolutionary movement, see also K. Marx, *The Eighteenth Brumaire of Louis Bonaparte*. In this connection, Marx writes of the emergence of independent state or executive power.

The workers remain wage-workers—proletarians. The capitalist relation is not done away with. It is rather brought to a head. But, brought to a head, it topples over. State ownership of the productive forces is not the solution of the conflict, but concealed within it are the technical conditions that form the elements of that solution.

This solution can only consist in the practical recognition of the social nature of the modern forces of production, and therefore in the harmonising of the modes of production, appropriation, and exchange with the socialised character of the means of production. And this can only come about by society openly and directly taking possession of the productive forces which have outgrown all control except that of society as a whole. The social character of the means of production and of the products today reacts against the producers, periodically disrupts all production and exchange, acts only like a law of nature working blindly, forcibly, destructively. But with the taking over by society of the productive forces, the social character of the means of production and of the products will be utilised by the producers with a perfect understanding of its nature, and instead of being a source of disturbance and periodical collapse, will become the most powerful lever of production itself.

Active social forces work exactly like natural forces: blindly, forcibly, destructively, so long as we do not understand, and reckon with, them. But when once we understand them, when once we grasp their action, their direction, their effects, it depends only upon ourselves to subject them more and more to our own will, and by means of them to reach our own ends. And this holds quite especially of the mighty productive forces of today. As long as we obstinately refuse to understand the nature and the character of these productive forces—and this understanding goes against the grain of the capitalist mode of production and its defenders—so long these forces are at work in spite of us, in opposition to us, so long they master us, as we have shown above in detail.

But when once their nature is understood, they can, in the hands of the producers working together, be transformed from master demons into willing servants. The difference is as that between the destructive force of electricity in the lightning of the storm, and electricity under command in the telegraph and the voltaic arc; the difference between a conflagration, and fire working in the service of man. With this recognition, at last, of the real nature of the productive forces of today, the social anarchy of production gives place to a social regulation of production upon a definite plan, according to the needs of the community and of each individual. Then the capitalist mode of appropriation, in which the product enslaves first the producer and then the appropriator, is replaced by the mode of appropriation of the products that is based upon the nature of the modern means of production; upon the one hand, direct social appropriation, as means to the maintenance and extension of production—on the other, direct individual appropriation, as means of subsistence and of enjoyment.

Whilst the capitalist mode of production more and more completely transforms the great majority of the population into proletarians, it creates the power which, under penalty of its own destruction, is forced to accomplish this revolution. Whilst it forces on more and more the transformation of the vast means of production, already socialised, into state property, it shows itself the way to accomplishing this revolution. *The proletariat seizes political power and turns the means of production in the first instance into state property.*

But, in doing this, it abolishes itself as proletariat, abolishes all class distinctions and class antagonisms, abolishes also the state as state. Society thus far, based upon class antagonisms, had need of the state, that is, of an organisation of the particular class, which was *pro tempore* the exploiting class, for the maintenance of its external conditions of production, and, therefore, especially, for the purpose of forcibly keeping the exploited classes in the condition of oppression corresponding with the given mode of production (slavery, serfdom, wage-labour). The state was the official representative of society as a whole; the gathering of it together into a visible embodiment. But it was this only in so far as it was the state of that class which itself represented, for the time being, society as a whole: in ancient times, the state of slave-owning citizens; in the Middle Ages, the feudal lords; in our own time, the bourgeoisie. When at last it becomes the real representative of the whole of society, it renders itself unnecessary. As soon as there is no longer any social class to be held in subjection; as soon as class rule, and the individual struggle for existence based upon our present anarchy in production, with the collisions and excesses arising from these, are removed, nothing more remains to be repressed, and a special repressive force, a state, is no longer necessary. The first act by virtue of which the state really constitutes itself the representative of the whole of society—the taking possession of the means of production in the name of society—this is, at the same time, its last independent act as a state. State interference in social relations becomes, in one domain after another, superfluous, and then dies out of itself; the government of persons is replaced by the administration of things, and by the conduct of processes of production. The state is not 'abolished'. *It dies out.*[1] This gives the measure of the value of the phrase 'a free people's state', both as to its justifiable use at times by agitators, and as to its ultimate scientific insufficiency; and also of the demands of the so-called anarchists for the abolition of the state out of hand.

From *Anti-Dühring* (1877), pt. III, ch. II, pp. 386-9 (Foreign Languages Publishing House, Moscow, 1954).

LENIN, *The State and the Revolution*

In his *Critique of the Gotha Programme* Marx gave one of his tantalisingly brief references to the state in a communist society, which Lenin used later as his text of Chapter V of *The State and the Revolution.*

The question then arises: what transformation will the state undergo in communist society? In other words, what social functions will remain in existence there that are analogous to the present functions of the state? This question can only be answered scientifically and one does not get a flea-hop nearer to the problem by a thousand-fold combination of the word people with the word state.

Between capitalist and communist society lies the period of the revolutionary transformation of the one into the other. There corresponds to this also a political transition period in which the state can be nothing but the revolutionary dictatorship of the proletariat.

Lenin quotes this famous passage, repeats Marx's own analysis of the sham of bourgeois democracy and continues:

[1] 'Is this proposition of Engels' correct?'

'Yes, it is correct, but only on one of two conditions: (1) *if* we study the socialist state only from the angle of the internal development of the country, abstracting ourselves in advance from the international factor, isolating, for the convenience of investigation, the country and the state from the international situation; or (2) *if* we assume that socialism is already victorious in all countries, or in the majority of countries, that a socialist encirclement exists instead of a capitalist encirclement, that there is no more danger of foreign attack, and that there is no more need to strengthen the army and the state.' Stalin, Speech at 18th Congress of C.P.S.U. (B), 1939.

But the dictatorship of the proletariat, i.e. the organisation of the vanguard of the oppressed as the ruling class for the purpose of crushing the oppressors, cannot result merely in an expansion of democracy. Simultaneously with an immense expansion of democracy, which for the first time becomes democracy for the poor, democracy for the people, and not democracy for the rich, the dictatorship of the proletariat imposes a series of restrictions on the freedom of the oppressors, the exploiters, the capitalists. We must crush them in order to free humanity from wage-slavery; their resistance must be broken by force; it is clear that where there is suppression, where there is coercion, there is no freedom, no democracy.

Engels expressed this splendidly in his letter to Bebel when he said, as the reader will remember, that 'so long as the proletariat still uses the state, it does not use it in the interests of freedom but in order to hold down its adversaries, and as soon as it becomes possible to speak of freedom, the state as such ceases to exist.'

Democracy for the vast majority of the people, and suppression by force, i.e., exclusion from democracy, of the exploiters and oppressors of the people—this is the change democracy undergoes during the transition from capitalism to communism.

Only in communist society, when the resistance of the capitalists has been completely broken, when the capitalists have disappeared, when there are no classes (i.e. when there is no difference between the members of society as regards their relation to the social means of production), only then 'the state . . . ceases to exist', and it 'becomes possible to speak of freedom'. Only then will really complete democracy, democracy without any exceptions, be possible and be realised. And only then will democracy begin to wither away owing to the simple fact that, freed from capitalist slavery, from the untold horrors, savagery, absurdities and infamies of capitalist exploitation, people will gradually become accustomed to observing the elementary rules of social intercourse that have been known for centuries and repeated for thousands of years in all copy-book maxims; they will become accustomed to observing them without force, without compulsion, without subordination, without the special apparatus for compulsion which is called the state.

The expression 'the state withers away' is very well chosen, for it indicates both the gradual and the spontaneous nature of the process. Only habit can, and undoubtedly will, have such an effect; for we see around us millions of times how readily people become accustomed to observing the necessary rules of social intercourse if there is no exploitation, if there is nothing that causes indignation, that calls forth protest and revolt or evokes the necessity for suppression.

From *The State and the Revolution* (1917), ch. v.

STALIN, *The Withering Away of the State*

It is sometimes asked: 'We have abolished the exploiting classes; there are no longer any hostile classes in the country; there is nobody to suppress; hence there is no more need for the state; it must die away. Why, then, do we not help our socialist state to die away? . . .'.

Or further: 'The exploiting classes have already been abolished in our country; socialism has been built in the main; we are advancing towards communism . . . . Why, then, do we not help our socialist state to die away? . . .'.

These questions show that those who ask them have conscientiously memorised certain propositions contained in the doctrine of Marx and Engels about the state. But they also show that these comrades have failed to understand the essential meaning of this doctrine; that they have failed to realise in what historical conditions the various propositions of this doctrine were elaborated; and, what is more, that they do not understand present-day international conditions, have overlooked the capitalist encirclement and the dangers it entails for the socialist country. These questions not only betray an underestimation of the capitalist encirclement, but also an underestimation of the role and significance of the bourgeois states and their organs, which send spies, assassins and wreckers into our country and are waiting for a favourable opportunity to attack it by armed force. They likewise betray an underestimation of the role and significance of our socialist state and of its military, punitive and intelligence organs, which are essential for the defence of the socialist land from foreign attack. It must be confessed that the comrades mentioned are not the only ones to sin in this underestimation. All the Bolsheviks, all of us without exception, sin to a certain extent in this respect. Is it not surprising that we learnt about the espionage and conspiratorial activities of the Trotskyite and Bukharinite leaders only quite recently, in 1937 and 1938, although, as the evidence shows, these gentry were in the service of foreign espionage organisations and carried on conspiratorial activities from the very first days of the October Revolution? How could we have failed to notice so grave a matter? . . . How is this blunder to be explained? It is to be explained by an underestimation of the strength and consequence of the mechanism of the bourgeois states surrounding us and of their espionage organs, which endeavour to take advantage of people's weaknesses, their vanity, their slackness of will, to enmesh them in their espionage nets and use them to surround the organs of the Soviet state. It is to be expected by an underestimation of the role and significance of the mechanism of our socialist state and of its intelligence service, by an underestimation of this intelligence service, by the twaddle that an intelligence service in a Soviet state is an unimportant trifle, and that the Soviet intelligence service and the Soviet state itself will soon have to be relegated to the museum of antiquities . . . .

Since the October Revolution, our socialist state has passed through two main phases in its development

The first phase was the period from the October Revolution to the elimination of the exploiting classes. The principal task in that period was to suppress the resistance of the overthrown classes, to organise the defence of the country against the attack of the interventionists, to restore industry and agriculture, and to prepare the conditions for the elimination of the capitalist elements. Accordingly, in this period our state performed two main functions. The first function was to suppress the overthrown classes inside the country . . . The second function was to defend the country from foreign attack . . . Our state had yet a third function: this was the work of economic organisation and cultural education performed by our state bodies with the purpose of developing the infant shoots of the new, socialist economic system and re-educating the people in the spirit of socialism. But this new function did not attain to any considerable development in that period.

The second phase was the period from the elimination of the capitalist elements in town and country to the complete victory of the socialist economic system and the adoption of the new Constitution. The principal task in this period was to establish the socialist economic system all over the country and to eliminate the last remnants of the capitalist elements, to bring about a cultural revolution, and to form a thoroughly modern army for the defence of the country. And the functions of our socialist state changed accordingly. The function of military suppression inside the country ceased, died away; for exploitation had been abolished, there were no more exploiters left, and so there was no one to suppress. In place of this function of suppression, the state acquired the function of protecting socialist property from thieves and pilferers of the people's property. The function of defending the country from foreign attack fully remained; consequently, the Red Army and the Navy also fully remained, as did the punitive organs and the intelligence service, which are indispensable for the detection and punishment of the spies, assassins and wreckers sent into our country by foreign espionage services. The function of economic organisation and cultural education by the state organs also remained, and was developed to the full . . . .

As you see, we now have an entirely new, socialist state, without precedent in history and differing considerably in form and functions from the socialist state of the first phase.

But development cannot stop there. We are going ahead, towards communism. Will our state remain in the period of communism also?

Yes, it will, unless the capitalist encirclement is liquidated, and unless the danger of foreign military attack has disappeared. Naturally, of course, the forms of our state will again change in conformity with the change in the situation at home and abroad.

No, it will not remain and will atrophy if the capitalist encirclement is liquidated and a socialist encirclement takes its place.

That is how the question stands with regard to the socialist state.

From *Speech to 18th Congress of the Communist Party of the Soviet Union* (1939).

SECTION E

POLITICAL ACTION

LENIN, *How the Working Class can make use of a Bourgeois Revolution*

Lenin wrote *Two Tactics of Social Democracy in the Democratic Revolution* immediately after the Third Congress of the Russian Social-Democratic Labour Party (which was attended only by the Bolsheviks) and the Conference of the Mensheviks at Geneva. Lenin attacked the Mensheviks on their tactics towards the democratic revolution which was eagerly awaited in Russia. If it was a democratic, bourgeois revolution, destined to hasten the development not of socialism but of capitalism, what ought to be the attitude of Revolutionary Marxists? Lenin argues that although it is a bourgeois revolution, it can be exploited by the Social Democrats who can use the revolutionary situation to hasten the arrival of a genuine proletarian revolution and the dictatorship of the proletariat.

Marxists are absolutely convinced of the bourgeois character of the Russian revolution. What does this mean? It means that the democratic changes in the political regime and the social and economic changes which have become necessary for Russia do not in themselves imply the undermining of capitalism, the undermining of bourgeois domination; on the contrary, they will, for the first time, properly clear the ground for a wide and rapid European, and not Asiatic, development of capitalism, they will, for the first time, make it possible for the bourgeoisie to rule as a class .... It is extremely important for Social-Democracy, both from the theoretical and the practical-political standpoint, to insist on this truth, for from it logically arises the necessity of the complete class independence of the party of the proletariat in the present 'general democratic' movement. But it does not at all follow from this that the *democratic* revolution (bourgeois in its social and economic content) is not of *enormous* interest for the proletariat. It does not at all follow that the democratic revolution could not take place in a form advantageous mainly to the big capitalist, the financial magnate, the 'enlightened' landlord, and in a form advantageous to the peasant and to the worker ....

Since, under capitalism, the domination of the bourgeoisie over the working class is inevitable, we are entitled to say that the bourgeois revolution expresses not so much the interests of the proletariat as those of the bourgeoisie. But the idea that the bourgeois revolution does not express the interests of the proletariat is altogether absurd . . . . Theoretically, this idea ignores the elementary postulates of Marxism concerning the inevitability of capitalist development on the basis of commodity production. Marxism teaches that at a certain stage of its development a society that is based on commodity production, and having commercial intercourse with civilised capitalist nations, inevitably takes the road of capitalism itself . . . In countries like Russia, the working class suffers not so much from capitalism as from the lack of capitalist development. The working class is therefore undoubtedly interested in the widest, freest and speediest development of capitalism . . . .

Therefore, the *bourgeois* revolution is in the *highest degree advantageous to the proletariat.* The bourgeois revolution is *absolutely* necessary in the interests of the proletariat. The more complete, determined and consistent the bourgeois revolution is, the more secure will the proletarian struggle against the bourgeoisie and for socialism become. Such a conclusion may appear new, or strange, or even paradoxical only to those who are ignorant of the rudiments of scientific socialism. And from this conclusion, among other things, follows the postulate that, *in a certain sense,* the bourgeois revolution is more *advantageous* to the proletariat than it is to the bourgeoisie . . . . It is to the advantage of the bourgeoisie if the necessary bourgeois-democratic changes take place more slowly, more gradually, more cautiously, with less determination, by means of reforms and not by means of revolution; if these changes spare the 'venerable' institutions of feudalism (such as the monarchy); if these reforms develop as little as possible the revolutionary initiative, the initiative and the energy of the common people, i.e. the peasantry, and especially the workers, for otherwise it will be easier for the workers, as the French say, 'to pass the rifle from one shoulder to the other,' i.e. to turn the guns which the bourgeois revolution will place in their hands, the liberty which the revolution will bring, the democratic institutions which will spring up on the ground that will be cleared of feudalism, against the bourgeoisie.

On the other hand, it is more advantageous for the working

class if the necessary bourgeois-democratic changes take place in the form of revolution and not reform; for the latter is the road of delay, procrastination, of painfully slow decomposition of the putrid parts of the national organism . . . The revolutionary way is one of quick amputation, least painful to the proletariat, the way of direct amputation of the decomposing parts, the way of fewest concessions to and least consideration for the monarchy and the disgusting, vile, contaminating institutions which correspond to it . . . .

The very position the proletariat as a class occupies compels it to be consistently democratic. The bourgeoisie looks behind, is afraid of democratic progress which threatens to strengthen the proletariat. The proletariat has nothing to lose but its chains, but by means of democracy it has the whole world to win. Therefore, the more consistent the bourgeois revolution is in its democratic reforms the less will it limit itself to those measures which are advantageous only to the bourgeoisie. The more consistent the bourgeois revolution is, the more does it guarantee the advantages which the proletariat and the peasantry will derive from a democratic revolution . . . .

What is needed is to give a *democratic lead* in a real revolution, . . . to state straightforwardly and trenchantly the immediate tasks of the actual revolutionary struggle of the proletariat and the peasantry, as distinguished from the liberal broker tactics of the landlords and manufacturers. At the present time the crux of the matter lies in the following, . . . whether our revolution will result in a real, great victory, or in a miserable bargain, whether it will go as far as the revolutionary-democratic dictatorship of the proletariat and the peasantry, or whether it will exhaust itself in a liberal constitution . . . .

A Social-Democrat must never, even for an instant, forget that the proletarian class struggle for socialism against the most democratic and republican bourgeoisie and petty bourgeoisie is inevitable. This is beyond doubt. From this logically follows the absolute necessity of a separate, independent and strictly class party of Social-Democracy. From this logically follows the provisional character of our tactics to 'strike together' with the bourgeoisie and the duty to carefully watch 'our ally, as if he were an enemy'. All this is also beyond doubt. But it would be ridiculous and reactionary to deduce from this that we must forget, ignore or neglect those tasks which, although transient and temporary, are vital at the present time. The struggle against autocracy is a temporary and transient task of the Socialists, but to ignore or neglect this task would be tantamount to betraying socialism and rendering a service to reaction. Certainly, the revolutionary-democratic dictatorship of the proletariat and the peasantry is only a transient, provisional task of the Socialists, but to ignore this task in the period of a democratic revolution would be simply reactionary . . . .

The time will come when the struggle against Russian autocracy will be over, when the period of democratic revolution in Russia will also be over, and then it will be ridiculous to talk about 'unity of will' of the proletariat and the peasantry, about a democratic dictatorship, etc. When that time comes we shall take up the question of the socialist dictatorship of the proletariat and deal with it at greater length. But at present the party of the advanced class cannot help striving in a most energetic manner for a decisive victory of the democratic revolution over tsarism. And a decisive victory is nothing else than the revolutionary-democratic dictatorship of the proletariat and the peasantry.

From *Two Tactics of Social Democracy in the Democratic Revolution* (1905), chs. VI, X.
(Little Lenin Library, vol. 17, Lawrence and Wishart.)

STALIN, *Problems of Leninism*

Formerly it was the accepted thing to speak of the existence or absence of objective conditions for the proletarian revolution in individual countries, or, to be more precise, in one or another developed country. Now this point of view is no longer adequate. Now we must speak of the existence of objective conditions for the revolution in the entire system of world imperialist economy as an integral unit; the existence within this system of some countries that are not sufficiently developed industrially cannot serve as an insurmountable obstacle to the revolution, *if* the system as a whole, or, more correctly, *because* the system as a whole is already ripe for revolution . . . .

Where will the revolution begin? Where, in what country, can the front of capital be pierced first?

Where industry is more developed, where the proletariat constitutes the majority, where there is more culture, where there is more democracy—that was the reply usually given formerly.

No, objects the Leninist theory of revolution; *not necessarily where industry is more developed* .... The front of capital will be pierced where the chain of imperialism is weakest, for the proletarian revolution is the result of the breaking of the chain of the world imperialist front at its weakest link; and it may turn out that the country which has started the revolution, which has made a breach in the front of capital, is less developed in a capitalist sense than other, more developed, countries, which have, however, remained within the framework of capitalism.

In 1917 the chain of the imperialist world front proved to be weaker in Russia than in the other countries. It was there that the chain gave way and provided an outlet for the proletarian revolution. Why? Because in Russia a great popular revolution was unfolding, and at its head marched the revolutionary proletariat, which had such an important ally as the vast mass of the peasantry who were oppressed and exploited by the landlords. Because the revolution there was opposed by such a hideous representative of imperialism as tsarism, which lacked all moral prestige and was deservedly hated by the whole population. The chain proved to be weaker in Russia, although that country was less developed in a capitalist sense than, say, France or Germany, England or America ....

The heroes of the Second International asserted (and continue to assert) that between the bourgeois-democratic revolution and the proletarian revolution there is a chasm, or at any rate a Chinese Wall, separating one from the other by a more or less protracted interval of time, during which the bourgeoisie, having come into power, develops capitalism, while the proletariat accumulates strength and prepares for the 'decisive struggle' against capitalism. This interval is usually calculated to extend over many decades, if not longer. It is hardly necessary to prove that this Chinese Wall 'theory' is totally devoid of scientific meaning under the conditions of imperialism, that it is and can be only a means of concealing and camouflaging the counter-revolutionary aspirations of the bourgeoisie. It is hardly necessary to prove that under the conditions of imperialism, which is pregnant with collisions and wars; under the conditions of the 'eve of the Socialist revolution', when 'flourishing' capitalism is becoming 'moribund' capitalism (Lenin) and the revolutionary movement is growing in all countries of the world; when imperialism is allying itself with all reactionary forces without exception, down to and including tsarism and serfdom, thus making imperative the coalition of all revolutionary forces, from the proletarian movement of the West to the national liberation movement of the East; when the overthrow of the survivals of the regime of feudal serfdom becomes impossible without a revolutionary struggle against imperialism—it is hardly necessary to prove that the bourgeois-democratic revolution, in a more or less developed country, must under such circumstances verge upon the proletarian revolution, that the former must pass into the latter. The history of the revolution in Russia has provided palpable proof that this thesis is correct and incontrovertible. It was not without reason that Lenin, as far back as 1905, on the eve of the first Russian revolution, in his pamphlet *Two Tactics*, depicted the bourgeois-democratic revolution and the Socialist revolution as two links in the same chain, as a single and integral picture of the sweep of the Russian revolution:

> The proletariat must carry to completion the democratic revolution, by allying to itself the mass of the peasantry in order to crush by force the resistance of the autocracy and to paralyse the instability of the bourgeoisie. The proletariat must accomplish the Socialist revolution by allying to itself the mass of the semi-proletarian elements of the population in order to crush by force the resistance of the bourgeoisie and to paralyse the instability of the peasantry and the petty bourgeoisie. (Lenin, *Selected Works*, vol. III, pp. 110-11.)

I do not even mention other, later works of Lenin's, in which the idea of the bourgeois revolution passing into the proletarian revolution stands out in greater relief than in *Two Tactics* as one of the cornerstones of the Leninist theory of revolution. . . .

Very well, we may be told; but if this be the case, why did Lenin combat the idea of 'permanent (uninterrupted) revolution'?

Because Lenin proposed that the revolutionary capacities of the peasantry be utilised 'to the utmost' and that the fullest use be made of their revolutionary energy for the complete liquidation of tsarism and for the transition to the proletarian revolution, whereas the adherents of 'permanent revolution' did not understand the important role of the peasantry in the Russian revolution, underestimated the strength of the revolutionary energy of the peasantry, underestimated the strength and capacity of the Russian proletariat to lead the peasantry, and thereby hampered the work of emancipating the peasantry from the influence of the bourgeoisie, the work of rallying the peasantry around the proletariat.

Because Lenin proposed that the work of the revolution *be crowned* with the transfer of power to the proletariat, whereas the adherents of 'permanent' revolution wanted to *begin* at once with the establishment of the power of the proletariat, failing to realise that in so doing they were closing their eyes to such a 'minor detail' as the survivals of serfdom and were leaving out of account so important a force as the Russian peasantry, failing to understand that such a policy could only retard the winning of the peasantry to the side of the proletariat.

Consequently, Lenin fought the adherents of 'permanent' revolution, not over the question of uninterruptedness, for he himself maintained the point of view of uninterrupted revolution, but because they underestimated the role of the peasantry, which is an enormous reserve force for the proletariat, because they failed to understand the idea of the hegemony of the proletariat.

The idea of 'permanent' revolution is not a new idea. It was first advanced by Marx at the end of the forties in his well-known *Address to the Communist League* (1850). It is from this document that our 'permanentists' took the idea of uninterrupted revolution. It should be noted, however, that in taking it from Marx our 'permanentists' altered it somewhat, and in altering it spoilt it and made it unfit for practical use. The experienced hand of Lenin was needed to rectify this mistake, to take Marx's idea of uninterrupted revolution in its pure form and make it a cornerstone of his theory of revolution.

Here is what Marx, in his *Address*, after enumerating a number of revolutionary-democratic demands which he calls upon the Communists to win, says about uninterrupted revolution:

While the democratic petty bourgeois wish to bring the revolution to a conclusion as quickly as possible, and with the achievement, at most, of the above demands, it is our interest and our task to make the revolution permanent, until all more or less possessing classes have been displaced from domination, until the proletariat has conquered state power, and the association of proletarians, not only in one country but in all the dominant countries of the world, has advanced so far that competition among the proletarians of these countries has ceased and that at least the decisive productive forces are concentrated in the hands of the proletarians.

In other words:

(*a*) Marx did not propose to *begin* the revolution in the Germany of the fifties with the immediate establishment of the proletarian power—*contrary* to the plans of our Russian 'permanentists'.

(*b*) Marx proposed only that the work of the revolution *be crowned* with the establishment of proletarian state power, by hurling, step by step, one section of the bourgeoisie after another from the heights of power, in order, after the attainment of power by the proletariat, to kindle the fire of revolution in every country—and everything that Lenin taught and carried out in the course of our revolution in pursuit of his theory of the proletarian revolution under the conditions of imperialism was *fully in line* with that proposition . . .

Formerly, the victory of the revolution in one country was considered impossible, on the assumption that it would require the combined action of the proletarians of all or at least of a majority of the advanced countries to achieve victory over the bourgeoisie. Now this point of view no longer accords with the facts. Now we must proceed from the possibility of such a victory, for the uneven and spasmodic character of the development of the various capitalist countries under the conditions of imperialism, the development, within imperialism, of catastrophic contradictions leading to inevitable wars, the growth of the revolutionary movement in all countries of the world—all this leads, not only to the possibility, but also to the necessity of the victory of the proletariat in individual countries. The history of the Russian Revolution is direct proof of this. At the same time, however, it must be borne in mind that the overthrow of the bourgeoisie can be successfully accomplished only when certain absolutely necessary conditions exist, in the absence of which there can be even no question of the proletariat taking power.

Here is what Lenin says about these conditions in his pamphlet '*Left-Wing' Communism, an Infantile Disorder:*

The fundamental law of revolution, which has been confirmed by all revolutions, and particularly by all three Russian revolutions in the twentieth century, is as follows: it is not enough for revolution that the exploited and oppressed masses should understand the impossibility of living in the old way and demand changes; it is essential for revolution that the exploiters should not be able to live and rule in the old way. Only when the 'lower classes' do not want the old way, and when the 'upper classes' cannot carry on in the old way—only then can revolution triumph. This truth may be expressed in other words: Revolution is impossible without a nation-wide crisis (affecting both the exploited and the exploiters). It follows that for revolution it is essential, first, that a majority of the workers (or at least a majority of the class conscious, thinking, politically active workers) should fully understand that revolution is necessary and be ready to sacrifice their lives for it; secondly, that the ruling classes should be passing through a governmental crisis, which draws even the most backward masses into politics . . . weakens the government and makes it possible for the revolutionaries to overthrow it rapidly. (Lenin, *Selected Works*, vol. x, p. 127.)

But the overthrow of the power of the bourgeoisie and establishment of the power of the proletariat in one country does not yet mean that the complete victory of Socialism has been ensured. After consolidating its power and taking the peasantry in tow, the proletariat of the victorious country can and must build up a Socialist society. But does this mean that it will thereby achieve the complete and final victory of Socialism, i.e. does it mean that with the forces of only one country it can finally consolidate Socialism and fully guarantee that country against intervention and, consequently, also against restoration? No, it does not. For this victory of the revolution in at least several countries is needed. Therefore, the development and support of revolution in other countries is an essential task of the victorious revolution. Therefore, the revolution in the victorious country must regard itself not as a self-sufficient entity but as an aid, as a means of hastening the victory of the proletariat in other countries.

Lenin expressed this thought in a nutshell when he said that the task of the victorious revolution is to do 'the utmost possible in one country for the development, support and awakening of the revolution in all countries'.

From *Foundations of Leninism* (1924), ch. III
(Foreign Languages Publishing House, Moscow, 1945).

ENGELS, *Preface to Marx's 'The Class Struggles in France'*

In a preface which he wrote to the 1895 edition of K. Marx, *The Class Struggles in France 1848-1850*, Frederick Engels discussed the techniques of revolutionary action in the light of events since the time when Marx had written this book. After discussing the growth of the Social Democratic Party in Germany and the increasing Socialist representation in the Reichstag, he goes on (pp. 27-39):

The *Communist Manifesto* had already proclaimed the winning of universal suffrage, of democracy, as one of the first and most important tasks of the militant proletariat, and Lassalle had again taken up this point. Now, when Bismarck found himself compelled to introduce this franchise as the only means of interesting the mass of the people in his plans, our workers immediately took it in earnest and sent August Bebel to the first, constituent Reichstag. And from that day on, they have used the franchise in a way which has paid them a thousandfold and has served as a model to the workers of all countries . . . .

With this successful utilisation of universal suffrage, however, an entirely new method of proletarian struggle came into operation, and this method quickly developed further. It was found that the state institutions, in which the rule of the bourgeoisie is organised, offer the working class still further opportunities to fight these very state institutions. The workers took part in elections to particular Diets, to municipal councils and to trades courts; they contested with the bourgeoisie every post in the occupation of which a sufficient part of the proletariat had a say. And so it happened that the bourgeoisie and the government came to be much more afraid of the legal than of the illegal action of the workers' party, of the results of elections than of those of rebellion.

For here, too, the conditions of the struggle had essentially changed. Rebellion in the old style, street fighting with barricades, which decided the issue everywhere up to 1848, was to a considerable extent obsolete . . .

. . . The irony of world history turns everything upside down. We, the 'revolutionists', the 'overthrowers'—we are thriving far better on legal methods than on illegal methods and overthrow. The parties of Order, as they call themselves, are perishing under the legal conditions created by themselves. They cry despairingly with Odilon Barrot: *la légalité nous tue*, legality is the death of us; whereas we, under this legality, get firm muscles and rosy cheeks and look like life eternal. And if *we* are not so crazy as to let ourselves be driven to street fighting in order to please them, then in the end there is nothing left for them to do but themselves break through this fatal legality.

From the preface to 1895 edition of *The Class Struggles in France* (Marx) published by Wilhelm Liebkrecht in *Vorwärts*. (Full text available in the Library of Marxist-Leninist Classics, Foreign Languages Publishing House, Moscow, 1952.)

SECTION F

MARXISM AND COLONIAL AND DEPENDENT TERRITORIES

STALIN, *The National Question*

Formerly, the principle of self-determination of nations was usually wrongly interpreted, not infrequently being narrowed down to mean the right of nations to autonomy. Certain leaders of the Second International even went so far as to convert the right of self-determination into the right to cultural autonomy, i.e. the right of oppressed nations to have their own cultural institutions while the whole political power was to remain in the hands of the dominant nation. The result of this was that the idea of self-determination stood in danger of being transformed from a means of fighting annexations into a means of justifying them. Now this confusion must be regarded as eliminated. Leninism has broadened the conception of self-determination, interpreting it as the right of the oppressed peoples in dependent countries and colonies to complete secession, as the right of nations to independent political existence. This has precluded the possibility of justifying annexations by representing the right of self-determination as the right to autonomy. As to the principle of self-determination itself, it was thus changed from the means of deceiving the masses it undoubtedly was in the hands of the social-chauvinists during the imperialist war into a means of exposing all imperialist aspirations or chauvinist machinations, a means of politically educating the masses in the spirit of internationalism.

Formerly, the question of the oppressed nations was usually regarded purely as a juridical question. The solemn proclamation of 'national equality of status' and innumerable declarations of the 'equality of nations' were what sustained the parties of the Second International, which slur over the fact that 'equality of nations' under imperialism, when one group of nations (a minority) lives by exploiting another group of nations, is an insult to the oppressed nations. This bourgeois juridical view of the national question must now be considered exposed. Leninism brought the national question down from the lofty heights of high-sounding declarations to solid ground and declared that declarations regarding the 'equality of nations' which are not reinforced by the proletarian parties giving direct support to the struggle for emancipation of the oppressed nations are meaningless and false. In this way the question of the oppressed nations became a question of rendering support and assistance, genuine and constant assistance, to the oppressed nations in their struggle against imperialism, in their struggle for a true equality of nations and for their independent existence as states.

Formerly, the national question was regarded in a reformist way, it was regarded as an independent question separate from the general question of capitalist rule, of the overthrow of imperialism and the proletarian revolution. It was tacitly assumed that the victory of the proletariat in Europe was possible without a direct alliance with the movement for emancipation in the colonies, that the national and colonial question could be solved surreptitiously, that it would solve itself, off the highroad of the proletarian revolution, without a revolutionary struggle against imperialism. Now this anti-revolutionary point of view must be considered exposed. Leninism has proved, and the imperialist war and the revolution in Russia have confirmed, that the national question can be solved only in connection with and on the basis of the proletarian revolution, and that the road to the victory of the revolution in the West lies through a revolutionary alliance with the liberation movement of the colonies and dependent countries against imperialism. The national question is part and parcel of the general question of the proletarian revolution, part and parcel of the question of the dictatorship of the proletariat.

The question is as follows: are the revolutionary possibilities inherent in the revolutionary movement for emancipation of the oppressed countries *already exhausted* or not; and if not, is there any hope, any basis for believing that these possibilities may be utilised for the proletarian revolution, that the dependent and colonial countries may be transformed from a reserve of the imperialist bourgeoisie into a reserve of the revolutionary proletariat, into an ally of the latter?

Leninism replies to this question in the affirmative, that is, it recognises that there are revolutionary capabilities inherent in the national liberation movement of the oppressed countries, and that they can be utilised for the purpose of overthrowing the common enemy, for the purpose of overthrowing imperialism. The mechanics of the development of imperialism, the imperialist war and the revolution in Russia entirely confirm the deductions made by Leninism in this respect.

Hence the necessity for the proletariat supporting, vigorously and actively supporting, the national liberation movement of the oppressed and dependent peoples.

This of course does not mean that the proletariat must support *every* national movement, everywhere and always, in every single, concrete instance. The point is that support must be given to those national movements which tend to weaken imperialism and not to strengthen and preserve it . . . .

Lenin was right in saying that the national movement of the oppressed countries should be judged not from the point of view of formal democracy, but from the point of view of the actual results in the sum total of the struggle against imperialism, that is to say, 'not in an isolated way, but on a world scale'.

Extract from a Series of Lectures on the Foundations of Leninism delivered at the Sverdlov University, April 1924. Published in *Marxism and the National and Colonial Question.*

SECTION G

PEACEFUL CO-EXISTENCE

KHRUSHCHEV, *Some Fundamental Questions of Present-Day International Development*

Comrades, I should like to dwell on some fundamental questions concerning present-day international development which determine not only the present course of events, but also the prospects for the future.

These questions are the peaceful co-existence of the two systems, the possibility of preventing wars in the present era, and the forms of transition to socialism in different countries. Let us examine these questions in brief.

THE PEACEFUL CO-EXISTENCE OF THE TWO SYSTEMS

The Leninist principle of peaceful co-existence of states with different social systems has always been and remains the general line of our country's foreign policy.

It has been alleged that the Soviet Union puts forward the principle of peaceful co-existence merely out of tactical considerations, considerations of expediency. Yet it is common knowledge that we have always, from the very first years of Soviet power, stood with equal firmness for peaceful co-existence. Hence, it is not a tactical move, but a fundamental principle of Soviet foreign policy.

This means that if there is indeed a threat to the peaceful co-existence of countries with differing social and political systems, it by no means comes from the Soviet Union or the rest of the socialist camp. Is there a single reason why a socialist state should want to unleash aggressive war? Do we have classes and groups that are interested in war as a means of enrichment? We do not. We abolished them long ago. Or, perhaps, we do not have enough territory or natural wealth, and perhaps we lack sources of raw materials or markets for our goods? No, we have enough and to spare of all those. Why then should we want war? We do not want it, and as a matter of principle we renounce any policy that might lead to millions of people being plunged into war for the sake of the selfish interests of a handful of multi-millionaires. Do those who shout about the 'aggressive intentions' of the U.S.S.R. know all this? Of course they do. Why then do they keep up the old monotonous refrain about some imaginary 'Communist aggression'? Only to stir up mud, to conceal their plans for world domination, a 'crusade' against peace, democracy and socialism.

To this day the enemies of peace allege that the Soviet Union is out to overthrow capitalism in other countries by 'exporting' revolution. It goes without saying that among us Communists there are no supporters of capitalism. But this does not mean that we have interfered, or plan to interfere, in the internal affairs of countries where capitalism still exists. Romain Rolland was right when he said that 'freedom is not brought in from abroad in baggage trains like Bourbons'. It is ridiculous to think that revolutions are made to order. We often hear representatives of bourgeois countries reasoning thus: 'The Soviet leaders claim that they are for peaceful co-existence between the two systems. At the same time they declare that they are fighting for communism, and say that communism is bound to win in all countries. Now if the Soviet Union is fighting for communism, how can there be any peaceful co-existence with it?' This view is the result of bourgeois propaganda. The ideologists of the bourgeoisie distort the facts and deliberately confuse questions of ideological struggle with questions of relations between states, in order to make the Communists of the Soviet Union look like advocates of aggression.

When we say that the socialist system will win in the competition between the two systems—the capitalist and the socialist systems—this by no means signifies that its victory will be achieved through armed interference by the socialist countries in the internal affairs of the capitalist countries. Our certainty of the victory of communism is based on the fact that the socialist mode of production possesses decisive advantages over the capitalist mode of production. Precisely because of this, the ideas of Marxism-Leninism are more and more capturing the minds of the broad masses of the working people in the capitalist countries, just as they have captured the minds of millions of men and women in our country and the people's democracies. We believe that all working men in the world, once they have become convinced of the advantages communism brings, will sooner or later take the road of struggle for the construction of socialist society. Building communism in our country, we are resolutely against war. We have always held and continue to hold that the establishment of a new social system in this or that country is the internal affair of the peoples of the countries concerned. This is our attitude, based on the great Marxist-Leninist teaching.

The principle of peaceful co-existence is gaining ever wider international recognition. This principle is one of the cornerstones of the foreign policy of the Chinese People's Republic and the other people's democracies. It is being actively implemented by the Republic of India, the Union of Burma and a number of other countries. And this is natural, for in present-day conditions there is no other way out. Indeed, there are only two ways: either peaceful co-existence or the most destructive war in history. There is no third way.

We believe that countries with differing social systems can do more than exist side by side. It is necessary to proceed further, to improve relations, strengthen confidence between countries and co-operate. The historical significance of the famous five principles, put forward by the Chinese People's Republic and the Republic of India and supported by the Bandung Conference and the world public in general, lies in the fact that they provide the best form for relations between countries with differing social systems in present-day conditions. Why not make these principles the foundation for peaceful relations among all countries in all parts of the world? It would meet the vital interests and demands of the peoples if all countries subscribed to these five principles.

THE POSSIBILITY OF PREVENTING WAR IN THE PRESENT ERA

Millions of people all over the world are asking whether another war is really inevitable, whether mankind, which has already experienced two devastating world wars, must still go through a third one? Marxists must answer this question, taking into consideration the epoch-making changes of the last decades.

There is, of course, a Marxist-Leninist precept that wars are inevitable as long as imperialism exists. This precept was evolved at a time when (i) imperialism was an all-embracing world system, and (ii) the social and political forces which did not want war were weak, poorly organised, and hence unable to compel the imperialists to renounce war.

People usually take only one aspect of the question and examine only the economic basis of wars under imperialism. This is not enough. War is not only an economic phenomenon. Whether there is to be a war or not depends in large measure on the correlation of class, political forces, the degree of organisation and the awareness and determination of the people. Moreover, in certain conditions the struggle waged by progressive social and political forces may play a decisive role. Hitherto the state of affairs was such that the forces that did not want war and opposed it were poorly organised and lacked the means to check the schemes of the war-makers. Thus it was before the First World War, when the main force opposed to the threat of war—the world proletariat—was disorganised by the treachery of the leaders of the Second International. Thus it was on the eve of the Second World War, when the Soviet Union was the only country that pursued an active peace policy, when the other great powers to all intents and purposes encouraged the aggressors, and the right-wing Social-Democratic leaders had split the labour movement in the capitalist countries.

In that period this precept was absolutely correct. At the present time, however, the situation has changed radically. Now there is a world camp of socialism, which has become a mighty force. In this camp the peace forces find not only the moral, but also the material means to prevent aggression. Moreover, there is a large group of other countries with a population running into many hundreds of millions which are actively working to avert war. The labour movement in the capitalist countries has today become a tremendous force. The movement of peace supporters has sprung up and developed into a powerful factor.

In these circumstances certainly the Leninist precept that so long as imperialism exists, the economic basis giving rise to wars will also be preserved, remains in force. That is why we must display the greatest vigilance. As long as capitalism survives in the world, the reactionary forces representing the interests of the capitalist monopolies will continue their drive towards military gambles and aggression, and may try to unleash war. But war is not fatalistically inevitable. Today there are mighty social and political forces possessing formidable means to prevent the imperialists from unleashing war, and if they actually do try to start it, to give a smashing rebuff to the aggressors and frustrate their adventurist plans. In order to be able to do this, all the anti-war forces must be vigilant and prepared, they must act as a united front and never relax their efforts in the battle for peace. The more actively the peoples defend peace, the greater will be the guarantees that there will be no new war.

FORMS OF TRANSITION TO SOCIALISM IN DIFFERENT COUNTRIES

In connection with the radical changes in the world arena new prospects are also opening up as regards the transition of countries and nations to socialism.

As long ago as the eve of the Great October Socialist Revolution, Lenin wrote: 'All nations will arrive at socialism—this is inevitable, but not all will do so in exactly the same way, each will contribute something of its own in one or another form of democracy, one or another variety of the dictatorship of the proletariat, one or another rate at which socialist transformations will be effected in the various aspects of social life. There is nothing more primitive from the viewpoint of theory or more ridiculous from that of practice than to paint, "in the name of historical materialism", *this* aspect of the future in a monotonous grey. The result will be nothing more than Suzdal daubing' [*Works*, Russian edition, vol. XXIII, p. 58].

The experience of history has fully confirmed Lenin's brilliant precept. Alongside the Soviet form of reconstructing society on socialist lines, we now have the form of people's democracy.

In Poland, Bulgaria, Czechoslovakia, Albania and the other European people's democracies this form sprang up and is being utilised in conformity with the concrete historical, social and economic conditions and peculiarities of each of these countries. It has been thoroughly tried and tested in the course of ten years and has fully proved its worth.

Much that is unique in socialist construction is being contributed by the People's Republic of China, whose economy prior to the victory of the revolution was exceedingly backward, semi-fuedal and semi-colonial in character. Having taken over the decisive commanding positions, the people's democratic state is using them in the social revolution to implement a policy of peaceful reorganisation of private industry and trade and their gradual transformation into a component of socialist economy.

The leadership of the great cause of socialist reconstruction by the Communist Party of China and the Communist and Workers' Parties of the other people's democracies, exercised in keeping with the peculiarities and specific features of each country, is creative Marxism in action.

In the Federal People's Republic of Yugoslavia, where state power belongs to the working people, and society is founded on public ownership of the means of production, specific concrete forms of economic management and organisation of the state apparatus are arising in the process of socialist construction.

It is probable that more forms of transition to socialism will appear. Moreover, the implementation of these forms need not be associated with civil war under all circumstances. Our enemies like to depict us Leninists as advocates of violence always and everywhere. True, we recognise the need for the revolutionary transformation of capitalist society into socialist society. It is this that distinguishes the revolutionary Marxists from the reformists, the opportunists. There is no doubt that in a number of capitalist countries the violent overthrow of the dictatorship of the bourgeoisie and the sharp aggravation of class struggle connected with this are inevitable. But the forms of social revolution vary. It is not true that we regard violence and civil war as the only way to remake society.

It will be recalled that in the conditions that arose in April 1917 Lenin granted the possibility that the Russian Revolution might develop peacefully, and that in the spring of 1918, after the victory of the October Revolution, Lenin drew up his famous plan for peaceful socialist construction. It is not our fault that the Russian and international bourgeoisie organised counter-revolution, intervention and civil war against the young Soviet state and forced the workers and peasants to take to arms. It did not come to civil war in the European people's democracies, where the historical situation was different.

Leninism teaches us that the ruling classes will not surrender their power voluntarily. And the greater or lesser degree of intensity which the struggle may assume, the use or the non-use of violence in the transition to socialism, depends on the resistance of the exploiters, on whether the exploiting class itself resorts to violence, rather than on the proletariat.

In this connection the question arises of whether it is possible to go over to socialism by using parliamentary means. No such course was open to the Russian Bolsheviks, who were the first to effect this transition. Lenin showed us another road, that of the establishment of a republic of Soviets—the only correct road in those historical conditions. Following that course, we achieved a victory of world-wide historical significance.

Since then, however, the historical situation has undergone radical changes which make possible a new approach to the question. The forces of socialism and democracy have grown immeasurably throughout the world, and capitalism has become much weaker. The mighty camp of socialism with its population of over 900 million is growing and gaining in strength. Its gigantic internal forces, its decisive advantages over capitalism, are being increasingly revealed from day to day. Socialism has a great power of attraction for the workers, peasants and intellectuals of all countries. The ideas of socialism are indeed coming to dominate the minds of all working mankind.

At the same time the present situation offers the working class in a number of capitalist countries a real opportunity to unite the overwhelming majority of the people under its leadership and to secure the transfer of the basic means of production into the hands of the people. The right-wing bourgeois parties and their governments are suffering bankruptcy with increasing frequency. In these circumstances the working class, by rallying around itself the working peasantry, the intelligentsia, all patriotic forces, and resolutely repulsing the opportunist elements who are incapable of giving up the policy of compromise with the capitalists and landlords, is in a position to defeat the reactionary forces opposed to the interests of the people, to capture a stable majority in parliament, and transform the latter from an organ of bourgeois democracy into a genuine instrument of the people's will. In such an event this institution, traditional in many highly developed capitalist countries, may become an organ of genuine democracy—democracy for the working people.

The winning of a stable parliamentary majority backed by a mass revolutionary movement of the proletariat and of all the working people could create for the working class of a number of capitalist and former colonial countries the conditions needed to secure fundamental social changes.

In the countries where capitalism is still strong and has a huge military and police apparatus at its disposal, the reactionary forces will, of course, inevitably offer serious resistance. There the transition to socialism will be attended by a sharp class, revolutionary struggle.

Whatever the form of transition to socialism, the decisive and indispensable factor is the political leadership of the working class headed by its vanguard. Without this there can be no transition to socialism.

It must be strongly emphasised that the more favourable conditions for the victory of socialism created in other countries are due to the fact that socialism has won in the Soviet Union and is winning in the people's democracies. Its victory in our country would have been impossible had Lenin and the Bolshevik Party not upheld revolutionary Marxism in battle against the reformists, who broke with Marxism and took the path of opportunism.

Such are the considerations which the central committee of the Party considers it necessary to set out with regard to the forms of transition to socialism in present-day conditions.

From *Report of the Central Committee to the 20th Congress of the Communist Party of the Soviet Union* (February 1956). (*Soviet News Booklet No.* 4).

PART III

PAPAL POLITICAL THEORY

INTRODUCTION

This section deals in the main with statements on social, economic and political questions by three Popes—Leo XIII, Pius XI and the present pontiff, Pius XII. It is not, nor can it be, a statement of the political philosophy of the Roman Catholic Church; nor is it the political creed of every Catholic citizen. It is well known that Roman Catholics differ widely on political matters—that they can be found on both sides of the house at Westminster; that on the Continent there are liberal and conservative Catholics of every hue in the political spectrum; that prominent Catholic philosophers are to be found supporting radically different political theories. But to admit all this is not to deny that in recent years a body of papal political theory has been expounded, mainly through encyclical letters, which, while not binding on Roman Catholics as part of their faith, forms a coherent and consistent view of political affairs.

One of the most outstanding developments in post war European politics has been the rising influence of Christian Democratic parties which are predominantly Roman Catholic in composition. In practice, however, the Christian Democratic Movement does not stand for any uniform body of political and social principles. It takes its colour from its environment. In Germany today, for example, its economic policy is one of extreme *laissez-faire* while, in France, Christian Democrats have been moderately socialistic in their approach to economic questions. In so far as the Christian Democratic Movement professes a social and political philosophy, it reflects with differences of emphasis the broad themes of papal pronouncements of politics and society. Hence, it has been decided to concentrate in this section on illustrating these themes, which form a framework of Catholic thought on these subjects. It must be emphasised, however, that this is a broad framework which leaves ample scope for diversity.[1]

The root of all Catholic political thinking, as the papal pronouncements published here show, is the idea of natural law.

[1] In this connection mention should be made of the 'Worker-Priest' Movement in France and the controversy which it has aroused; but strictly, this is a controversy about the proper function of a priest, not an excursion into political theory.

This idea is itself flexible, and the progress of Catholic social and political thought can largely be traced by reference to its development. Accordingly, the first document has been chosen to illustrate, from a recent work of M. Jacques Maritain, the principal contemporary Catholic philosopher of politics and one of the leaders of Christian Democratic thought, the prevailing view of the theory of natural law. The main idea which the concept of natural law carries is that it is possible, by considering the different instincts and emotions which make up human nature, to discover a latent harmony between them; each instinct and each general human inclination has, it is asserted, a purpose which can be fulfilled in harmony with the rest; conflict and disorder is the consequence of sin; and the business of the state, in the sphere which is entrusted to it, is to create the conditions in which this harmony—a harmony of man with himself and of men with each other—can be most easily achieved.

In the past, it has been the tendency of Catholic political thinkers to state the doctrine of natural law in rigid, *a priori* terms, to assume that the provisions of natural law are immediately accessible to reason and that the act of expressing them in positive law is, to a very large extent, simply one of deductive logic. The present tendency, as represented by M. Maritain is to a much more empirical view. By contemporary Catholic scholars, natural law is seen as something which reveals itself in history and the task of applying it to human affairs is seen as one of infinite complexity, involving continual adaptations of settled principles to changing circumstances. Nevertheless, the theory of natural law is still concerned with what is common to human nature; its aim, with however much modesty it may be pursued, is to affirm absolutes. In form, therefore, Catholic political thought is *a priori* rather than empirical.

Leo XIII claimed to do no more than apply this theory of natural law to the problems of the late nineteenth century—the highly industrialised era of the secular state, with the forces of capital and labour growing stronger and less reconcilable. The social policy he expounded in *Rerum Novarum* was an attempt to apply Thomist philosophy and Christian doctrine to the social disorders of the Europe of the 1890's. He saw the pitiful condition of the working classes as part of a wider industrial and political question. In attacking the secular state for its abdication of God-given responsibilities towards the widows and fatherless, the weak and the poor, he also defended property on grounds of natural law, against socialist detractors of the modern liberal state. He developed the conception of groups within and antecedent to the state—of which the family was the chief example—and on this based a defence of trade unions as latter-day guilds, and urged employers and other similar interests to form associations. This Pius XI carried a stage further in *Quadragesimo Anno* in which he described the elements of a corporate state, in which each industry governs itself by corporations composed of work-people and employers.

Papal social teaching attacks the extremes of poverty and wealth, and the godless character of the economic system which produces them, as roundly as might Socialist critics of capitalism. Leo XIII and Pius XI reject the conception of labour as a commodity in the market.

> It is inhuman to use men as things of gain and to put no more value on them than they are worth in muscle and energy. . . . Likewise, more work is not to be imposed than strength can endure, nor that kind of work which is unsuited to a worker's age and sex.[2]

And he went on to affirm that 'it is incontestable that the wealth of nations arises from no other source than from the labour of the workers'. Yet because property was held to be protected by natural law, and because the family could not attain this stature without the right to own and bequeath property, the socialist answer is rejected. Sound social legislation is to be encouraged, but in the last resort, the excesses of wealth and poverty can only be removed by charitable and purposeful almsgiving on the part of those whose needs are more than met.

Historically the state and the Church are contenders for power, and this is recognised in the conception of state power expressed in *Immortale Dei* and elaborated subsequently by Pius XI and Pius XII.

All Authority stems from God—this is the recurrent theme. Some of it is entrusted to the Church; some to the family, some to the other groups within society, some to the state. State power being delegated, is limited—not by a fictitious social contract, but by Divine dispensation, and by the sanctions of the natural law. This applies to all types of political organisation: it matters not whether a country has a monarchy, an oligarchy or a

[2] Leo XII, Encyclical *Rerum Novarum* (1891).

democracy, the nature of political authority will be the same. Political obligation flows from this divinely ordained and divinely limited state power—and with it, under certain circumstances, the duty to withhold obedience from unjust laws or governments which usurp powers not entrusted to them by God. Church and state are linked in the defence of order and the rule of law (so long as that law is kept in its place). Within the nation, the Church should stand co-equal with the state, established but not subservient—and should be the authority to which the state would look unquestioningly in spiritual matters.

The clash between the Church and the state in practical politics usually comes over such matters as education and marriage. Education is regarded as the primary responsibility of the parent—though the state may be legitimately interested in fostering skill among its subjects. And the parent's first responsibility is to the spiritual welfare of his children—which in many countries makes the question of Catholic schools a central issue in politics. All three agencies, Church, state and family have distinct responsibilities in education, of which the conjoined duties of parent and Church may be held to predominate. In regard to marriage and divorce, the Church holds that marriage is a sacrament of divine institution and denies the right to remarriage after divorce. Divorce undermines the family, the essential unit of social life and therefore the state, as well.

Such is the broad framework of Catholic political thought as defined in papal pronouncements. Its breadth and flexibility must again be emphasised. Particularly in relation to Church and state, there is among professing Catholics a variety of views, and the various concordats which different circumstances have necessitated, do not all conform to the ideal described in papal pronouncements. Nevertheless, in this as in other matters, the political and social theory of the papacy may be taken as representing, subject to differences of interpretation, the largest common measure of agreement between Catholics on the ordering of secular affairs. It also constitutes a distinctive and influential contribution to contemporary social and political theory.

JACQUES MARITAIN, *Natural Law*

Shall we try to re-establish our faith in human rights on the basis of a true philosophy? This true philosophy of the rights of the human person is based upon the true idea of natural law, regarded in an ontological perspective and as conveying through the essential structures and exigencies of created nature the wisdom of the Author of Being.

The genuine idea of natural law is a heritage of Greek and Christian thought.[1] It goes back not only to Grotius, who indeed began deforming it, but, before him to Suarez and Francisco de Vitoria; and further back to St Thomas Aquinas (who alone comprehended the matter in a wholly consistent doctrine, which unfortunately was expressed in an insufficiently clear vocabulary,[2] so that its most profound aspects were soon overlooked and disregarded); and still further back to St Augustine and the Church Fathers and St Paul (we remember St Paul's saying: 'When the Gentiles who have not the Law, *do by nature* the things contained in the Law, these, having not the Law, are a law unto themselves . . .');[3] and even further back to Cicero, to the Stoics, to the great moralists of antiquity and its great poets, particularly Sophocles. Antigone, who was aware that in transgressing the human law and being crushed by it she was obeying a higher commandment, the *unwritten and unchangeable laws*, is the eternal heroine of natural law: for, as she puts it, they were not, those unwritten laws, born out of today's or yesterday's sweet will, 'but they live always and forever, and no man knows from where they have arisen.'[4]

[1] See the interesting volume on *The Place of Hooker in the History of Thought* by Peter Munz (Routledge & Kegan Paul Ltd, 1952). (Ed.)

[2] Especially because the vocabulary of the *Commentary on the Sentences*, as concerns the 'primary' and 'secondary' precepts of Natural Law, is at variance with the vocabulary of the *Summa theologica* (I–II, 94). Thomas's respect for the stock phrases of the jurists also causes trouble, particularly when it comes to Utopia.

[3] Rom. 2. 14.

[4] Nor did I deem
Your ordinance of so much binding force,
As that a mortal man could overbear
The unchangeable unwritten code of Heaven;
This is not of today and yesterday,
But lives forever, having origin
Whence no man knows: whose sanctions I were loath
In Heaven's sight to provoke, fearing the will
Of any man.

(Sophocles, *Antigone*, II, 452-60, George Young's translation.)

THE FIRST ELEMENT (ONTOLOGICAL) IN NATURAL LAW

Since I have not time here to discuss nonsense (we can always find very intelligent philosophers, not to name Mr Bertrand Russell, who defend it most brilliantly) I take it for granted that we admit that there is a human nature, and that this human nature is the same in all men. I take it for granted that we also admit that man is a being who is gifted with intelligence, and who, as such, acts with an understanding of what he is doing, and therefore with the power to determine for himself the ends which he pursues. On the other hand, possessed of a nature, of an ontological structure which is a locus of intelligible necessities, man possesses ends which necessarily correspond to his essential constitution and which are the same for all—as all pianos, for instance, whatever their particular type and in whatever place they may be, have as their end the production of certain attuned sounds. If they do not produce these sounds they must be tuned, or discarded as worthless. But since man is endowed with intelligence and determines his own ends, it is for him to attune himself to the ends that are necessarily demanded by his nature. This means that there is, by force and virtue of human nature itself, an order or disposition which human reason can discover and according to which the human will must act in order to attune itself to the essential and necessary ends of the human being. The unwritten law, or natural law, is nothing more than that.

The example that I just used—taken from the world of human workmanship—was purposely crude and provocative: yet did not Plato himself have recourse to the idea of any work of human art whatever, the idea of the Bed, the idea of the Table, in order to make clear his theory (which I do not share) of eternal Ideas? What I mean is that every being has its own natural law, as it has its own essence. Any kind of thing produced by human industry has, like the stringed instrument, ornament of our middle-class drawing-rooms, that I mentioned a moment ago, its own natural law, that is, the *normality of its functioning*, the proper way in which, by reason of its specific construction, it requires to be put into action, it '*should*' be used. Confronted with any supposedly unknown gadget, be it a corkscrew or a peg-top or a calculating machine or an atom bomb, children or scientists, in their eagerness to discover how to use it, will not query the existence of that inner law of the type or kind.

Any kind of thing existing in nature, a plant, a dog, a horse, has its own natural law, that is, the *normality of its functioning*, the proper way in which, by reason of its specific structure and specific ends, it '*should*' achieve fullness of being either in its growth or in its behaviour. Washington Carver, when he was a child and healed sick flowers in his garden, had an obscure knowledge, both by intelligence and affinity, of their law of growth. Horse-breeders have an experiential knowledge, both by intelligence and affinity, of the natural law of horses, a natural law with respect to which a horse's behaviour makes him a *good horse* or a *vicious horse* in the troop. Well, horses do not enjoy free will, their natural law is but a part of the immense network of essential tendencies and rules that are involved in the movement of the cosmos, and the individual horse who fails to conform to that equine law only obeys the universal order of nature on which the deficiencies of his individual nature depend. If horses were free, there would be an ethical way of conforming to the specific natural law of horses, but that horsy morality is a dream because horses are not free.

When I said a moment ago that the natural law of all beings existing in nature is the proper way in which, by reason of their specific nature and specific ends, they *should* achieve fullness of being in their behaviour, this very word '*should*' had only a metaphysical meaning (as we say that a good or a normal eye 'should' be able to read letters on a blackboard from a given distance.) The same word '*should*' begins to have a *moral* meaning, that is, to imply moral obligation, when we pass the threshold of the world of free agents. Natural law for man is *moral* law, because man obeys or disobeys it freely, not necessarily, and because human behaviour pertains to a particular, privileged order which is irreducible to the general order of the cosmos and tends to a final end which is superior to the immanent common good of the cosmos.

What I am emphasising is the first basic element to be recognised in natural law, namely the *ontological* element; I mean the *normality of functioning* which is grounded on the essence of that being: man. Natural law in general, as we have just seen, is the ideal formula of development of a given being; it might be compared with an algebraical equation to which a curve develops in space, yet with man the curve has freely to conform to the equation. Let us say, then, that in its ontological aspect, natural law is an *ideal order* relating to human actions, a watershed between the fitting and the unfitting, the proper and the improper, which appertains to our human nature or essence and the unchanging necessities that are rooted in it. I do not mean that the proper rule for every possible human situation is contained in our human essence, as Leibniz believed that every event in the life of Caesar was contained beforehand in the idea of Caesar. Human situations belong to the existential order. Neither they nor their appropriate regulations are contained in the essence of man. I would say that they pose questions to that essence. Any given situation, for instance, the situation of Cain with regard to Abel, implies a relation to the essence of man, and the possible murder of the one by the other is incompatible with the general ends and normality of functioning of the rational essence. Murder is rejected by the rational essence. Hence the prohibition of murder is grounded on or required by the essence of man. The precept: thou shalt do no murder, is a precept of natural law. This can be inferred on reflection from the fact that a primordial and absolutely general end of human nature is to respect its own being in its own members, in that existent who is a person, and a universe unto himself; and from the fact that man as man has a right to live.

Suppose a completely new case or situation, unheard of in human history: suppose, for instance, that what we now call *genocide* were as new as that very name. In the way I have just explained, that possible behaviour will confront the human essence as incompatible with its general ends and normality of functioning: that is to say, as prohibited by natural law. The condemnation of genocide by the General Assembly of United Nations[5] has added a sanction to the prohibition of the crime in question by natural law—which does not imply that such a prohibition was eternally inscribed as a kind of metaphysical feature in the essence of man—nor that it was a notion recognised from the beginning by the conscience of mankind.

To sum up, let us say that natural law is something both *ontological* and *ideal*. It is something *ideal*, because it is grounded on the human essence and its unchangeable structure and the

[5] 11 December 1948.

intelligible necessities it involves. Natural law is something *ontological*, because the human essence is an ontological reality, which moreover does not exist separately, but in every human being, so that, by the same token, natural law dwells as an ideal order in the very being of all existing men.

In this first consideration, or in reference to the basic *ontological* element it implies, natural law is coextensive with the whole field of natural moral regulations, of natural morality. Not only the primary and fundamental precepts but the remotest regulations of natural ethics mean conformity to natural law—say, natural obligations or rights of which perhaps now we have no idea, and of which men may become aware in a distant future.

An angel who knew the human essence in his angelic manner and all the possible existential situations of man would know natural law in the infinity of its extension. But we do not: though the eighteenth-century theoreticians thought they did.

THE SECOND ELEMENT (GNOSEOLOGICAL) IN NATURAL LAW

We come to the *second* basic element in natural law, to natural law *as known*, and thus as measuring in actual fact our practical reason, which is in turn the measure of human acts.

Natural law is not a written law. Men know it with greater or less difficulty, and in different degrees, here as elsewhere being subject to error. The only practical knowledge all men have naturally and infallibly in common as a self-evident principle, intellectually perceived by virtue of the concepts involved, is that we must do good and avoid evil. This is the preamble and the principle of natural law; it is not the law itself. Natural law is the ensemble of things to do and not to do which follow therefrom in *necessary* fashion. That every sort of error and deviation is possible in the determination of these things merely proves that our sight is weak, our nature coarse, and that innumerable accidents can corrupt our judgment. Montaigne maliciously remarked that, among certain peoples, incest and theft were considered virtuous acts. Pascal was scandalised by it. All this proves nothing against natural law, any more than a mistake in addition proves anything against arithmetic, or the mistakes of certain primitive peoples, for whom the stars were holes in the tent which covered the world, prove anything against astronomy.

Natural law is an unwritten law. Man's knowledge of it has increased little by little as man's moral conscience has developed. The latter was at first in a twilight state.[6] Anthropologists have taught us within what structures of tribal life and in the midst of what half-conscious magic it was first formed. This proves merely that the knowledge men have had of the unwritten law has passed through more diverse forms and stages than certain philosophers or theologians have believed. The knowledge that our own moral conscience has of this law is doubtless still imperfect, and very likely it will continue to develop and to become more refined as long as mankind exists. Only when the Gospel has penetrated to the very depths of our human substance will natural law appear in its full flower and its perfection.

So the law and the knowledge of the law are two different things. Yet the law has force of law only when it is promulgated. It is only in so far as it is known and expressed in affirmations of practical reason that natural law has the force of law.

At this point let us stress that human reason does not discover the regulations of natural law in an abstract and theoretical manner, as a series of geometrical theorems. Nay more, it does not discover them through the conceptual exercise of the intellect, or by way of rational knowledge. I think that Thomas Aquinas's teaching, here, needs to be understood in a much deeper and more precise fashion than is common. When he says that human reason discovers the regulations of natural law through the guidance of the *inclinations* of human nature, he means that the very mode or manner in which human reason knows natural law is not rational knowledge, but knowledge *through inclination*.[7] That kind of knowledge is not clear knowledge through concepts and conceptual judgments; it is obscure, unsystematic, vital knowledge by connaturality or affinity, in which the intellect, in order to form its judgment, consults and listens to the inner melody that the vibrating strings of abiding tendencies awaken in us.

When one has clearly seen this basic fact, and when, moreover, one has realised that St Thomas's views on the matter call for an historical approach and a philosophical use of the idea of

[6] Cf. Raïssa Maritain, *Historie d' Abraham ou les premiers âges de la conscience morale* (Paris: Desclée De Brouwer, 1947).

[7] See over.

development that the Middle Ages were ill equipped to carry into effect, then at last one is enabled to get a completely comprehensive concept of natural law. And one understands that the human knowledge of natural law has been progressively shaped and moulded by the inclinations of human nature, starting from the most basic ones. I do not propose to offer an *a priori* picture of those genuine inclinations which are rooted in man's being as vitally permeated with the preconscious life of reason, and which either developed or were released with the progressive movement of mankind. They are evinced by the very history of human conscience. Those inclinations *were really genuine* which in the immensity of the human past have guided reason in becoming aware, little by little, of the regulations that have been most definitely and most generally recognised by the human race, starting from the most ancient social communities. For the knowledge of the primordial aspects of natural law was first expressed in social patterns rather than in personal judgments: so that we might say that such knowledge has developed within the double protecting tissue of human inclination and human society.

With regard to the second basic element, the element of knowledge which natural law implies in order to have force of law, it may accordingly be said that natural law *naturally known*, or, more exactly, natural law *the knowledge of which is embodied in the most general and most ancient heritage* of mankind covers only the field of ethical regulations of which men have become aware by virtue of knowledge *through inclination*. These are *basic principles*

[7] This is, in my opinion, the real meaning implied by St Thomas, even though he did not use the very expression when treating of Natural Law. Knowledge through inclination is generally understood in all his doctrine on Natural Law. It alone makes this doctrine perfectly consistent. It alone squares with such statements as the following: 'Omnia illa ad quae homo *habet naturalem inclinationem, ratio naturaliter apprehendit ut bona*, et per consequens ut opere prosequenda; et contraria eorum, ut mala et vitanda' (I–II, 94, 2); 'Ad legem naturae pertinet omne illud ad quod homo inclinatur secundum naturam . . . Sed, si loquamur de actibus virtuosis secundum seipsos, prout scilicet in propriis speciebus considerantur, sic *non* omnes actus virtuosi sunt de lege naturae. Multa enim secundum virtutem fiunt *ad quae natura non primo inclinat; sed per rationis inquisitionem ea homines adinvenerunt*, quasi utilia ad bene vivendum' (I-II, 94, 3). The matter has been somewhat obscured because of the perpetual comparison that St Thomas uses in these articles between the speculative and the practical intellect, and by reason of which he speaks of the *propria principia* of Natural Law as '*quasi conclusiones principiorum communium*' (I-II, 94, 4). As a matter of fact, those *propria principia* or specific precepts of Natural Law are in no way conclusions rationally deduced; they play in the practical realm a part *similar* to that of conclusions in the speculative realm. (And they appear as inferred conclusions to the 'after-knowledge' of the philosophers who have to reflect upon and explain the precepts of Natural Law.)

in moral life—progressively recognised from the most general principles to the more and more specific ones.

These remarks may help us to understand why, on the one hand, a careful examination of the data of anthropology shows that the fundamental *dynamic schemes* of natural law, if they are understood in their authentic, that is, still undetermined meaning,[8] are matters of much more universal awareness—everywhere and in every age—than would appear to a superficial glance; and why, on the other hand, an immense amount of relativity and variation is to be found in the particular rules, customs, and standards in which, among all the peoples of the earth, human reason has expressed its knowledge even of the most basic aspects of natural law. The reason is, as I have already indicated, that this spontaneous knowledge does not bear on moral regulations *conceptually* discovered and *rationally* deduced, but on moral regulations known *through inclination*, and, in the beginning, on general tendential forms or frameworks, I just said on *dynamic schemes* of moral regulation, such as can be obtained by the first, 'primitive' attainments of knowledge by way of inclination. And in such tendential frameworks or dynamic schemes many various, still defective contents may occur—not to speak of warped, deflected, or perverted inclinations which can mingle with the basic ones.

We may understand at once why natural law essentially involves a dynamic development, and why moral conscience, or the knowledge of natural law, has progressed from the age of the cave-man in a two-fold manner: first, as regards the way in which human reason has become aware in a less and less crepuscular, rude, and confused manner, of the primordial regulations of natural law; secondly, as regards the way in which it has become aware—always by means of knowledge through inclination—of its more advanced and higher regulations. And such knowledge is still progressing, it will progress as long as human history endures. The progress of moral conscience is indeed the most indisputable instance of progress in mankind.

I have said that natural law is unwritten law: it is unwritten law in the deepest sense of that expression, because our knowledge of it is no work of free conceptualisation, but results from a

[8] For instance: to take a man's life is not like taking another animal's life; or, the family group has to comply with some fixed pattern; or, sexual intercourse has to be contained within given limitations; or, we are bound to look towards the Invisible; or, we are bound to live together under certain rules and prohibitions.

conceptualisation *bound* to the essential inclinations of being, of living nature, of reason, which are at work in man, and because it develops in proportion to the degree of moral experience and self-reflection, and of social experience also, of which man is capable in the various stages of his history. Thus it is that in ancient and medieval times attention was paid, in natural law, to the *obligations* of man more than to his *rights*. The proper achievement—a great achievement indeed—of the eighteenth century has been to bring out in full light the *rights* of man also as required by natural law. That discovery was essentially due to a progress in moral and social experience, through which the root *inclinations* of human nature in regard to the rights of the human person were set free, and consequently, *knowledge through inclination* with regard to them developed. But, according to a sad law of human knowledge, that great achievement was paid for by the ideological errors, in the theoretical field, that I have stressed at the beginning of this chapter. Attention even shifted from the obligations of man to his rights only. A genuine and comprehensive view would pay attention *both* to the obligations and to the rights that are involved in the requirements of natural law.

From *Man and the State* (1954).

LEO XIII, *The State*

In *Immortale Dei*, Pope Leo XIII set out 'the form and character of the state were it governed according to the principles of Christian Philosophy'. It includes a discussion of authority in the state as God-given and God-supported; the relationship of Church and state as twin powers, spiritual and secular; and the attitude of the Church to the post-1789 conception of liberty.

It is not difficult to determine what would be the form and character of the state were it governed according to the principles of Christian philosophy. Man's natural instinct moves him to live in civil society, for he cannot, if dwelling apart, provide himself with the necessary requirements of life, nor procure the means of developing his mental and moral faculties. Hence, it is divinely ordained that he should lead his life—be it family, social, or civil—with his fellowmen, amongst whom alone his several wants can be adequately supplied. But as no society can hold together unless some one be over all, directing all to strive earnestly for the common good, every civilised community must have a ruling authority, and this authority, no less than society itself, has its source in nature, and has, consequently, God for its Author. Hence, it follows that all public power must proceed from God: for God alone is the true and supreme Lord of the world. Everything, without exception, must be subject to Him, and must serve Him, so that whosoever holds the right to govern holds it from one sole and single Source, namely God, the Sovereign Ruler of all. *There is no power but from God.*

The right to rule is not necessarily, however, bound up with any special mode of government. It may take this or that form, provided only that it be of a nature to insure the general welfare. But whatever be the nature of the government, rulers must ever bear in mind that God is the paramount Ruler of the world, and must set Him before themselves as their exemplar and law in the administration of the state. For, in things visible, God has fashioned secondary causes in which His divine action can in some wise be discerned, leading up to the end to which the course of the world is ever tending. In like manner in civil society, God has always willed that there should be a ruling authority, and that they who are invested with it should reflect the divine power and providence in some measure over the human race.

They, therefore, who rule should rule with even-handed justice, not as masters, but rather as fathers, for the rule of God over man is most just, and is tempered always with a father's kindness. Government should moreover be administered for the well-being of the citizens, because they who govern others possess authority solely for the welfare of the state. Furthermore, the civil power must not be subservient to the advantage of any one individual, or of some few persons; inasmuch as it was established for the common good of all. But if those who are in authority rule unjustly, if they govern overbearingly or arrogantly, and if their measures prove hurtful to the people, they must remember that the Almighty will one day bring them to account, the more strictly in proportion to the sacredness of their office and pre-eminence of their dignity. *The mighty shall be mightily tormented.* Then truly will the majesty of the law meet with the dutiful and willing homage of the people, when they are convinced that their rulers hold authority from God, and feel that it is a matter of justice and duty to obey them, and to show them reverence and fealty, united to a love not unlike that which children show their parents. *Let every soul be subject to higher powers.* To despise legitimate authority, in whomsoever vested, is unlawful, as a rebellion against the Divine Will; and whoever resists that rushes wilfully to destruction. *He that resisteth the power resisteth the ordinance of God, and they that resist, purchase to themselves damnation.* To cast aside obedience and by popular violence to incite to revolt, is, therefore, treason, not against man only, but against God . . . .

It is a public crime to act as though there were no God. So, too, is it a sin in the state not to have care for religion, as something beyond its scope, or as of no practical benefit; or out of many forms of religion to adopt that one which chimes in with the fancy; for we are bound absolutely to worship God in that way which He has shown to be His will. All who rule, therefore, should hold in honour the Holy Name of God, and one of their chief duties must be to favour religion, to protect it, to shield it under the credit and sanction of the laws, and neither to organise nor enact any measures that may compromise its safety. This is the bounden duty of rulers to the people over whom they rule: for one and all we are destined, by our birth and adoption, to enjoy, when this frail and fleeting life is ended, a supreme and final good in heaven, and to the attainment of this every endeavour should be directed. Since, then, upon this depends the full and perfect happiness of mankind, the securing of this end should be, of all imaginable interests, the most urgent. Hence, civil society, established for the common welfare, should not only safeguard the well-being of the community, but have also at heart the interests of its individual members, in such mode as not in any way to hinder, but in every manner to render as easy as may be, the possession of that highest and unchangeable good for which all should seek. Wherefore, for this purpose, care must especially be taken to preserve unharmed and unimpeded the religion whereof the practice is the link connecting man with his God . . . .

The Almighty, therefore, has appointed the charge of the human race between two powers, the ecclesiastical and the divine, the one being set over divine, and the other over human things. Each in its kind is supreme, each has fixed limits within which it is contained, limits which are defined by the nature and special object of the province of each, so that there is, we may say, an orbit traced out within which the action of each is brought into play by its own native right.

... There must, accordingly, exist, between these two powers, a certain orderly connection, which may be compared to the union of the soul and body in man. The nature and scope of the connection can be determined only, as We have laid down, by having regard to the nature of each power, and by taking account of the relative excellence and nobleness of their purpose. One of the two has for its proximate and chief object the well-being of this mortal life; the other the everlasting joys of heaven. Whatever, therefore, in things human is of a sacred character, whatever belongs either of its own nature or by reason of the end to which it is referred, to the salvation of souls, or to the worship of God, is subject to the power and judgment of the Church. Whatever is to be ranged under the civil and political order is rightly subject to the civil authority. Jesus Christ has Himself given command that what is Caesar's is to be rendered to Caesar, and that what belongs to God is to be rendered to God.

There are, nevertheless, occasions when another method of concord is available, for the sake of peace and liberty: We mean when rulers of the state and the Roman Pontiff come to an understanding touching some special matter. At such times the Church gives signal proof of her motherly love by showing the greatest possible kindliness and indulgence ...

... To exclude the Church, founded by God Himself, from the business of life, from the power of making laws, from the training of youth, from domestic society, is a grave and fatal error. A state from which religion is banished can never be well regulated; and already perhaps more than is desirable is known of the nature and tendency of the so-called *civil* philosophy of life and morals. The Church of Christ is the true and sole teacher of virtue and guardian of morals. She it is who preserves in their purity the principles from which duties flow, and by setting forth most urgent reasons for virtuous life, bids us not only to turn away from wicked deeds, but even to curb all movements of the mind that are opposed to reason even though they be not carried out in action.

To wish the Church to be subject to the civil power in the exercise of her duty is a great folly and a sheer injustice. Whenever this is the case, order is disturbed for things natural are put above things supernatural; the many benefits which the Church, if free to act, would confer on society are either prevented or at least lessened in number; and a way is prepared for enmities and contentions between the two powers; with how evil result to both the issue of events has taught us only too frequently . . .

In the same way the Church cannot approve of that liberty which begets a contempt of the most sacred laws of God, and casts off the obedience due to lawful authority, for this is not liberty so much as licence, and is most correctly styled by St Augustine the 'liberty of self-ruin', and by the Apostle, St Peter, the *cloak for malice.* Indeed, since it is opposed to reason, it is a true slavery, *for whosoever committeth sin is the servant of sin.* On the other hand, that liberty is truly genuine, and to be sought after, which in regard to the individual does not allow men to be the slaves of error and of passion, the worst of all masters; which, too, in public administration guides the citizens in wisdom and provides for them increased means of well-being; and which, further, protects the state from foreign interference.

This honourable liberty, alone worthy of human beings, the Church approves most highly and has never slackened her endeavour to preserve, strong and unchanged, among nations. And in truth whatever in the state is of chief avail for the common welfare; whatever has been usefully established to curb the licence of rulers who are opposed to the true interests of the people, or to prevent governments from unwarrantably interfering in municipal or family affairs;—whatever tends to uphold the honour, manhood and equal rights of individual citizens;—of all these things, as the monuments of past ages bear witness, the Catholic Church has always been the originator, the promoter, or the guardian. Ever, therefore, consistent with herself, while on the one hand she rejects that exorbitant liberty which in individuals and in nations ends in licence or in thraldom, on the other hand, she willingly and most gladly welcomes whatever improvements the age brings forth, if these really secure the prosperity of life here below, which is as it were a stage in the journey to the life that will know no ending . . .

All this, though so reasonable and full of counsel, finds little favour nowadays, when states not only refuse to conform to the rules of Christian wisdom, but seem even anxious to recede from them further and further on each successive day. Nevertheless, since truth when brought to light is wont, of its own nature, to spread itself far and wide, and gradually take possession of the minds of men, We, moved by the great and holy duty of Our Apostolic mission to all nations, speak, as We are bound to do, with freedom. Our eyes are not closed to the spirit of the times. We repudiate not the assured and useful improvements of our age, but devoutly wish affairs of state to take a safer course than they are now taking, and to rest on a more firm foundation without injury to the true freedom of the people. For the best parent and guardian of liberty amongst men is truth. *The truth shall make you free* . . . .

But in matters merely political, as for instance the best form of government, and this or that system of administration, a difference of opinion is lawful. Those, therefore, whose piety is in other respects known, and whose minds are ready to accept in all obedience the decrees of the Apostolic See, cannot in justice be accounted as bad men because they disagree as to subjects We have mentioned; and still graver wrong will be done them, if—as We have more than once perceived with regret—they are accused of violating, or of wavering in, the Catholic Faith.

From Encyclical *Immortale Dei* on the Christian constitution of States (1 November 1885). Printed in *Principles for Peace*, National Catholic Welfare Conference, Washington (1943).

Pius xii, *The Rights of Man*

The Rights of Man is the title which has been given to Pope Pius XII's Christmas message of 1942. He is concerned with the social and political institutions which will be set up after the war and in the two excerpts quoted here, he considers first 'the legal structure of society and its purpose', and second 'five fundamental points for the peaceful ordering of Human Society.'

I. THE LEGAL STRUCTURE OF SOCIETY AND ITS PURPOSE

If social life, such as God wills it, is to attain its end it needs a legal structure for its support, defence, and protection. The function of this structure is not to dominate, but to serve; to encourage the development and vital growth of society in the abundant variety of its aims, promoting the full achievement of private enterprise in harmonious collaboration, and protecting it by suitable and legitimate means against anything detrimental to its full expansion. Such structure, in order to secure the balance, the security, and the concord of society, has also the right of coercion against those who cannot in any other way be restrained within the honourable discipline of social life; but no authority worthy of the name can fail to feel, in the just exercise of this right, an anxious sense of responsibility in the sight of the Eternal Judge, before whose tribunal any unjust sentence, and especially any reversal of divinely established principles, will receive inevitable punishment and condemnation.

The ultimate, deep-rooted, lapidary principles which lie at the foundation of society cannot be abolished by any effort of human ingenuity; they may be denied, ignored, disregarded, or disobeyed, but they can never de deprived of their juridical validity. Admittedly conditions change with the passage of time, but there is never a complete gap, never entire discontinuity, between the law of yesterday and the law of today, between the disappearance of old forms of government and the introduction of new constitutions. Whatever happens, whatever change or transformation may take place, the purpose of all social life remains the same, ever sacred, ever obligatory: the development of the personal values of man, who is made in the image of God; whatever legislator or authority he may obey, every member of the human family remains bound to secure his immutable ends. He has therefore always the inalienable right—a right which no opposition can destroy and which all, friends and enemies alike, are bound to acknowledge—to a constitution and an administration of justice inspired by the conviction and understanding that it is their essential duty to serve the common good.

The legal structure has also the noble and arduous task of securing harmonious relations between individual citizens, between various associations within the State, and between their members. Legislators will accomplish this task successfully if they avoid dangerous theories and practices which are detrimental to the community and to its cohesion, and which owe their origin and wide diffusion to false postulates. Among these is to be counted a juridical positivism which invests purely human laws with a majesty to which they have no title, opening the way to a fatal dissociation of law from morality. Likewise to be banned is the theory which claims for a particular nation, or race, or class, a juridical instinct against whose law and command there is no appeal. Finally, all those theories are to be shunned which, though in themselves divergent and deriving from opposed ideologies, have this in common that they regard the state, or a group representing it, as an absolute and supreme entity exempt from all control and criticism, even when its theoretical and practical postulates result in open and clashing contradiction with essential data of the human and Christian conscience.

Those who clearly perceive the vital connection between genuine social order and a genuine juridical constitution, those who appreciate that interior unity in multiplicity depends upon the primacy of the spiritual, upon respect for human personality both in oneself and in others, upon a true love for society, and upon attachment to the ends for which God has ordained it, cannot wonder at the unhappy results of juridical conceptions which have departed from the royal road of truth to follow the slippery paths of materialism; and they must immediately see how urgently necessary it is to return to a conception of society which is spiritual and ethical, earnest and profound, instinct with the warmth of a true humanity, lit by the light of Christian faith which reveals in the juridical constitution a reflection of the social order as God has willed it, a luminous product of the spirit of man, which in its turn is an image of the spirit of God.

This organic conception of society, the only vital conception, combines a noble humanity with the genuine Christian spirit, and it bears the inscription from Holy Writ which St Thomas has explained:[1] 'The work of justice shall be peace'; a text applicable to the life of a people whether it be considered in itself or in its relations with other nations. In this view love and justice are not contrasted as alternatives; they are united in a fruitful synthesis. Both radiate from the spirit of God, both have their place in the programme which defends the dignity of man; they complement, help, support, and animate each other: while justice prepares the way for love, love softens the rigour of justice and ennobles it; both raise up human life to an atmosphere in which, despite the failings, the obstacles, and the harshness

[1] *S. Th.* 2a 2æ, q. 29, a. 3.

which earthly life presents, a brotherly intercourse becomes possible. But if the evil spirit of materialism gains the mastery, if the rough hands of power and tyranny are suffered to guide events, you will then see daily signs of the disintegration of human fellowship, and love and justice will disappear—presaging the catastrophes which must come upon a society that has apostatised from God....

II. FUNDAMENTAL POINTS

(*a*) *The Dignity and Rights of the Human Person*

He who would have the star of peace to shine permanently over society must do all in his power to restore to the human person the dignity which God conferred upon him from the beginning; he must resist the excessive herding together of human beings, as though they were a soulless mass; he must set his face against their disintegration in economic, social, political, intellectual, and moral life; against their lack of solid principles and firm convictions; against their excessive reliance upon instinct and emotion, and against their fickleness of mood; he must favour, by all legitimate means and in every sphere of life, social forms which render possible and guarantee full personal responsibility in regard to things both temporal and spiritual.

He must foster the observance and practical implementing of the following fundamental rights of the person: the right to maintain and develop physical, intellectual, and moral life, and in particular the right to a religious training and education; the right to worship God, both in private and in public, including the right to engage in religious works of charity; the right, in principle, to marriage and to the attainment of the purpose of marriage, the right to wedded society and home life; the right to work as an indispensable means for the maintenance of family life; the right to the free choice of a state of life, and therefore of the priestly and religious state; the right to a use of material goods, subject to its duties and to its social limitations.

(*b*) *The Protection of Social Unity, and especially of the Family*

He who would have the star of peace to shine permanently over society must reject all forms of materialism, which regard the people as nothing but a herd of individuals, disunited and lacking organic cohesion, and as the raw material for domination and arbitrary treatment.

He must endeavour to see society as an organic unity, growing to maturity under the government of divine Providence; a unity which, within the spatial limits assigned to it and in the measure of its peculiar endowments, is designed, through the collaboration of the various classes and vocational groups of the community, to achieve the eternal and ever new ends of culture and religion.

He must defend the indissolubility of marriage; he must give to the family, which is the irreplaceable unit of society, the space, light, and air that it needs in order to fulfil its mission of perpetuating new life, and of educating children in a spirit corresponding with its own true religious convictions; he must devote his energies to preserving, protecting, or restoring the economic, spiritual, moral, and juridical unity of the family: by ensuring that the material and spiritual advantages of the family shall be shared also by the domestic staff: by securing for every family a home in which a healthy family life, both physical and moral, may be maintained in all its vigour and dignity; by ensuring that home and place of work are not so distant from each other that the head of the family, the educator of his children, becomes almost a stranger in his own home; by ensuring, above all, that between school and family that bond of confidence and mutual assistance shall be restored which in times past produced such happy results, but which today has given place to mistrust, in cases where the school, under the influence or the control of a materialistic spirit, contaminates and corrupts the good which the parents have instilled into the minds of their children.

(*c*) *The Dignity and Prerogatives of Labour*

He who would have the star of peace to shine permanently over society must give to labour the place assigned to it by God from the beginning. All labour, as an indispensable means to the mastery of the earth, by which God wills to be glorified, has an inalienable dignity and at the same time an intimate connection with the development of the human person; nor does this noble dignity and prerogative of labour suffer any diminution from the burden of fatigue which, in consequence of original sin, must be endured in obedient submission to the will of God.

Those who are familiar with the great Encyclicals of Our

Predecessors and with Our own previous Messages will know that the Church does not hesitate to draw the practical conclusions which follow from the moral dignity of labour, or to give them the full weight of her authority. The dignity of labour demands, not only a just wage, adequate to the needs of the worker and his family, but also the maintenance and development of a social order which will render possible and secure a portion of private property, however modest, for all sections of the community; which will favour a higher education for children of the working classes who are exceptionally intelligent and well-disposed; and which will promote and give effect to a practical social spirit in the neighbourhood, in the district, and throughout the nation, thus mitigating hostility between various classes and interests, and giving to the workers, instead of a feeling of isolation from their fellow-men, the comforting experience of a truly human solidarity and Christian brotherhood.

The progress and extent of social reform will depend upon the economic power of each nation. It is only by a rational and generous exchange of resources between the strong nations and the weak that a state of world-wide peace will become possible, and all centres of conflagration and infection, which might give rise to new conflicts, be eliminated.

There are clear signs which lead Us to think that, amidst the ferment of prejudice and hate which are an inevitable but unhappy feature of the war mentality, peoples have not lost the consciousness of their intimate dependence upon one another for good or for ill; indeed that consciousness appears to have become even more lively and active. Is it not true that serious thinkers are coming to perceive more and more clearly that the way to world salvation lies in the renunciation of national egoism and isolation, ready as they are to ask their own people to bear a heavy burden of the sacrifices which will be needful to bring social peace to other nations? May this Christmas Message of Ours, addressed to all men of good will and generous heart, encourage and increase the army of social crusaders in every land! And may God grant to their peace-loving cause the victory which such a noble enterprise deserves!

(*d*) *The Restoration of the Juridical Constitution*

He who would have the star of peace to shine permanently

over social life must make every effort towards the restoration of a juridical constitution.

The modern idea of justice is often corrupted by a positivist and utilitarian theory and practice subservient to the interests of particular groups, sections, and movements; the course of legislation and the administration of justice being dictated by their policies.

This state of affairs can be remedied only by awakening the human conscience to the need of a juridical constitution based upon God's sovereign lordship and immune from human caprice; a constitution which will use its coercive authority to protect the inviolable rights of man against the aggression of any human power.

A constitution conformable with the divine will gives man a right to juridical security, and accordingly grants him a sphere of rights immune from all arbitrary attack.

The relation of man towards man, of individual towards society, towards authority, and towards civic duties, and the relation of society and authority towards individuals—all these must be based upon a clear juridical foundation and, where necessary, protected by the authority of the courts. This supposes:

(i) a tribunal and a judge taking their directions from law clearly defined;

(ii) clear principles which cannot be upset by unwarranted appeals to a supposed popular sentiment or by merely utilitarian considerations;

(iii) the recognition of the principle that the state also, and the officials and organisations dependent upon the state, are under the obligation of revising and withdrawing such measures as are incompatible with the liberty, the property, the honour, the advancement, or the welfare of individuals.

(e) The Christian Conception of the State

He who would have the star of peace to shine permanently upon human society must strive for the recognition of a political theory and practice based upon rational discipline, noble humanity, and a responsible Christian spirit.

He must assist in bringing back the state and the power of the state to its proper function of serving society, and to a full respect for the human person and for his activity in pursuit of his eternal destiny.

He must use every effort to stamp out the errors which cause the state and its authority to depart from the path of moral rectitude, repudiating the eminently ethical bond which connects them with individual and social life, and denying or in practice ignoring their essential dependence upon the will of the Creator.

He must promote the general recognition of the truth that, even in the temporal order, the deepest meaning, the ultimate moral basis, and the universal legitimacy of the right to govern, lies in the duty to serve.

From *The Rights of Man* (Christmas Message, 1942).

SOCIAL POLICY

(1) LEO XIII, *The Condition of the Working Classes*

RERUM NOVARUM

Leo XIII's great Encyclical on 'The Conditions of the Working Classes' was issued in 1891. As Pius XI and Pius XII have recognised by *Quadragesimo Anno* (1931) and *La Solennita della Pentecoste* (1941), it marked the beginning of the effective exposition of the Roman Catholic view on the socio-political questions of the modern state. Taking the conditions of life of the labouring masses as the starting point, the Encyclical discusses the nature of the relationship between employers and employed, examines and dismisses the socialist solution, expounds the social gospel of the Church, the doctrine of the just wage and the rightful role of trade unions.

That the spirit of revolutionary change, which has long been disturbing the nations of the world, should have passed beyond the sphere of politics and made its influence felt in the cognate sphere of practical economics is not surprising. The elements of the conflict now raging are unmistakable, in the vast expansion of industrial pursuits and the marvellous discoveries of science; in the changed relations between masters and workmen; in the enormous fortunes of some few individuals, and the utter poverty of the masses; in the increased self-reliance and closer mutual combination of the working classes; as also, finally, in the prevailing moral degeneracy ....

Some opportune remedy must be found quickly for the misery and wretchedness pressing so unjustly on the majority of the working class: for the ancient working-men's guilds were abolished in the last century, and no other protective organisation took their place. Public institutions and the laws set aside the ancient religion. Hence by degrees it has come to pass that working-men have been surrendered, isolated and helpless, to the hard-heartedness of employers and the greed of unchecked competition. The mischief has been increased by rapacious usury, which, although more than once condemned by the Church, is nevertheless, under a different guise, but with the like injustice, still practised by covetous and grasping men. To this must be added that the hiring of labour and the conduct of trade are concentrated in the hands of comparatively few; so that a small number of very rich men have been able to lay upon the teeming masses of the labouring poor a yoke little better than that of slavery itself.

SOCIALISM

To remedy these wrongs the Socialists, working on the poor man's envy of the rich, are striving to do away with private property, and contend that individual possessions should become the common property of all, to be administered by the state or by municipal bodies. They hold that by thus transferring property from private individuals to the community, the present mischievous state of things will be set to rights, inasmuch as each citizen will then get his fair share of whatever there is to enjoy. But their contentions are so clearly powerless to end the controversy that were they carried into effect the working-man himself would be among the first to suffer. They are moreover emphatically unjust, for they would rob the lawful possessor, distort the functions of the state, and create utter confusion in the community.

It is surely undeniable that, when a man engages in remunerative labour, the impelling reason and motive of his work is to obtain property, and thereafter to hold it as his very own. If one man hires out to another his strength or skill, he does so for the purpose of receiving in return what is necessary for the satisfaction of his needs; he therefore expressly intends to acquire a right full and real, not only to the remuneration, but also to the disposal of such remuneration, just as he pleases. Thus, if he lives sparingly, saves money, and, for greater security, invests his savings in land, the land, in such case, is only his wages under another form; and, consequently, a working-man's little estate thus purchased should be as completely at his full disposal as are the wages he receives for his labour. But it is precisely in such power of disposal that ownership obtains, whether the property consist of land or chattels. Socialists, therefore, by endeavouring to transfer the possessions of individuals to the community at large, strike at the interests of every wage-earner, since they would deprive him of the liberty of disposing of his wages, and thereby of all hope and possibility of increasing his resources and of bettering his condition in life.

PROPERTY A NATURAL RIGHT

What is of far greater moment, however, is the fact that the remedy they propose is manifestly against justice. For every man has by nature the right to possess property as his own. This is one of the chief points of distinction between man and the animal creation, for the brute has no power of self-direction, but is governed by two main instincts, which keep his powers on the alert, impel him to develop them in a fitting manner, and stimulate and determine him to action without any power of choice . . . . But with man it is wholly different . . . .

THE FAMILY

The natural rights here spoken of, belonging to each individual man, are seen in much stronger light when considered in relation to man's social and domestic obligations. In choosing a state of life, it is indisputable that all are at full liberty to follow the counsel of Jesus Christ as to observing virginity, or to bind themselves by the marriage tie. No human law can abolish the natural and original right of marriage, nor in any way limit the chief and principal purpose of marriage ordained by God's authority from the beginning: *Increase and multiply.*[1] Hence we have the family; the 'society' of a man's house—a society very small, one must admit, but none the less a true society, and one older than any state. Consequently it has rights and duties peculiar to itself which are quite independent of the state.

[1] Gen. i. 28.

THE RIGHT TO PRIVATE PROPERTY PROVED FROM THE FAMILY

That right to property, therefore, which has been proved to belong naturally to individual persons, must in like wise belong to a man in his capacity of head of a family; nay, that right is all the stronger in proportion as the human person receives a wider extension in the family group. It is a most sacred law of nature that a father should provide food and all necessaries for those whom he has begotten; and, similarly, it is natural that he should wish that his children, who carry on, so to speak, and continue his personality, should be by him provided with all that is needful to enable them to keep themselves decently from want and misery amid the uncertainties of this mortal life. Now in no other way can a father effect this except by the ownership of productive property, which he can transmit to his children by inheritance. A family, no less than a state, is, as We have said, a true society, governed by an authority peculiar to itself, that is to say, by the authority of the father. Provided, therefore, the limits which are prescribed by the very purposes for which it exists be not transgressed, the family has at least equal rights with the state in the choice and pursuit of the things needful to its preservation and its just liberty . . . .

The contention, then, that the civil government should at its option intrude into and exercise intimate control over the family and the household, is a great and pernicious error . . . The Socialists, therefore, in setting aside the parent and setting up a state supervision, act *against natural justice*, and break into pieces the stability of all family life . . . .

It must be first of all recognised that the condition of things inherent in human affairs must be borne with, for it is impossible to reduce civil society to one dead level. Socialists may in that intent do their utmost, but all striving against nature is in vain. There naturally exist among mankind manifold differences of the most important kind; people differ in capacity, skill, health, strength; and unequal fortune is a necessary result of unequal condition. Such inequality is far from being disadvantageous either to individuals or to the community. Social and public life can only be maintained by means of various kinds of capacity for business and the playing of many parts; and each man, as a rule, chooses the part which suits his own peculiar domestic condition. As regards bodily labour, even had man never fallen from *the state of innocence*, he would not have remained wholly unoccupied; but that which would then have been his free choice and his delight, became afterwards compulsory, and the painful expiation for his disobedience. *Cursed be the earth in thy work; in thy labour thou shalt eat of it all the days of thy life.*[2]

In like manner, the other pains and hardships of life will have no end or cessation on earth; for the consequences of sin are bitter and hard to bear, and they must accompany man so long as life lasts. To suffer and to endure, therefore, is the lot of humanity; let them strive as they may, no strength and no artifice will ever succeed in banishing from human life the ills and troubles which beset it. If any there are who pretend differently—who hold out to a hard-pressed people the boon of freedom from pain and trouble, an undisturbed repose, and constant enjoyment—they delude the people and impose upon them, and their lying promises will only one day bring forth evils worse than the present. Nothing is more useful than to look upon the world as it really is—and at the same time to seek elsewhere, as We have said, for the solace to its troubles.

AGAINST CLASS WAR

The great mistake made in regard to the matter now under consideration, is to take up with the notion that class is naturally hostile to class, and that the wealthy and the working men are intended by nature to live in mutual conflict. So irrational and so false is this view, that the direct contrary is the truth. Just as the symmetry of the human frame is the result of the suitable arrangement of the different parts of the body, so in a state is it ordained by nature that these two classes should dwell in harmony and agreement, so as to maintain the balance of the body politic. Each needs the other: Capital cannot do without Labour, nor Labour without Capital. Mutual agreement results in the beauty of good order; while perpetual conflict necessarily produces confusion and savage barbarity. Now, in preventing such strife as this, and in uprooting it, the efficacy of Christian

[2] Gen. III. 17.

institutions is marvellous and manifold. First of all, there is no intermediary more powerful than Religion (whereof the Church is the interpreter and guardian) in drawing the rich and the working class together, by reminding each of its duties to the other, and especially of the obligations of justice. Of these duties, the following bind the proletarian and the worker: fully and faithfully to perform the work which has been freely and equitably agreed upon: never to injure the property, nor to outrage the person, of an employer; never to resort to violence in defending their own cause, nor to engage in riot or disorder; and to have nothing to do with men of evil principles, who work upon the people with artful promises of great results, and excite foolish hopes which usually end in useless regrets and grievous loss. The following duties bind the wealthy owner and the employer: not to look upon their workpeople as their bondsmen, but to respect in every man his dignity and worth as a man and as a Christian. They are reminded that, according to natural reason and Christian philosophy, working for gain is creditable, not shameful, to a man, since it enables him to earn an honourable livelihood; but to misuse men as though they were things in the pursuit of gain, or to value them solely for their physical powers—that is truly shameful and inhuman. Again justice demands that, in dealing with the working man religion and the good of his soul must be kept in mind. Hence the employer is bound to see that the worker has time for his religious duties; that he be not exposed to corrupting influences and dangerous occasions; and that he be not led away to neglect his home and family, or to squander his earnings. Furthermore, the employer must never tax his work-people beyond their strength, or employ them in work unsuited to their sex and age. His great and principal duty is to give every one what is just . . . .

STATE AND WORKING CLASS

Although all citizens, without exception, can and ought to contribute to that common good in which individuals share so advantageously to themselves, yet it should not be supposed that all can contribute in the like way and to the same extent. No matter what changes may occur in forms of government, there will ever be differences and inequalities of condition in the state. Society cannot exist or be conceived of without them. Some there must be who devote themselves to the work of the commonwealth, who make the laws or administer justice, or whose advice and authority govern the nation in times of peace, and defend it in war. Such men clearly occupy the foremost place in the state, and should be held in highest estimation, for their work concerns most nearly and effectively the general interests of the community. Those who labour at a trade or calling do not promote the general welfare in such measure as this; but they benefit the nation, if less directly, in a most important manner. We have insisted, it is true, that, since the end of society is to make men better, the chief good that society can possess is Virtue. Nevertheless, it is the business of all well-constituted states to see to the provision of those material and external helps *the use of which is necessary to virtuous action.*[3] Now for the provision of such commodities, the labour of the working class—the exercise of their skill, and the employment of their strength, in the cultivation of the land, and in the workshops of trade—is especially responsible and quite indispensable. Indeed, their co-operation is in this respect so important that it may be truly said that it is only by the labour of working-men that states grow rich. Justice, therefore, demands that the interests of the working classes should be carefully watched over by the administration, so that they who contribute so largely to the advantage of the community may themselves share in the benefits which they create—that being housed, clothed, and bodily fit, they may find their life less hard and more endurable. It follows that whatever shall appear to prove conducive to the well-being of those who work should obtain favourable consideration. There is no fear that solicitude of this kind will be harmful to any interest: on the contrary, it will be to the advantage of all; for it cannot but be good for the commonwealth to shield from misery those on whom it so largely depends for the things that it needs.

We have said that the state must not absorb the individual or the family; both should be allowed free and untrammelled action so far as is consistent with the common good and the interests of others. Rulers should, nevertheless, anxiously safeguard the community and all its members; the community, because the conservation thereof is so emphatically the business

[3] St Thomas, *De Regimine Principum*, I, 15.

of the supreme power, that the safety of the commonwealth is not only the first law, but it is a government's whole reason of existence; and the members, because both philosophy and the Gospel concur in laying down that the object of the government of the state should be, not the advantage of the ruler, but the benefit of those over whom he is placed. As the power to rule comes from God, and is, as it were, a participation in His, the highest of all sovereignties, it should be exercised as the power of God is exercised—with a fatherly solicitude which not only guides the whole, but reaches also to details . . . .

When there is question of defending the rights of individuals, the poor and badly-off have a claim to especial consideration. The richer class have many ways of shielding themselves, and stand less in need of help from the state; whereas the mass of the poor have no resources of their own to fall back upon, and must chiefly depend upon the assistance of the state. And it is for this reason that wage-earners, since they mostly belong to that class, should be specially cared for and protected by the Government . . . .

A JUST WAGE

Let the working man and the employer make free agreements, and in particular let them agree freely as to the wages; nevertheless, there underlies a dictate of natural justice more imperious and ancient than any bargain between man and man, namely, that wages ought not to be insufficient to support a frugal and well-behaved wage-earner. If through necessity or fear of a worse evil the workman accept harder conditions because an employer or contractor will afford him no better, he is made the victim of force and injustice . . . .

If a workman's wages be sufficient to enable him comfortably to support himself, his wife, and his children, he will find it easy, if he be a sensible man, to practise thrift; and he will not fail, by cutting down expenses, to put by some little savings and thus secure a modest source of income. Nature itself would urge him to this. We have seen that this great labour question cannot be solved save by assuming as a principle that private ownership must be held sacred and inviolable. The law, therefore, should favour ownership, and its policy should be to induce as many as possible of the people to become owners.

TRADE UNIONS

In the last place—employers and workmen may of themselves effect much in the matter We are treating, by means of such associations and organisations as afford opportune aid to those who are in distress, and which draw the two classes more closely together . . . .

The most important of all are Working-men's Unions; for these virtually include all the rest . . . It is gratifying to know that there are actually in existence not a few associations of this nature, consisting either of workmen alone, or of workmen and employers together; but it were greatly to be desired that they should become more numerous and more efficient. We have spoken of them more than once; yet it will be well to explain here how notably they are needed, to show that they exist of their own right, and what should be their organisation and their mode of action . . . .

Private societies, then, although they exist within the state, and are severally part of the state, cannot nevertheless be absolutely, and as such, prohibited by the state. For to enter into a 'society' of this kind is the natural right of man; and the state is bound to protect natural rights, not to destroy them; and if it forbid its citizens to form associations, it contradicts the very principle of its own existence; for both they and it exist in virtue of the like principle, namely, the natural tendency of man to dwell in society . . . .

DUTIES OF ASSOCIATIONS

To sum up, then, We may lay it down as a general and lasting law, that working-men's associations should be so organised and governed as to furnish the best and most suitable means for attaining what is aimed at, that is to say, for helping each individual member to better his condition to the utmost in body, soul, and property.

From Encyclical *Rerum Novarum* (1891).

(2) Pius xi, *The Social Order*

Forty years after *Rerum Novarum*, Pope Pius XI issued the Encyclical *Quadragesimo Anno* to celebrate the Leonine social doctrine and restate it in terms of the 1930's. In particular this dealt again with the formation of trade unions and employers' associations, discussing briefly the corporative state, and bringing Leo's condemnation of socialism up to date by distinguishing between social democracy and Communism, while condemning both.

WORKING-MEN'S UNIONS

Worthy of all praise, therefore, are the directions authoritatively promulgated by Leo XIII, which served to break down this opposition and dispel these suspicions. They have a still higher distinction, however; that of encouraging Christian working-men to form unions according to their various trades, and of teaching them how to do it. Many were thus confirmed in the path of duty, in spite of the vehement attractions of socialist unions, which claimed to be the sole defenders and champions of the lowly and oppressed . . . .

ORGANISATIONS AMONG OTHER CLASSES

The doctrine concerning the innate right of association, which Leo XIII treated so learnedly and defended so vigorously, began to find ready application to associations other than those of working-men. It would seem therefore that the Encyclical is in no small measure responsible for the gratifying prosperity and increase of associations amongst farmers and others of the middle classes. These excellent organisations, with others of a similar kind, happily combine economic advantages with spiritual culture.

DISTRIBUTION OF WEALTH

It is easy to see that in order to keep these false doctrines from blocking for them the path that leads to justice and peace, both parties had only to hearken to the wise words of Our Predecessor: 'The earth even though apportioned amongst private owners, ceases not thereby to minister to the needs of all.'[1] This teaching We Ourselves have reaffirmed above, when We wrote

[1] Encyclical, *Rerum Novarum*, § 7.

that the division of goods, which is effected by private ownership, is confirmed by nature itself, to the end that created things may minister to man's needs in an orderly and stable fashion; and this must be constantly borne in mind, if we would not wander from the path of truth.

Now, not every kind of distribution of wealth and property amongst men is such that it can at all, and still less can properly, attain the end intended by God. Wealth therefore, which is constantly being augmented by social and economic progress, must be so distributed amongst the various individuals and classes of society, that the needs of all, of which Leo XIII spoke, be thereby satisfied. In other words, the good of the whole community must be safeguarded. By this principle of social justice, one class is forbidden to exclude the other from a share of the benefits. This principle is violated by those of the wealthy who, practically free from care in their own possessions, consider it perfectly right that they should receive everything and the worker nothing; it is violated also by those of the proletariat who demand for themselves all the fruits of production, as being the work of their hands. Such men, vehemently incensed by the violation of justice, go too far in vindicating the one right of which they are conscious; they attack and seek to abolish all forms of ownership and all incomes not obtained by labour, whatever be their nature or whatever social function they represent, for the sole reason that they are not obtained by labour. In this connection it must be noted that the appeal made by some to the words of the Apostle: 'If any man will not work, neither let him eat,'[2] is as inept as it is unfounded. The Apostle is here passing judgment on those who refuse to work though they can and ought to work; he admonishes us to use diligently our time and our powers of body and mind, and not to become burdensome to others as long as we are able to provide for ourselves. In no sense does he teach that labour is the sole title which gives a right to a living or to an income.[3]

Each one, therefore, must receive his due share, and the distribution of created goods must be brought into conformity with the demands of the common good or social justice. For every sincere observer is conscious that, on account of the vast difference between the few who hold excessive wealth and the many

[2] II Thess. III. 10.

[3] Cf. II Thess. III. 8-10.

who live in destitution, the distribution of wealth is to-day gravely defective.

EMANCIPATION OF THE PROLETARIAT

This is the aim which Our Predecessor urged as the necessary object of our efforts: the emancipation of the proletariat. It calls for more emphatic assertion and more insistent repetition, because these salutary injunctions of the Pontiff have not infrequently been forgotten, deliberately ignored, or deemed impracticable, though they were both feasible and imperative. They have lost none of their force or wisdom for our own age, even though the horrible pauperism of Leo's time is less prevalent today. The condition of the working-man has indeed been improved and rendered more equitable, particularly in the larger and more civilised states, where the workers can no longer be said to be universally in misery and want. But, when the use of machinery and the expansion of industry progressed with astonishing speed and overran and took possession of many countries in the new world, no less than of the ancient civilisations of the Far East, the number of needy proletarians, whose groans rise from earth to heaven, increased beyond all measure. Moreover, there is the immense army of agricultural wage-earners whose condition is depressed in the extreme, and who have no hope of ever obtaining 'any share in the land'.[4] These also, unless appropriate and efficacious remedies be applied, will remain perpetually sunk in their proletarian condition.

It is very true that proletarianism must be carefully distinguished from pauperism; nevertheless, the immense number of proletarians on the one hand, and the enormous wealth of the very rich on the other, are an unanswerable argument that the material goods so abundantly produced in this age of industrialism are far from rightly distributed and equitably shared among the various classes of men.

Every effort therefore must be made that at least in future a just share only of the fruits of production be permitted to accumulate in the hands of the wealthy, and that an ample sufficiency be supplied to the workers. The purpose is not that these become negligent about working, for man is born to labour as the bird to fly, but that by thrift they may increase their possessions, and by the prudent management of the same may be

[4] Encyclical, *Rerum Novarum*, § 35.

enabled to bear family burdens with greater ease and security; and that being freed from that uncertainty which is the lot of the proletarian, they may not only be in a position to support life's changing fortunes, but may also have the confidence that, when their own lives are ended, some provision will remain for those whom they leave behind them.

These ideas were not merely suggested, but stated in frank and open terms, by Our Predecessor. We emphasise them with renewed insistence in this present Encyclical; for unless serious attempts be made, with all energy and without delay, to put them into practice, let nobody persuade himself that public order and the peace and tranquillity of human society can be effectively defended against the forces of revolution.

SOCIAL ORDER

When We speak of the reform of institutions, it is principally the state that comes to mind. Not indeed that all salvation is to be hoped from its intervention; but because on account of the evil of 'individualism', as We called it, things have come to such a pass that the highly developed social life which once flourished in a variety of associations organically linked with each other, has been damaged and all but ruined, leaving thus virtually only individuals and the state, to the no small detriment of the state itself. Social life has entirely lost its organic form; the state, today encumbered with all the burdens once borne by those associations now destroyed, has been submerged and overwhelmed by an infinity of occupations and duties . . . .

Order, as St Thomas well defines,[5] is unity arising from the proper arrangement of a number of objects; hence, true and genuine social order demands that the various members of a society be joined together by some firm bond. Such a bond of union is provided both by the production of goods or the rendering of services in which employers and employees of one and the same vocational group collaborate; and by the common good which all such groups should unite to promote, each in its own sphere, with friendly harmony. Now this union will become powerful and efficacious in proportion to the fidelity with which the individuals and the vocational groups strive to discharge their professional duties and to excel in them . . . .

[5] St Thomas, *Cont. Gent.* III, 71; cf. *Summ. Theol.* Ia, q. 65, art. 2c.

Within recent times, as all are aware, a special syndical and corporative organisation has been inaugurated which, in view of the subject of the present Encyclical, demands of Us some mention and opportune comment.

The state here grants juridical personality to the union, and thereby confers on it some of the features of a monopoly; for in virtue of this grant, it alone can uphold the rights of the workers or employers (according to the kind of union), and it alone can negotiate wage-terms and make labour agreements. Membership of the union is optional, but only to this extent can the union be said to be voluntary; because contribution to the union and other special taxes are obligatory for all who belong to each trade or profession, whether workers or employers, and the labour agreements made by the legally established union are likewise binding on all. It is true that it has been authoritatively declared that the legally established union does not exclude the existence of other professional associations, which, however, are not legally recognised.

The corporations are composed of delegates of the unions of workers and employers of the same trade or profession, and, as true and genuine organs and institutions of the state, they direct and co-ordinate the activities of the unions in all matters of common interest.

Strikes and lock-outs are forbidden. If the contending parties cannot come to an agreement, public authority intervenes.

Little reflection is required to perceive the advantage of the institution thus summarily described: peaceful collaboration of various classes, repression of socialist organisations and efforts, the moderating influence of a special magistracy. But in order to overlook nothing in a matter of such importance, and in the light of the general principles stated above, as well as of those shortly to be added, We feel bound to say that to Our knowledge there are some who fear that the state is substituting itself in the place of private initiative, instead of limiting itself to necessary and sufficient assistance. It is feared that the new syndical and corporative organisation tends to have an excessively bureaucratic and political character, and that, notwithstanding the general advantages referred to above, it ends in serving particular political aims rather than in contributing to the initiation and promotion of a better social order.

We believe that to attain this last named lofty purpose, for the true and permanent advantage of the commonwealth, there is need before and above all else of the blessing of God, and in the second place of the co-operation of all men of good will. We believe, moreover, as a necessary consequence, that the end intended will be the more certainly attained, the greater the number of those who are ready to contribute their technical, professional and social competence to this, and, more still, the greater the contribution made by Catholic principles and their practical application.

SOCIALISM AND COMMUNISM

Since the days of Leo XIII, socialism, . . . the chief enemy with which his battles were waged, has, no less than the economic regime, undergone profound changes. At that time socialism could almost be termed a single system, which defended certain definite and mutually coherent doctrines. Nowadays it has in the main become divided into two opposing and often bitterly hostile camps, neither of which, however, has abandoned the anti-Christian basis which was ever characteristic of socialism.

One section of socialism has undergone approximately the same change as that through which, as we have described, the capitalist economic regime has passed; it has degenerated into communism. Communism teaches and pursues a twofold aim: merciless class warfare, and complete abolition of private ownership; and this it does, not in secret and by hidden methods, but openly, publicly, and by every means, even the most violent. To obtain these ends, communists shrink from nothing and fear nothing; and when they have acquired power, it is monstrous beyond belief how cruel and inhuman they show themselves to be. Evidence for this is the ghastly destruction and ruin with which they have laid waste immense tracts of Eastern Europe and Asia; while their antagonism and open hostility to Holy Church and to God Himself are too well, alas! only too well proved by facts and perfectly known to all. We do not think it necessary to warn upright and faithful children of the Church against the impious and nefarious character of communism. But We cannot contemplate without sorrow the heedlessness of those who seem to despise these imminent dangers, and with a sort of indolent apathy allow the propagation far and wide of those doctrines, which seek by violence and bloodshed the destruction of the whole of society. Even more severely must be condemned the foolhardiness of those who neglect to remove or modify such conditions as exasperate the hearts of the people, and so prepare the way for the overthrow and ruin of the social order.

The other section, which has retained the name of socialism, is much less radical in its views. Not only does it condemn recourse to violence; it even mitigates class warfare and the abolition of private property and qualifies them to some extent, if it does not actually reject them. It would seem as if socialism were afraid of its own principles and of the conclusions drawn therefrom by communists, and in consequence were tending towards the truths which Christian tradition has always held in respect; for it cannot be denied that its opinions sometimes closely approach the just demands of Christian social reformers.

For class warfare, provided it abstains from enmities and mutual hatred, changes little by little into a justifiable dispute, based upon the desire of justice. If this is by no means the happy social peace which we all long for, it can be and ought to be a point of departure for the mutual co-operation of vocational groups. The war waged against private ownership has more and more abated, and is being so limited that ultimately it is not the possession of the means of production which is attacked, but a form of social authority which property has usurped in violation of all justice. This authority in fact pertains not to individual owners, but to the state. If these changes continue, it may well come about that gradually these tenets of mitigated socialism will no longer be different from the programme of those who seek to reform human society according to Christian principles. For it is rightly contended that certain forms of property must be reserved to the state, since they carry with them a power too great to be left to private individuals without injury to the community at large.

Just demands and desires of this kind contain nothing opposed to Christian truth; much less are they peculiar to socialism. Those therefore who look for nothing else, have no reason for becoming socialists . . .

Our pronouncement is as follows: Whether considered as a doctrine, or as an historical fact, or as a movement, socialism, if it really remains socialism, cannot be brought into harmony with the dogmas of the Catholic Church, even after it has yielded to truth and justice on the points we have mentioned: the reason being that it conceives human society in a way utterly alien to Christian truth.

For according to Christian doctrine man, endowed with a social nature, is placed here on earth in order that, spending his life in society, and under an authority ordained by God,[6] he may cultivate and evolve to the full all his faculties to the praise and glory of his Creator; and that, by fulfilling faithfully the functions of his trade or other calling, he may attain both to temporal and eternal happiness. Socialism, on the contrary, entirely ignorant of and unconcerned about this sublime end both of individuals and of society, affirms that human society was instituted merely for the sake of material well-being . . . .

If, like all errors, socialism contains a certain element of truth (and this the Sovereign Pontiffs have never denied), it is nevertheless founded upon a doctrine of human society peculiarly its own, which is opposed to true Christianity. Religious socialism, Christian socialism, are expressions implying a contradiction in terms. No one can be at the same time a sincere Catholic and a socialist properly so called.

From Encyclical *Quadragesimo Anno* (1931).

(3) Pius XII, *Social and Economic Policy*

Pope Pius XII in his discourse *La Solennita della Pentecoste* marked the fiftieth anniversary of *Rerum Novarum* with a further discussion of social and economic policy.

The Encyclical, *Rerum Novarum*, expounds, on the question of property and man's sustenance, principles which have lost nothing of their inherent vigour with the passage of time, and today, fifty years after, strike their roots deeper and retain their innate vitality. Every man, as a living being gifted with reason, has in fact from nature the fundamental right to make use of the material goods of the earth, while it is left to the will of man and to the juridical statutes of nations to regulate in greater detail the actuation of this right. This individual right cannot in any way be suppressed, even by other clear and undisputed rights over material goods. Undoubtedly the natural order,

[6] Cf. Rom. XIII. 1.

deriving from God, demands also private property and the free reciprocal commerce of goods by interchange and gift, as well as the functioning of the state as a control over both these institutions. But all this remains subordinated to the natural scope of material goods and cannot emancipate itself from the first and fundamental right which concedes their use to all men; but it should rather serve to make possible the actuation of this right in conformity with its scope. Only thus can we and must we secure that private property and the use of material goods bring to society peace and prosperity and long life, that they no longer set up precarious conditions which will give rise to struggles and jealousies, and which are left to the mercy of the blind interplay of force and weakness.

The native right to the use of material goods, intimately linked as it is to the dignity and other rights of the human person, together with the statutes mentioned above, provides man with a secure material basis of the highest import, on which to rise to the fulfilment, with reasonable liberty, of his moral duties. The safe guardianship of this right will ensure the personal dignity of man, and will facilitate for him the attention to and fulfilment of that sum of stable duties and decisions for which he is directly responsible to his Creator. Man has in truth the entirely personal duty to preserve and order to perfection his material and spiritual life, so as to secure the religious and moral scope which God has assigned to all men, and has given them as the supreme norm obliging always and everywhere, before all other duties.

To safeguard the inviolable sphere of the rights of the human person and to facilitate the fulfilment of his duties should be the essential office of every public authority. Does not this flow from that genuine concept of the common good which the state is called upon to promote? Hence, it follows that the care of such a *common good* does not imply a power so extensive over the members of the community that in virtue of it the public authority can interfere with the evolution of that individual activity which we have just described, decide directly on the beginning or—excepting the case of legitimate capital punishment—the ending of human life, determine at will the manner of his physical, spiritual, religious and moral movements in opposition to the personal duties or rights of man, and to this end abolish or deprive of efficacy his natural rights to material goods. To deduce such extension of power from the care of the common good would be equivalent to overthrowing the very meaning of the word common good, and falling into the error that the proper scope of man on earth is society, that society is an end in itself, that man has no other life which awaits him beyond that which ends here below. Likewise the national economy, as it is the product of the men who work together in the community of the state, has no other end than to secure without interruption the material conditions in which the individual life of the citizens may fully develop. Where this is secured in a permanent way, a people will be, in a true sense, economically rich because the general well-being, and consequently the personal right of all to the use of worldly goods, is thus actuated in conformity with the purpose willed by the Creator.

From this, beloved children, it will be easy for you to conclude that the economic riches of a people do not properly consist in the abundance of goods, measured according to a purely and solely material calculation of their worth, but in the fact that such an abundance represents and offers really and effectively the material basis sufficient for the proper personal development of its members. If such a just distribution of goods were not secured, or were effected only imperfectly, the real scope of national economy would not be attained; for, although there were at hand a lucky abundance of goods to dispose of, the people, in not being called upon to share them, would not be economically rich but poor. Suppose, on the other hand, that such a distribution is effected genuinely and permanently, and you will see a people, even if it disposes of less goods, making itself economically sound.

These fundamental concepts regarding the riches and poverty of peoples, it seems to Us particulary opportune to set before you today, when there is a tendency to measure and judge such riches and poverty by balance sheets and by purely quantitative criteria of the need or the redundance of goods. If, instead, the scope of the national economy is correctly considered, then it will become a guide for the efforts of statesmen and peoples, and will enlighten them to walk spontaneously along a way which does not call for continual exactions in goods and blood, but will give fruits of peace and general welfare.

With the use of material goods you yourselves, dear children, see how labour is connected. *Rerum Novarum* teaches that there are two essential characteristics of human labour: it is personal and it is necessary. It is personal, because it is achieved through the exercise of man's particular forces; it is necessary, because without it one cannot secure what is indispensable to life; and man has a natural, grave, individual obligation to maintain life. To the personal duty to labour imposed by nature corresponds and follows the natural right of each individual to make of labour the means to provide for his own life and that of his children; so profoundly is the empire of nature ordained for the preservation of man.

But note that such a duty and the corresponding right to work is imposed on and conceded to the individual in the first instance by nature, and not by society, as if man were nothing more than a mere slave or official of the community. From that it follows that the duty and the right to organise the labour of the people belongs above all to the people immediately interested: the employers and the workers. If they do not fulfil their functions, or cannot because of special extraordinary contingencies fulfil them, then it falls back on the state to intervene in the field of labour and in the division and distribution of work according to the form and measure that the common good properly understood demands.

In any case, every legitimate and beneficial interference of the state in the field of labour should be such as to safeguard and respect its personal character, both in the broad outlines, and, as far as possible, in what concerns its execution; and this will happen, if the norms of the state do not abolish or render impossible the exercise of other rights and duties equally personal; such as the right to give God His due worship; the right to marry; the right of husband and wife, of father and mother to lead a married domestic life; the right to a reasonable liberty in the choice of a state of life and fulfilment of a true vocation; a personal right, this last, if ever there was one, belonging to the spirit of man, and sublime when the higher imprescriptible rights of God and of the Church meet, as in the choice and fulfilment of the priestly and religious vocations.

According to the teaching of *Rerum Novarum*, nature itself has closely joined private property with the existence of human society and its true civilisation, and in a very special manner with the existence and development of the family. Such a link appears more than obvious. Should not private property secure for the father of a family the healthy liberty he needs in order to fulfil the duties assigned him by the Creator regarding the physical, spiritual and religious welfare of the family? In the family the nation finds the natural and fecund roots of its greatness and power. If private property has to conduce to the good of the family, all public standards, and especially those of the state which regulate its possession, must not only make possible and preserve such a function—a function in the natural order under certain aspects superior to all others—but must also perfect it ever more. A so-called civil progress would, in fact, be unnatural, which—either through the excessive burdens imposed, or through exaggerated direct interference—were to render private property void of significance, practically taking from the family and its head the freedom to follow the scope set by God for the perfection of family life.

Of all the goods that can be the object of private property, none is more conformable to nature, according to the teaching of *Rerum Novarum*, than the land, the holding on which the family lives, and from the products of which it draws all or part of its subsistence. And it is in the spirit of *Rerum Novarum* to state that, as a rule, only that stability which is rooted in one's own holding, makes of the family the vital and most perfect and fecund cell of society, joining up in a brilliant manner in its progressive cohesion the present and future generations. If today the concept and the creation of vital spaces is at the centre of social and political aims, should not one, before all else, think of the vital space of the family and free it of the fetters of conditions which do not permit one even to formulate the idea of a homestead of one's own?

Our planet, with all its extent of oceans and seas and lakes, with mountains and plains covered with eternal snows and ice, with great deserts and tractless lands is not, all the same, without habitable regions and vital spaces, now abandoned to wild natural vegetation, and well suited to be cultivated by man to satisfy his needs and civil activities; and more than once it is inevitable that some families, migrating from one spot or another, should go elsewhere in search of a new homeland. Then, according to the teaching of *Rerum Novarum*, the right of the family to a vital space is recognised. When this happens, emigration attains its natural scope, as experience often shows; We mean the more favourable distribution of men on the earth's surface, suitable to colonies of agricultural workers; that surface which God created and prepared for the use of all. If the two parties, those who agree to leave their native land, and those who agree to admit the newcomers, remain anxious to eliminate as far as possible all obstacles to the birth and growth of real confidence between the country of emigration and that of immigration, all those affected by such a transference of people and places will profit by the transaction: the families will receive a plot of ground which will be native land for them in the true sense of the word; the thickly inhabited countries will be relieved, and their peoples will acquire new friends in foreign countries; and the states which receive the emigrants will acquire industrious citizens. In this way the nations which give and those which receive will both contribute to the increased welfare of man and the progress of human culture.

From Discourse *La Solennita della Pentecoste* (1 June 1941), commemorating the fiftieth anniversary of the Encyclical *Rerum Novarum* of Pope Leo XIII. Printed in *Principles for Peace*, National Catholic Welfare Conference, Washington (1943).

Pius xi, *Communism*

In his Encyclical Letter *Divini Redemptoris* dated 19 March 1937, Pope Pius XI set out categorically to state the Roman Catholic view of Communism, and Roman Catholic answer to the questions of politics and social life from which Communism springs. He begins by describing briefly the main tenets of Marxism, and then goes on to the 'fruits of Communism', by which he means atrocities in Russia, Mexico and Spain, lawlessness and impiety. Then comes a section on 'The doctrine of the Church contrasted with Communism' which provides a short exposition of Roman Catholic doctrine on natural law, the family, civil society, the rights and duties of man, the principles of social order, and the limits of state authority.

THE DOCTRINE OF THE CHURCH

Having thus fully exposed the false doctrines of the bolshevistic atheists and their lying and violent methods, We must now, Venerable Brethren, contrast with them the true notion of the *Civitas humana*, and set forth briefly the concept of the civil society as it is made known to us by reason and revelation through the mouth of the Church, Teacher of all nations.

God the sovereign reality. The first fact to be borne in mind is that there exists above all things one Supreme Being, God, who is the almighty creator of the whole universe and the all-wise and all-just judge of mankind. This sovereign reality, God, is the utter and complete refutation of the arrogant and baseless falsehoods of the communists. And, mark it well, it is not because men believe in God that God exists. No, it is because He really exists that all men, at any rate all who are not wilfully blind to the truth, believe in Him and pray to Him.

Man and his rights. Concerning man, the teaching of the Catholic faith and of the human reason has been explained in its main features in Our Encyclical on Christian Education.[1] Man has a spiritual and immortal soul, and, being a person and endowed by the Creator with quite marvellous gifts of mind and body, he is rightly called a 'microcosm' (to use the expression of the ancients) because in perfection he far transcends the whole measureless world of inanimate nature. His final end, not only in this life but also in the everlasting life to come, is God alone; and because he has been raised up by sanctifying grace to the dignity of a son of God, he is united to the kindgom of God in the mystical Body of Jesus Christ. In consequence of this God has bestowed upon him various prerogatives, such as the right to integrity of life and body; the right to acquire the necessities of life and duly pursue the end which God has appointed to him; the right of association, and the right to own and use private property.

The family. Moreover, marriage and the natural use of marriage being of divine institution, the constitution of the family and its chief functions likewise have their origin in the sovereign Creator of all, and not in the will of man or in any economic system. These are matters which we have explained fully enough in Our Encyclical on the sanctity of Christian Marriage as well as in the aforesaid Encyclical on Christian Education.

Civil society divinely instituted for the sake of man. But God has also destined man for the civil society which his nature requires. In the Creator's plan society is the natural means which every citizen can and must use for the attainment of his appointed

[1] *Divini illius Magistri*, 31 Dec. 1929 (see above, p. 231).

end; and therefore society exists for the sake of man, not man for the sake of society. But this principle is not to be understood in the individualistic sense of the liberals, who subordinate the community to the selfish interests of each single citizen. What it means is that their organic union in society enables all citizens, through their mutual collaboration, to attain true earthly prosperity. The grouping of human beings in society also develops and fosters in man those individual and social qualities with which he is naturally endowed, and which, transcending as they do the immediate and selfish interests of the individual, exhibit in human society an aspect of the divine perfection which man living in solitude could never display. In this respect too society is a benefit to man, enabling him to recognise this reflection of the divine goodness and to render thanks for it to the Creator by praise and worship. For it is only individual human beings, not any association of them, that are endowed with reason and moral freedom.

Reciprocal rights and duties of man and society. From this it follows that a man cannot repudiate the duties which by God's commandment bind him to the civil society; its rulers have accordingly the right to constrain him to his duty should he unlawfully refuse to obey. But it follows equally that society cannot deprive the citizen of his God-given rights, the chief of which We have mentioned above, nor by its decree make the exercise of them impossible. It is therefore a conclusion of the human reason itself that all earthly things are given to man for his use and benefit, so that he may thus direct them back to the Creator who is their source; and this accords with what the Apostle of the Nations wrote to the Corinthians concerning the Christian economy of salvation: 'Everything is for you . . . and you for Christ, and Christ for God.'[2] See, then, how communism, by inverting the true relation of man to society, debases human personality, and how reason and revelation exalt it!

General economic and social principles. As for the economic and social order and the cause of the workers, the guiding principles to be observed on these matters have been expounded by Leo XIII in his Encyclical *Rerum novarum*,[3] and We Ourself, in Our Encyclical on the Social Order,[4] have adapted them to the

[2] I Cor. III, 22, 23.

[3] 15 May 1891 (see below, p. 201).

[4] 15 May 1931 (see below, p. 210).

conditions and needs of modern times. In this same letter, closely adhering to the ancient doctrine of the Church on the nature of private property in its relation to the individual and to society, We clearly and distinctly emphasised the rights and dignity of human labour, the mutual relations of help and support which should subsist between those who provide capital and those who supply their labour, and the worker's right in strict justice to the wage necessary for himself and his family.

The only hope for the salvation of society. We showed, further, that there can be no hope of saving human society from the ruin and disaster to which an amoral liberalism is driving it, unless the economic and social order is inspired and guided by the principles of social justice and Christian charity; no salvation, certainly, is to be found for it in class warfare, in terrorism, or in the arbitrary and tyrannical use of the power of the state. We indicated also that the true welfare of the people should be secured through a properly devised system of corporations which would acknowledge and respect the different ranks of social authority; that all workers' associations should combine in friendly collaboration to pursue the common good of society; and that therefore the true and proper function of the public authority consists in doing everything possible to encourage such mutual co-operation and harmony.

Authority of the state and rights of citizens. With a view to the attainment of social peace by means of this universal co-operation, the principles of Catholic doctrine recognise in the government such dignity and authority as it needs in order to keep vigilant guard over those divine and human rights upon which the Scriptures and the Fathers of the Church so greatly insist. It is utterly untrue, and mere empty talk, to say that all citizens have equal rights and that there are no ruling ranks in society. On this subject we need only mention the aforesaid Encyclicals of Leo XIII, especially those on Civil Authority[5] and on the Christian Constitution of States,[6] where Catholics may find clearly expounded the principles of reason and revelation which will arm them against the beguiling and dangerous doctrines of communism.

To deprive citizens of their personal rights and thus reduce them to slavery; to deny the first and primary origin of civil

[5] *Diuturnum illud*, 29 June 1861. *Acta Leonis XIII*, vol. II, pp. 269-287.

[6] *Immortale Dei*, 1 Nov. 1885. *Acta Leonis XIII*, vol. V, pp. 118-150 (see below, p. 189)

society and its authority; iniquitously to use the authority of the state as the tool of a criminal conspiracy—all this is completely opposed to natural ethics and to the will of the divine Creator. The community as well as the citizen is of divine origin, and each is adapted to the other; therefore neither citizen nor society can repudiate each other's obligations nor deny or reduce each other's rights. In their fundamentals these mutual relations of citizen and community have been established and regulated by God Himself; and therefore the arrogant claim of the communists to substitute for the divine law, based upon the principles of truth and charity, a political party programme inspired by hate and devised by the wit of man, is beyond all doubt a most unjust and iniquitous usurpation.

Aim of the Church's social doctrine. In proclaiming her clear teaching on this subject the Catholic Church has but one object: to realise on earth that glory for God and peace for men[7] of which the angels sang in their joyous message over the cave of Bethlehem; to establish true peace and true happiness so far as these can be attained, at any rate by men of good will, even during this mortal life, in preparation for the perfect happiness of heaven.

Rights and duties reconciled. It is a doctrine opposed equally to all erroneous extremes and to the violent methods and policies of those who embrace them. Today as ever in the past, the Church pursues the even path of truth and justice, vindicating her teaching by argument and promoting its realisation in practice. This she does by harmonising rights and duties with each other: authority with liberty; the dignity of the state with the dignity of the individual; the human personality of the subject and his consequent duty of obedience, with the function of those who wield authority in God's name; and finally by reconciling an ordinate love of self, family, and country with that charity towards other families and other nations which is based upon the love of God, the common Father of all, the source of all things and their final goal.

From Encyclical *Divini Redemptoris* (19 March 1937).

[7] Cf. Luke II, 14.

Pius xi, *Church, State and Family in Education*

It is the inalienable right as well as the indispensable duty of the Church, to watch over the entire education of her children, in all institutions, public or private, not merely in regard to the religious instruction there given, but in regard to every other branch of learning and every regulation in so far as religion and morality are concerned.

Nor should the exercise of this right be considered undue interference, but rather maternal care on the part of the Church in protecting her children from the grave danger of all kinds of doctrinal and moral evil. Moreover, this watchfulness of the Church not only can create no real inconvenience, but must, on the contrary, confer valuable assistance in the right ordering and well-being of families and of civil society; for it keeps far away from youth the moral poison which at that inexperienced and changeable age more easily penetrates the mind and more rapidly spreads its baneful effects. For it is true, as Leo XIII has wisely pointed out, that without proper religious and moral instruction 'every form of intellectual culture will be injurious; for young people not accustomed to respect God, will be unable to bear the restraint of a virtuous life, and never having learned to deny themselves anything, they will easily be incited to disturb the public order.' ....

The family, therefore, holds directly from the Creator the mission and, hence, the right to educate the offspring, a right inalienable because inseparably joined to the strict obligation, a right anterior to any right whatever of civil society, and of the state, and therefore, inviolable on the part of any power on earth ...

It must be borne in mind also that the obligation of the family to bring up children, includes not only religious and moral education, but physical and civic education as well, principally in so far as it touches upon religion and morality. This incontestable right of the family has at various times been recognised by nations anxious to respect the natural law in their civil enactments. Thus, to give one recent example, the Supreme Court of the United States of North America, in a decision on an important controversy, declared that it is not in the competence of the state to fix any uniform standard of education by forcing children to receive instruction exclusively in public schools, and it bases its decision on the natural law: the child is not the mere creature of the state; those who nurture him and direct his destiny have the right, coupled with the high duty, to educate him and prepare him for the fulfilment of his obligations . . . .

These rights have been conferred upon civil society by the Author of nature Himself, not by title of fatherhood, as in the case of the Church and of the family, but in virtue of the authority which it possesses to promote the common temporal welfare, which is precisely the purpose of its existence. Consequently, education cannot pertain to civil society in the same way in which it pertains to the Church and to the family, but in a different way corresponding to its own particular end and object.

Now this end and object, the common welfare in the temporal order, consists in that peace and security in which families and individual citizens have the free exercise of their rights, and at the same time enjoy the greatest spiritual and temporal prosperity possible in this life, by the mutual union and co-ordination of the work of all. The function, therefore, of the civil authority residing in the state is twofold, to protect and to foster, but by no means to absorb the family and the individual, or to substitute itself for them . . . .

In general, then, it is the right and duty of the state to protect, according to the rules of right reason and faith, the moral and religious education of youth, by removing public impediments that stand in the way. In the first place, it pertains to the state, in view of the common good, to promote in various ways the education and instruction of youth. It should begin by encouraging and assisting, of its own accord, the initiative and activity of the Church and the family, whose successes in this field have been clearly demonstrated by history and experience. It should, moreover, supplement their work whenever this falls short of what is necessary, even by means of its own schools and institutions. For the state, more than any other society, is provided with the means put at its disposal for the needs of all, and it is only right that it use these means to the advantage of those who have contributed them.

Over and above this, the state can exact, and take measures to secure that all its citizens have the necessary knowledge of their civic and political duties, and a certain degree of physical, intellectual and moral culture, which, considering the conditions of our times, is really necessary for the common good.

However, it is clear that in all these ways of promoting education and instruction, both public and private, the state should respect the inherent rights of the Church and of the family concerning Christian education, and, moreover, have regard for distributive justice. Accordingly, unjust and unlawful is any monopoly, educational or scholastic, which, physically or morally, forces families to make use of government schools, contrary to the dictates of their Christian conscience, or contrary even to their legitimate preferences.

This does not prevent the state from making due provision for the right administration of public affairs and for the protection of its peace, within or without the realm. These are things which directly concern the public good and call for special aptitudes and special preparation. The state may, therefore, reserve to itself the establishment and direction of schools intended to prepare for certain civic duties and especially for military service, provided it be careful not to injure the rights of the Church or of the family in what pertains to them. It is well to repeat this warning here; for in these days there is spreading a spirit of nationalism which is false and exaggerated, as well as dangerous to true peace and prosperity. Under its influence various excesses are committed in giving a military turn to the so-called physical training of boys (sometimes even of girls, contrary to the very instincts of human nature); or again in usurping unreasonably, on Sunday, the time which should be devoted to religious duties and to family life at home. It is not Our intention, however, to condemn what is good in the spirit of discipline and legitimate bravery promoted by these methods; We condemn only what is excessive, as, for example, violence, which must not be confounded with courage nor with the noble sentiment of military valour in defence of country and public order; or again exaltation of athleticism which even in classic pagan times marked the decline and downfall of genuine physical training . . . .

While treating of education, it is not out of place to show here how an ecclesiastical writer, who flourished in more recent times, during the Renaissance, the holy and learned Cardinal Silvio Antoniano, to whom the cause of Christian education is greatly indebted, has set forth most clearly this well-established point of Catholic doctrine. He had been a disciple of that wonderful educator of youth, St Philip Neri; he was teacher and Latin secretary to St Charles Borromeo, and it was at the latter's suggestion and under his inspiration that he wrote his splendid treatise on *The Christian Education of Youth.* In it he argues as follows:

> The more closely the temporal power of a nation aligns itself with the spiritual, and the more it fosters and promotes the latter, by so much the more it contributes to the conservation of the commonwealth. For it is the aim of the ecclesiastical authority, by the use of spiritual means, to form good Christians in accordance with its own particular end and object; and in doing this it helps at the same time to form good citizens, and prepares them to meet their obligations as members of a civil society. This follows of necessity because in the City of God, the Holy Roman Catholic Church, a good citizen and an upright man are absolutely one and the same thing. How grave, therefore, is the error of those who separate things so closely united, and who think that they can produce good citizens by ways and methods other than those which make for the formation of good Christians. For, let human prudence say what it likes and reason as it pleases, it is impossible to produce true temporal peace and tranquillity by things repugnant or opposed to the peace and happiness of eternity.

... Parents, therefore, and all who take their place in the work of education, should be careful to make right use of the authority given them by God, Whose vicars, in a true sense, they are. This authority is not given for their own advantage, but for the proper up-bringing of their children in a holy and filial 'fear of God, the beginning of wisdom,' on which foundation alone all respect for authority can rest securely; and without which, order, tranquillity and prosperity, whether in the family, or in society, will be impossible ....

And let no one say that in a nation where there are different religious beliefs, it is impossible to provide for public instruction otherwise than by neutral or mixed schools. In such a case it becomes the duty of the state; indeed, it is the easier and more reasonable method of procedure, to leave free scope to the initiative of the Church and the family, while giving them such assistance as justice demands. That this can be done to the full satisfaction of families and to the advantage of education and of public peace and tranquillity, is clear from the actual experience of some countries comprising different religious denominations. There the school legislation respects the rights of the family and Catholics are free to follow their own system of teaching in schools that are entirely Catholic. Nor is distributive justice lost sight of, as is evidenced by the financial aid granted by the state to these schools . . . .

From Encyclical Divini Illius Magistri on the Christian Education of Youth (31 December 1929).

From the *Constitution of the Republic of Ireland*

PREAMBLE:

In the Name of the Most Holy Trinity, from Whom is all authority and to Whom, as our final end, all actions both of men and States must be referred,

We, the people of Eire,

Humbly acknowledging all our obligations to our Divine Lord, Jesus Christ, Who sustained our fathers through centuries of trial,

Gratefully remembering their heroic and unremitting struggle to regain the rightful independence of our Nation,

And seeking to promote the common good, with due observance of Prudence, Justice and Charity, so that the dignity and freedom of the individual may be assured, true social order attained, the unity of our country restored, and concord established with other nations,

Do hereby adopt, enact, and give to ourselves this Constitution.

Article 6

(1) All powers of government, legislative, executive and judicial, derive, under God, from the people, whose right it is to designate the rulers of the state and, in final appeal, to decide all questions of national policy, according to the requirements of the common good.

INTERNATIONAL RELATIONS

Article 29

(1) Ireland affirms its devotion to the ideal of peace and friendly co-operation amongst nations founded on international justice and morality.

(2) Ireland affirms its adherence to the principle of the pacific settlement of international disputes by international arbitration or judicial determination.

EDUCATION

Article 42

(1) The state acknowledges that the primary and natural educator of the child is the Family and guarantees to respect the inalienable right and duty of parents to provide, according to their means, for the religious and moral, intellectual, physical and social education of their children.

(2) Parents shall be free to provide this education in their homes or in private schools or in schools recognised or established by the state.

(3) 1° The state shall not oblige parents in violation of their conscience and lawful preference to send their children to schools established by the state, or to any particular type of school designated by the state.

2° The state shall, however, as guardian of the common good, require in view of actual conditions that the children receive a certain minimum education, moral, intellectual and social.

(4) The state shall provide for free primary education and shall endeavour to supplement and give reasonable aid toprivate and corporate educational initiative, and, when the public good requires it, provide other educational facilities or institutions with due regard, however, for the rights of parents, especially in the matter of religious and moral formation.

(5) In exceptional cases, where the parents for physical or moral reasons fail in their duty towards their children, the state as guardian of the common good, by appropriate means shall endeavour to supply the place of the parents, but always with due regard for the natural and imprescriptible rights of the child.

PRIVATE PROPERTY

Article 43

(1) 1° The state acknowledges that man, in virtue of his rational being, has the natural right, antecedent to positive law, to the private ownership of external goods.

2° The state, accordingly, guarantees to pass no law attempting to abolish the right of private ownership or the general right to transfer, bequeath, and inherit property.

(2) 1° The state recognises, however, that the exercise of the rights mentioned in the foregoing provisions of this Article ought, in civil society, to be regulated by the principles of social justice.

2° The state, accordingly, may as occasion requires delimit by law the exercise of the said rights with a view to reconciling their exercise with the exigencies of the common good.

THE FAMILY

Article 41

(1) 1° The state recognises the Family as the natural primary and fundamental unit group of Society, and as a moral institution possessing inalienable and imprescriptible rights, antecedent and superior to all positive law.

2° The state, therefore, guarantees to protect the Family in its constitution and authority, as the necessary basis of social order and as indispensable to the welfare of the nation and the state.

(2) 1° In particular, the state recognises that by her life within the home, woman gives to the state a support without which the common good cannot be achieved.

2° The state shall, therefore, endeavour to ensure that mothers shall not be obliged by economic necessity to engage in labour to the neglect of their duties in the home.

(3) 1° The state pledges itself to guard with special care the institution of Marriage, on which the Family is founded, and to protect it against attack.

2° No law shall be enacted providing for the grant of a dissolution of marriage.

3° No person whose marriage has been dissolved under the civil law of any other state but is a subsisting valid marriage, under the law for the time being in force within the jurisdiction of the Government and Parliament established by this Constitution shall be capable of contracting a valid marriage within that jurisdiction during the lifetime of the other party to the marriage so dissolved.

RELIGION

Article 44

(1) 1° The state acknowledges that the homage of public worship is due to Almighty God. It shall hold His Name in reverence, and shall respect and honour religion.

2° The state recognises the special position of the Holy Catholic Apostolic and Roman Church as the guardian of the Faith professed by the great majority of the citizens.

3° The state also recognises the Church of Ireland, the Presbyterian Church in Ireland, the Methodist Church in Ireland, the Religious Society of Friends in Ireland, as well as the Jewish Congregations and the other religious denominations existing in Ireland at the date of the coming into operation of this Constitution.

(2) 1° Freedom of conscience and the free profession and practice of religion are, subject to public order and morality, guaranteed to every citizen.

2° The state guarantees not to endow any religion.

3° The state shall not impose any disabilities or make any discrimination on the ground of religious profession, belief or status.

4° Legislation providing state aid for schools shall not discriminate between schools under the management of different religious denominations, nor be such as to affect prejudicially the right of any child to attend a school receiving public money without attending religious instruction at that school.

5° Every religious denomination shall have the right to manage its own affairs, own, acquire and administer property, movable and immovable, and maintain institutions for religious or charitable purposes.

6° The property of any religious denomination or any educational institution shall not be diverted save for necessary works of public utility and on payment of compensation.

DIRECTIVE PRINCIPLES OF SOCIAL POLICY

Article 45

The principles of social policy set forth in this Article are intended for the general guidance of the Oireachtas. The application of those principles in the making of laws shall be the care of the Oireachtas exclusively, and shall not be cognisable by any Court under any of the provisions of this Constitution.

(1) The state shall strive to promote the welfare of the whole people by securing and protecting as effectively as it may a social order in which justice and charity shall inform all the institutions of the national life.

(2) The state shall, in particular, direct its policy towards securing:

(i) That the citizens (all of whom, men and women equally, have the right to an adequate means of livelihood) may through their occupations find the means of making reasonable provision for their domestic needs.

(ii) That the ownership and control of the material resources of the community may be so distributed amongst private individuals and the various classes as best to subserve the common good.

(iii) That, especially, the operation of free competition shall not be allowed so to develop as to result in the concentration of the ownership or control of essential commodities in a few individuals to the common detriment.

(iv) That in what pertains to the control of credit the constant and predominant aim shall be the welfare of the people as a whole.

(v) That there may be established on the land in economic security as many families as in the circumstances shall be practicable.

(3) 1° The state shall favour and, where necessary, supplement private initiative in industry and commerce.

2° The state shall endeavour to secure that private enterprise shall be so conducted as to ensure reasonable efficiency in the production and distribution of goods and as to protect the public against unjust exploitation.

(4) 1° The state pledges itself to safeguard with especial care the economic interests of the weaker sections of the community, and, where necessary, to contribute to the support of the infirm, the widow, the orphan, and the aged.

2° The state shall endeavour to ensure that the strength and health of workers, men and women, and the tender age of children shall not be abused and that citizens shall not be forced by economic necessity to enter avocations unsuited to their sex, age or strength.

Dublin, December 1937.

PART IV

ROMANTIC AUTHORITARIANISM

ROMANTIC AUTHORITARIANISM

When Professor Oakeshott wrote his book in 1938, a large part of Europe was dominated by two political creeds, Nazism and Fascism, which, because of their extreme confusion, it is extremely difficult to classify. As his book admirably illustrated, they were not internally consistent doctrines of politics. Today, their influence is negligible, and, in a book about the contemporary state of political thought, they plainly do not deserve detailed treatment.

It would nevertheless be hazardous to neglect them altogether. The imposition of 'unconditional surrender' on Germany and Italy destroyed the political regimes of those countries and discredited the ideas on which they rested. With the return of Italy to the comity of nations and the steady advance of Western Germany towards equality with the victorious powers, however, there have been some signs of the re-emergence of these theories or something like them, particularly in Germany. If these trends continue, it is perfectly possible that what now seems to be an extinct attitude towards politics may again be of the greatest practical importance.

Furthermore, political thinking today is very largely a reaction against these attitudes, and these attitudes themselves are of a kind which tends to recur in the history of politics. When a proud nation has been humiliated and its social order has disintegrated certain well-defined tendencies will probably appear in its political thought; the state of mind of which Fascism and Nazism was a symptom is, therefore, a phenomenon which the political scientist cannot afford to ignore.

We believe that the most accurate phrase by which this phenomenon can be described is 'romantic authoritarianism'. Romanticism is an attitude towards life which exalts the emotions at the expense of reason, and authoritarianism is used here to signify the habit of making a presumption in favour of the power of central governments.

In the light of this definition, some of the salient characteristics of Fascist and Nazi thought may be briefly enumerated, subject always to the proviso that any attempt to see a consistent pattern in these characteristics would be an act of falsification. No attempt is here made to distinguish between Fascism and Nazism; many such attempts have been made and have been the occasions for considerable intellectual subtlety, but they have little relevance to the contemporary state of things. All that can now be done is to distinguish certain themes common to this type of political thinking.

(i) Romantic authoritarianism is anti-rationalist, that is to say it denies the validity of all universal systems of political rights and duties which profess to apply to men everywhere by virtue of their common humanity and of their place in the order of nature.

(ii) It is anti-individualist in the sense that it denies that the individual can for any purpose be considered apart from the community to which he belongs.

(iii) It exalts the nation or the race, regarding it as the unit to which men owe ultimate allegiance. Whether everyone owes allegiance to his own nation or race or merely the members of the 'superior' nation or race owe such allegiance is a question which is usually left in some doubt.

(iv) It denies the existence of any collective duty on the part of the nation or race towards other nations and races. It regards international relations as a struggle for survival, but it does not always see this struggle ending in the triumph of the fittest. On the contrary, it holds that there is an intrinsic virtue in the struggle, that it will go on indefinitely, and that sometimes the supreme moment of a nation's existence will be the hour of its extinction, provided that this takes place in suitably heroic circumstances.

(v) By 'race' it means a biological entity and by 'nation' an historical entity in which common race is the principal element. Some nation, for example Germany, is usually represented as demonstrating the peak of the race's development and as charged with the defence of the whole race.

(vi) Romantic authoritarianism is opposed to economic liberalism, regarding it as a disintegrating force, and to socialism regarding it as a creature of abstract intelligence. It borrows from Catholic political thought the idea of a corporate organisation of the economy, but prevents this from being realised in practice by demanding the greatest possible concentration of power in a central government dedicated to warlike preparations.

(vii) It is opposed to government by discussion and consent and to the independence of the judicature, regarding the first as a force making for national disunity and the second as a tribute to the false doctrine that the individual can have rights against the community.

(viii) It nevertheless frequently professes to be democratic, finding a natural affinity with the democratic idea of popular sovereignty and regarding the people as a mystical entity whose will is expressed in the commands of governmental authority.

(ix) It has a strong disposition in favour of personal leadership culminating in the rule of a single dictator.

(x) As a consequence of these views, it denies the legitimacy of any autonomous sphere of activity within the nation, regarding all art, science and letters as expressions of the national genius subject to the regulation of the national state.

Propositions of this sort plainly have a strong appeal to defeated countries with powerful national traditions. In Germany today various political groups and groups avowedly directed towards moral regeneration show some of these characteristics but they have not yet assumed the shape of a political philosophy or of anything which claims to be a political philosophy. They are all part of the empirical reaction against occupation. They are typified, for example, in attempts to excuse the Nazis for racial persecution by alleging that they killed fewer Jews than they are said to have killed, and by suggestions that Nazism gave social security and full employment while the revival of liberal capitalism has meant unemployment and insecurity. The anti-Communism of the Nazi Party obviously has a powerful appeal today, and extreme nationalism and militarism will obviously continue to be potential developments so long as Germany remains divided.

The circumstances in which General Franco rose to power in Spain—and the international implications of the clash between the Republicans and the Insurgents—have led some to attribute to the present Spanish dictatorship, a theoretical coherence which it does not possess. General Franco enjoyed the active support of Fascist Italy and Nazi Germany, and the politics of the Falange, the single political party allowed in Franco's Spain, have much in common with those of Mussolini's Fascist Party. But General Franco himself has been extremely guarded in his expressions of political theory, and to regard Spain as a working model of a Fascist State would be to repeat the error of the 1930's, when local and exclusively Spanish problems were interpreted by the rest of Europe in universal terms. Spanish political theory is better expressed and understood as a reflection of local circumstances influenced throughout by a strong and always individual Roman Catholic tradition.

At present, however, the status of the theories described above is very low everywhere. It is fair to point out, however, that this is in part due to a change in the political thinking of the liberal democracies. Fascism and Nazism were protests against the rationalistic and cosmopolitan flavour of liberal thought from the American and French revolutions onwards. They were hostile to abstract statements of political right; they emphasised the importance of the particular over the general, of national over international society, of personality over humanity. They condemned liberalism as having produced universal chaos and socialism as proposing a universal tyranny maintained by and for the intelligentsia. Today, the political thought by which representative democracy is defended is far more empirical than it was before the war. It accordingly is sceptical of abstractions and generalities, ready to draw distinctions, to admit the necessity of tensions, and to give a due regard to the diversities produced by history. It, therefore, makes concessions to some of the discontents which the Nazi and Fascist revolutions exploited. It stops short, of course, of that annihilation of reason and repudiation of the idea of justice to which these doctrines led; indeed the ideas of reason and justice are still the foundations of its creed, but, because it recognises the complexity of the just order and the impossibility of doing more than approximating to it, and because it recognises that universal principles are capable of an infinite variety of expressions, it is less exposed to anti-rational criticism than it used to be. Indeed, it finds its chief enemy now in Marxian Communism, which is an ultimate development of the rationalistic tradition of the French Revolution. The Fascist and Nazi protests have, therefore, produced an effect.

At first sight, there appears to be one exception to the view that romantic authoritarianism is virtually dead: the combination in South African nationalism of the ideas of popular sovereignty, nationalism and race, appears to suggest affinities with the

Fascist and Nazi attitudes. The analogy, however, is false: the desire to build a South African nation and to achieve separation from the Commonwealth does not spring from doctrinal sources. In its attitude towards race, the South African government would appear to be governed by empirical considerations or, at least, to assert that it is so governed. Its claim is that *apartheid*—the separation of the black and white races—is the most practical and mutually satisfactory solution of the race problem in South Africa. This may be a prejudiced view springing from subconscious assumptions which bear some relation to those of Fascism and Nazism, but the exploration of the subconscious is not the object of this book.

It must be noted here, however, that among the supporters of *apartheid*, is a group of theologians of the Dutch Reformed Church who advance a racial theory purporting to be based on scripture. This differs from Dr Rosenberg's view fundamentally: it is not based on biological science but on theology. It is not likely to achieve acceptance outside the Dutch Reformed Church where it has not been unanimously accepted, and it has already been strongly condemned by other Christian bodies. Above all, it does not involve a denial of the idea that all men have rights, and this sharply distinguishes it from the attitudes described earlier in this chapter. Since it has the status of a political theory, however, and, indeed, a remarkable degree of internal consistency, a brief extract illustrative of it is given below:

> We know God the Creator in Scripture as Hammabdil, as the Maker of Separations. To create a cosmos God separated things: light from darkness, waters above the firmament from waters under the firmament, dry land from the sea. From the very beginning it was the intention of the Lord that mankind should live in separate nations, St Paul said that God made out of one blood *all the nations* of men (Acts xvii. 26). In his sinful self-conceit man wished to frustrate this intention as much as to say: 'Let us not part, let us remain together. Let us build a tower to reach into heaven'. And then God came as the Maker of Separations and said: 'Behold the people is one and they have all one language .... Go to, let us go down and there confound their language—So the Lord scattered them abroad' (Gen. xi. 6-8). Mankind desired a unity that was sinful in the eyes of the Lord; the Lord intervened and caused an increase in peoples which, according to Scripture, must continue until the completion of all things, and possibly even after. The rise and continuance of separate peoples and nations is, according to Scripture, in accordance with the Will of God. Attempts at unification, the equalitarian idea, are a revival of the Babylonian spirit. God willed the separate existence of nations.

It is not only for practical reasons that the Dutch Reformed Churches in their mission policy aim at the establishment of separate non-white Churches which must finally become completely independent. It is claimed that the mission policy of these Churches rests on Scriptural grounds. The Christian Churches must be careful not to deprive the whole of Africa's Nativedom of the privilege to make its own contributions to the development of the Christian truths. There is first the possibility that the truths of Christian religion can be used to build an artificial, unnatural, sinful unity out of all sorts of heterogeneous elements. This would be equivalent to the building of a Tower of Babel and the characteristic of such unity may be best described by the words in Rev. xvii. 13, 'They have one mind . . . '. This way holds the one possibility that man, and even the Church, however well-meaningly, will convert the natural order, the cosmos willed and brought into being by God in such diversity, into a chaos, an interfusion of species and types where no order can any longer exist. The other possibility is to respect God's handiwork, to pay heed to all natural distinctions and to strive to come to the oneness of the Spirit of Christ. This, the much more difficult fact, is aimed at by the Dutch Reformed Churches. The primary duty of the Churches is to bring the gospel to the black man, to help him to build his own Churches, self-supporting, self-governing, self-propagating. Unity in Christ is not to be confused with unity as a human ideal. They are not the truly oecumenical Christians who blur the differences or facilely glide over them, but on the contrary those who, *each for himself in his Church*, are quite concretely a Church.

From *The Round Table* (March 1954),
'Apartheid and the Scriptures'.

PART V

PROTESTANT POLITICAL THOUGHT

INTRODUCTION

The documents reproduced in this section do not illustrate or profess to illustrate a coherent philosophy of politics. They are examples of the distinctive contribution which Protestant (in the sense of non-Roman Catholic) thought is today making to the political discussion.

An important part of the Protestant tradition in political thought has been the doctrine of passive obedience; the idea that Christians should accept the existing political and social order as inevitable and concentrate on preserving or achieving the opportunity to practise the faith as individuals. Today, however, this aspect of the Protestant tradition, though still represented, is no longer in the forefront. Most influential Protestants now accept the notion that the Gospel has social and political implications.

As will be seen from the documents reproduced below, however, this Protestant approach to society and politics has certain distinctive characteristics. It is marked by the belief that the problems of public morality, though of direct concern to Christians, are different in kind from those of private morality. This idea of a 'double standard' and of an ultimate reconciliation between these two standards has been most thoroughly worked out in the writing of Dr Niebuhr of which a typical extract appears below. Protestant political thought is sceptical of general, abstract propositions which claim to be universally valid, and recommends Christians to apply themselves diligently to the study of particular historical situations in an effort to discover how they illustrate God's purpose for the world—an attitude of mind which is well exemplified by the writing of Mr Herbert Butterfield. Protestants are particularly concerned to protect the Church from identifying itself with controversial political and social policies which cannot claim to derive directly from the New Testament, and to urge Christians, as a necessary preliminary to seeking agreement, to define political and social differences clearly and charitably, avoiding a dogmatic spirit. They uphold the view that the same ends may be served by many institutions, that there may be a hidden harmony behind apparently opposite views and that even while a doctrine, like atheistic materialism, may be pronounced un-Christian, it may be more valuable to see it as a judgment on the failings of Christians and as the exaggeration of some neglected aspect of Christian truth than to concentrate on condemning it. These points are illustrated in the quotations from the reports of the World Council of Churches and from the Presbyterian Commission on Communism.

The potential, practical importance of these views arises largely from the activity of the World Council of Churches, an organisation in whose work representatives of all churches with the exception of the Roman and Russian Orthodox Communions have participated. These views are also important because of the existence in central and eastern Europe of Protestant churches some of whose members, while rejecting Marxism, have found themselves in sympathy with certain features of the Communist revolution and strongly critical of certain features of capitalism and of the old order of agrarian society. It would be wrong to take the examples quoted here as typical of all Protestant political thought today. It must also be emphasised that the influence of this approach is diffuse and does not find expression in any organised political movement, though it may fairly be regarded as an important factor in the shaping of public opinion particularly in Britain and in the U.S.A.

REINHOLD NIEBUHR, *The Conflict between Individual and Social Morality*

A realistic analysis of the problems of human society reveals a constant and seemingly irreconcilable conflict between the needs of society and the imperatives of a sensitive conscience. This conflict, which could be most briefly defined as the conflict between ethics and politics, is made inevitable by the double focus of the moral life. One focus is in the inner life of the individual, and the other in the necessities of man's social life. From the perspective of society the highest moral ideal is justice. From the perspective of the individual the highest ideal is unselfishness. Society must strive for justice even if it is forced to use means, such as self-assertion, resistance, coercion and perhaps resentment, which cannot gain the moral sanction of the most sensitive moral spirit. The individual must strive to realise his life by losing and finding himself in something greater than himself.

These two moral perspectives are not mutually exclusive and the contradiction between them is not absolute. But neither are they easily harmonised. Efforts to harmonise them were analysed in the previous chapter. It was revealed that the highest moral insights and achievements of the individual conscience are both relevant and necessary to the life of society. The most perfect justice cannot be established if the moral imagination of the individual does not seek to comprehend the needs and interests of his fellows. Nor can any non-rational instrument of justice be used without great peril to society, if it is not brought under the control of moral goodwill. Any justice which is only justice soon degenerates into something less than justice. It must be saved by something which is more than justice. The realistic wisdom of the statesman is reduced to foolishness if it is not under the influence of the foolishness of the moral seer. The latter's idealism results in political futility and sometimes in moral confusion, if it is not brought into commerce and communication with the realities of man's collective life. This necessity and possibility of fusing moral and political insights does not, however, completely eliminate certain irreconcilable elements in the two types of morality, internal and external, individual and social. These elements make for constant confusion but they also add to the richness of human life. We may best bring our study of ethics and politics to a close by giving them some consideration . . . .

The distinction between individual and group morality is a sharper and more perplexing one. The moral obtuseness of human collectives makes a morality of pure disinterestedness impossible. There is not enough imagination in any social group to render it amenable to the influence of pure love. Nor is there a possibility of persuading any social group to make a venture in pure love, except, as in the case of the Russian peasants, the recently liberated Negroes and other similar groups, a morally dubious social inertia should be compounded with the ideal. The selfishness of human communities must be regarded as an inevitability. Where it is inordinate it can be checked only by competing assertions of interest; and these can be effective only if coercive methods are added to moral and rational persuasions. Moral factors may qualify, but they will not eliminate, the resulting social contest and conflict. Moral goodwill may seek to relate the peculiar interests of the group to the ideal of a total and final harmony of all life. It may thereby qualify the self-assertion of the privileged, and support the interests of the disinherited, but it will never be so impartial as to persuade any group to subject its interests completely to an inclusive social ideal. The spirit of love may preserve a certain degree of appreciation for the common weaknesses and common aspirations which bind men together above the areas of social conflict. But again it cannot prevent the conflict. It may avail itself of instruments of restraint and coercion, through which a measure of trust in the moral capacities of an opponent may be expressed and the expansion rather than contraction of those capacities is encouraged. But it cannot hide the moral distrust expressed by the very use of the instruments of coercion. To some degree the conflict between the purest individual morality and an adequate political policy must therefore remain . . . .

Individuals, even when involved in their communities, will always have the opportunity of loyalty to the highest canons of personal morality. Sometimes, when their group is obviously bent upon evil, they may have to express their individual ideals by dissociating themselves from their group. Such a policy may easily lead to political irresponsibility, as in the case of the more extreme sects of non-resisters. But it may also be socially useful. Religiously inspired pacifists who protest against the violence of their state in the name of a sensitive individual conscience may never lame the will-to-power of a state as much as a class-conscious labour group. But if their numbers grew to large proportions, they might affect the policy of the government. It is possible, too, that their example may encourage similar non-conformity among individuals in the enemy nation and thus mitigate the impact of the conflict without weakening the comparative strength of their own community.

The ideals of a high individual morality are just as necessary when loyalty to the group is maintained and its general course in relation to other groups is approved. There are possibilities for individual unselfishness, even when the group is asserting its interests and rights against other communities. The interests of the individual are related to those of the group, and he may therefore seek advantages for himself when he seeks them for his group. But this indirect egoism is comparatively insignificant beside the possibilities of e xpressing or disciplining his egoism in relation to his group. If he is a leader in the group, it is necessary to restrain his ambitions. A leadership, free of self-seeking, improves the morale of the whole group. The leaders of disinherited groups, even when they are avowed economic determinists and scorn the language of personal idealism, are frequently actuated by high moral ideals. If they sought their own personal advantage they could gain it more easily by using their abilities to rise from their group to a more privileged one. The temptation to do this among the abler members of disinherited groups is precisely what has retarded the progress of their class or race. . . .

There is, furthermore, always the possibility that an intelligent member of a social group will begin his career in unselfish devotion to the interests of his community, only to be tempted by the personal prizes to be gained, either within the group or by shifting his loyalty to a more privileged group. The interests of individuals are, in other words, never exactly identical with those of their communities. The possibility and necessity of individual moral discipline is therefore never absent, no matter what importance the social struggle between various human communities achieves . . . .

Whether the co-operative and moral aspects of human life, or the necessities of the social struggle, gain the largest significance, depends upon time and circumstance. There are periods of social stability, when the general equilibrium of social forces is taken for granted, and men give themselves to the task of making life more beautiful and tender within the limits of the established social system. The Middle Ages were such a period. While they took injustices for granted, such as would affront the conscience of our day, it cannot be denied that they elaborated amenities, urbanities and delicate refinements of life and art which must make our age seem, in comparison, like the recrudescence of barbarism.

Our age is, for good or ill, immersed in the social problem. A technological civilisation makes stability impossible. It changes the circumstances of life too rapidly to incline any one to a reverent acceptance of an ancestral order. Its rapid developments and its almost daily changes in the physical circumstances of life destroy the physical symbols of stability and therefore make for restlessness, even if these movements were not in a direction which imperil the whole human enterprise. But the tendencies of an industrial era are in a definite direction. They tend to aggravate the injustices from which men have perennially suffered; and they tend to unite the whole of humanity in a system of economic interdependence. They make us more conscious of the relations of individuals within their communities. They obsess us therefore with the brutal aspects of man's collective behaviour. They, furthermore, cumulate the evil consequences of these brutalities so rapidly that we feel under a tremendous urgency to solve our social problem before it is too late. As a generation we are therefore bound to feel harassed as well as disillusioned.

In such a situation all the highest ideals and tenderest emotions which men have felt all through the ages, when they became fully conscious of their heritage and possible destiny as human beings, will seem from our perspective to be something of a luxury. They will be under a moral disadvantage because they appear as a luxury which only those are able to indulge who are comfortable enough to be comparatively oblivious to the desperate character of our contemporary social situation....

All this is rather tragic. For what the individual conscience feels when it lifts itself above the world of nature and the system of collective relationships in which the human spirit remains under the power of nature, is not a luxury but a necessity of the soul. Yet there is beauty in our tragedy. We are, at least, rid of some of our illusions. We can no longer buy the highest satisfactions of the individual life at the expense of social injustice. We cannot build our individual ladders to heaven and leave the total human enterprise unredeemed of its excesses and corruptions.

In the task of that redemption the most effective agents will be men who have substituted some new illusions for the abandoned ones. The most important of these illusions is that the collective life of mankind can achieve perfect justice. It is a very valuable illusion for the moment; for justice cannot be approximated if the hope of its perfect realisation does not generate a sublime madness in the soul. Nothing but such madness will do battle with malignant power and 'spiritual wickedness in high places'. The illusion is dangerous because it encourages terrible fanaticisms. It must therefore be brought under the control of reason. One can only hope that reason will not destroy it before its work is done.

From *Moral Man and Immoral Society* (1932), ch. x.

HERBERT BUTTERFIELD, *History, Religion and the Present Day*

It would follow from various things which we have studied in these lectures that there is hardly reason for regarding the problem of contemporary Russia as radically different for the diplomatist from what it would have been if the regime had been a Tsarist one, or if that country had even been democratically governed. The general predicament would have been much the same supposing the Tsars had still been on the throne, possessing the territory, the satellite states, and the sphere of influence now belonging to the Soviet Union; and this would virtually have been the situation in 1919 (save that they would have held Constantinople too), if the Revolution had not cut across the avowed aims and cancelled the commitments of allied diplomacy. The history of Europe does not suggest that the adoption of a policy of aggression, when the distribution of power made such a policy feasible, would have been prevented if Russia had still been numbered amongst the Christian states, in the sense in which she was so numbered (along with Germany) in 1914.

It is not always realised—though once again the eighteenth century showed clear consciousness of the point—that the existence of a number of states intermediate in size but authentically controlling their own policy, so that they could shift their weight from one side to another, long served to provide ball-bearings for the European states-system, and made self-adjustments in that system more easy. The virtual elimination of this order of things after two World Wars, and the reduction of effective diplomacy to the transactions of very few great powers, keeps everything taut, so that every episode is a crisis, and it is difficult to see how the tension can be relaxed. If after 1945 things were so balanced that the predicament of Hobbesian fear was produced and all had to feel that the future of Europe depended on Germany—the Western Powers unable to tolerate Communism in that country, Russia determined not to be checkmated by the formation of an anti-Communist government there, and neither side able to afford to withdraw and allow the Germans authentically to determine their own future—such a predicament, viewed as the culmination of forty years of diplomacy and war, would look very much like the judgment of God on the victor nations themselves.

It is the tendency of contemporaries to estimate a revolution too exclusively by its atrocities, while posterity always seems to err through its inability to take these into account or vividly appreciate them. Many of the atrocities in various countries in the twentieth century would appear to be the concomitant of almost any order that has come into existence through violent revolution; and we find them in history even when the revolution avows itself liberal, like that of 1789, even indeed when it called itself Christian. On the other hand it is not certain whether such things as mass slavery are not to be associated with Russia and a backward civilisation rather than with anything inherent in the Communist teaching; though, through sympathetic attraction, they are liable to be brought into the West wherever Communism is successful. Many of the cruelties and the degradation of personality are at the same time a feature of what we have called modern barbarism, wherever the phenomenon may appear; and it is possible that there is no cure for this save peace and a continuity of development, during which men may grow in reasonableness. It is modern technique and organisation, rather than any change in the quality of human nature—save, possibly such change as the technical developments themselves almost inevitably produce—which have altered the scale of atrocities in the modern world. Revolution tears up the traditions, withers the urbanities and destroys the subtler values of a cultured society, falling heavily upon the imponderable things which spring from an uninterrupted history, and sacrificing a present generation for an end which must be postponed and highly contingent, if practicable at all. But war is the father of modern revolution and there may be justice in the argument that when a country has already been torn up by war, and government has broken down (as possibly in the case of Tsarist Russia) the best that can be hoped for is a revolutionary party which knows what it wants and has the firmness to seize and hold the reins.

It is not clear that egalitarianism or the classless society are involved as such in any of these questions, or that such principles are specifically anti-Christian, even if, like many bodies and movements (including liberalism at one time) they are connected with an anti-religious cause—a cause which Russia has only adopted, in any case, through the influence of the West. They represent a utopianism concerning which the Christian may have many misgivings; but even those of us who believe that an hierarchical society has conferred (save perhaps in material things) many benefits even upon the very class which appeared to be victimised, may be seriously perturbed if Christianity as such should be marshalled against a programme which, whatever its enemies might say, has taken up the interests of what in some respects are the disinherited. Men are often governed more by their hatreds than their loves, and some men have more surely hated the capitalists than they have loved the poor; but we should not wish Christianity to be judged by the faults of its more unworthy adherents. Even if all present-day Russia were still governed by the Tsars the situation would be such that war might humanly speaking be unavoidable. In view of all these facts, and supposing it to be legitimate to envisage history in the framework which these lectures have described, a serious problem would be presented to churchmen if war broke out and an attempt were made to erect the issue into a conflict of Christianity versus Communism. So long as there are discontented groups within the Western nations, the Soviet Union is perhaps clear-sighted in its recognition of the interest it has in keeping diplomacy on an ideological basis. In any case we who talk so easily about what would happen if this or that power were the victor in a war, are only just beginning to measure the portentous and far-reaching consequences of war itself, and to see how it emerges as the chief solvent of the very order of things we wish to preserve.

In regard to some of the most important things in life it is remarkable how little human beings know their liberty—how little they realise that the grand discoveries of the various inductive sciences still leave us free to range with the upper parts of our minds. In these days also when people are so much the prisoners of systems—especially the prisoners of those general ideas which mark the spirit of the age—it is not always realised that belief in God gives us greater elasticity of mind, rescuing us from too great subservience to intermediate principles, whether these are related to nationality or ideology or science. It even enables us to leave more play in our minds for the things that nature or history may still have to reveal to us in the near future. Similarly Christianity is not tied to regimes—not compelled to regard the existing order as the very end of life and the embodiment of all our values. Christians have too often tried to put the brake on things in the past, but at the critical turning-points in history they have less reason than others to be afraid that a new kind of society or civilisation will leave them with nothing to live for. We are told by many people that our new age needs a new mentality, but so often when one reads writers further all that they really say is that if we don't do now the things they have been continually telling us to do since 1919 we shall have the atomic bomb and presumably deserve it. I have nothing to say at the finish except that if one wants a permanent rock in life and goes deep enough for it, it is difficult for historical events to shake it. There are times when we can never meet the future with sufficient elasticity of mind, especially if we are locked in the contemporary systems of thought. We can do worse than remember a principle which both gives us a firm Rock and leaves us the maximum elasticity for our minds: the principle: Hold to Christ, and for the rest be totally uncommitted.

From *Christianity and History* (1949), ch. VII.

WORLD COUNCIL OF CHURCHES, *Social Questions*

PROBLEMS OF ECONOMIC LIFE

New Trends. One of the most important features of the modern world is the way in which society has increasingly taken the control of economic affairs out of the sphere of 'automatic responses'. Full employment policies, the spread of state action in economic life, and the growing economic power of organised groups of employers, employees, farmers, and professional people have brought great changes in the highly industrialised countries.

The need for inter-governmental co-operation in economic affairs accompanies the increase in domestic state action. In some areas, such as Europe, social reconstruction and supranational integration go hand in hand and challenge many old political and economic ideas. At the same time, the priority given to full employment policies in many countries strengthens tendencies towards economic self-sufficiency and can threaten international economic co-operation.

The new emphasis on state initiative and international organisation in the development of economic life has been accompanied by a fresh recognition of the importance of relative freedom in enterprise and of the regulating role of the price system. Many socialists have come to appreciate the importance of the private sector of the economy and the necessity for the energetic, enterprising and expert business man as well as being aware of the dangers of centralised government.

New Problems. These developments suggest that disputes about 'capitalism' and 'socialism' disguise the more important issues in the field of economic and social policy. Each word is applied to many different social forms and economic systems. It is not the case that we have merely a choice between two easily distinguishable types of economic organisation. Private enterprise takes many shapes in different countries at different stages and in different parts of one economy and is profoundly affected by the forms of government regulations. The operations of the state in business also takes various forms, such as post offices run by government departments, supply of electric power or gas by local authorities, and national or state public corporations. In all types of economy there is to be found a variety of forms; there is no one pattern that is universally valid. There are also various types of co-operative organisation. In some countries the 'welfare state' or the 'mixed economy' suggests a new pattern of economic life; others may be regarded as 'capitalist', but the capitalism of today is very different from the capitalism of even twenty or thirty years ago. The concrete issues in all countries concern the newly-evolving forms of economic organisation, and the relative roles of the state, organised groups and private enterprises.

The Church's Role. The Church is concerned with economic life, because of God's concern for human beings who work to produce goods and services, who use them, and for whom business exists. The Church cannot uncritically support any particular form of organisation as it exists in any particular country, but should be especially concerned with the following moral implications of economic life:

(i) State action in recent years has taken many new forms. The state must do those things for the economy that private industry cannot do properly, such as planning for urban development, stimulating industrial expansion and soil conservation, some types of large-scale industrial and agricultural research, and guidance of the distribution of industry. But state action needs to be decentralised, limited, and adaptable. The Christian should be ready to welcome fruitful new experiments, whether in the field of state action, private business or co-operative endeavour.

(ii) Efficient production is important as well as fair distribution. Much Christian social thought in the past has tended to ignore the former and stress primarily the latter. Laziness and waste are sins before God no less than selfishness and greed.

(iii) The Churches have been properly critical of monopolistic practices, and of the effects of many irresponsible business practices on people and society generally. But they also need to understand and lay stress on the valuable contribution which the skilled executive has to make to society, irrespective of the form of ownership or organisation. At its best the business system has provided incentives for the responsible initiative and hard work which produces economic progress, and has embodied the wisdom of decentralised decisions and widely distributed power. These are virtues needed in any system.

(iv) The Churches must never fail to recognise that the worker should have a status in society which accords with his responsibilities and his human dignity. Much has been done in recent years, but Christians are too ready to forget how much needs to be done, even in countries where social security and redistribution of income and power have gone far.

(v) One of the most important economic roles is that played by the world's farmers. In some countries they have met urgent needs by extraordinary advances in productivity. For the feeding of increasing populations with a better diet, radical changes in farming methods will have to be carried through in many other countries, but always with due regard to the human consequences. The Churches should recognise the justice of the farmers' demand for a reasonable measure of security of income; but even as they advance their legitimate demands for justice, farmers must resist the temptations to exhaust the soil, to exploit those who work for them, or to take unfair advantage of the consumers.

There are a number of places where our Christian concern for society makes us uneasy about the existing situation or where there is a demand for positive action.

(i) We can never forget the warnings in the Bible about the

dangers to the rich man. In our day these warnings must be applied to the temptations facing everyone in a rich society. The tendencies to create unlimited wants, to over-emphasise material values and to appeal to motives of social pride, envy and lust, stimulated by irresponsible salesmanship and advertising, are dangerous and need curbing.

(ii) Not only increased production but a stronger regard for equity in the distribution of wealth and income is also required. At the same time such factors as the place of incentive and the desire to avoid regimentation necessitate a measure of inequality in modern economic life. But every society should recognise the extent to which great contrasts between rich and poor destroy fellowship and undercut the political institutions of a responsible society.

(iii) The Churches have a duty to promote adequate assistance on the national and international level for children, the sick, the old, the refugees, and other economically weak groups, by means of church organisations, voluntary societies, and local or national governments. It is the duty of the Christian to work for improved national or local welfare legislation and for the provision of adequate medical care. It may also be his duty to fight against any tendency for the state to monopolise social welfare activity.

(iv) Serious problems arise from the great importance of organised groups, such as trade unions and associations of employers, farmers, or professional people. Christians can bear witness that these groups must be responsible to the whole of society, that their leadership must be responsible to their members, and that the members must participate responsibly in the organisation.

We welcome the role of responsible trade unions in fighting exploitation and promoting a humane environment for workers, and also the growing co-operation between labour and management to increase the material resources available for human welfare.

(v) Christians have a duty to bring to the attention of their governments that national policies have effects on the lives and welfare of peoples in other countries. National economic and political stability, justice, freedom and peace are dependent upon world economic and political stability. National and international policies are far more closely inter-related than ever before.

Excessive barriers to trade can create economic crises elsewhere. The greater the economic power, the larger is the responsibility in this field. The richer countries particularly must remember that one test of their policies is their effect on the under-developed areas of the world.

From *Social Questions: The responsible society in a world perspective.* A Report from the Second Assembly of the World Council of Churches, Evanston, U.S.A. (August 1954).

World Council of Churches, *Inter-Group Relations*

RESOLUTIONS ADOPTED BY THE ASSEMBLY

Resolution I: The Second Assembly of the World Council of Churches declares its conviction that any form of segregation based on race, colour, or ethnic origin is contrary to the gospel, and is incompatible with the Christian doctrine of man and with the nature of the Church of Christ. The Assembly urges the Churches within its membership to renounce all forms of segregation or discrimination and to work for their abolition within their own life and within society.

In doing so the Assembly is painfully aware that, in the realities of the contemporary world, many Churches find themselves confronted by historical, political, social, and economic circumstances which may make the immediate achievement of this objective extremely difficult. But under God the fellowship of the œcumenical movement is such as to offer to these Churches the strength and encouragement to help them and individuals within them to overcome these difficulties with the courage given by faith, and with the desire to testify ever more faithfully to our Master.

From its very beginning the œcumenical movement by its very nature has been committed to a form of fellowship in which there is no segregation or discrimination. The Assembly of the World Council of Churches rejoices in this fact and confirms this practice as the established policy of the Council.

Resolution II: This Second Assembly of the World Council of Churches recognises that one of the major problems of social justice in situations involving racial and ethnic tensions is that of securing for all the opportunities for the free exercise of responsible citizenship and for effective participation by way of franchise in both local and central government activity. It commends this matter to the attention of all Christian people for such action as, under God, they may be led to take in order to secure the solution of this problem.

Resolution III: While the questions of the Christian approach to the Jews and of anti-semitism present certain problems in the realm of racial and ethnic tensions, this section was, by its terms of reference, precluded from giving attention to them. It nevertheless reaffirms that anti-semitic prejudice is incompatible with Christian faith, and it recommends to the Central Committee that the study of anti-semitism be pressed forward in conjunction with the International Committee on the Christian Approach to the Jews.

Resolution IV: The Second Assembly recommends to the Central Committee that, in consultation with the International Missionary Council, it make structural provision for an organisation, preferably a department, giving assistance to the constituent Churches in their efforts to bring the gospel to bear more effectively upon relations between racial and ethnic groups. Such organisation should provide leadership and assistance not only in (*a*) continuing study of the problems of inter-group relations, especially of racial and ethnic tensions; (*b*) exchanging information on the matter of racial and ethnic groups and on the positions and work of the Churches; and (*c*) producing and distributing reports and educational materials to increase concern and understanding with regard to these matters in the constituency of the Council; but should also be the means whereby the various contributions of the rich cultural heritages of the groups within the Council's constituency may strengthen the life and witness of all the Churches and of this Council as a whole.

From *Inter-Group Relations—The Church amid Racial and Ethnic Tensions*. A Report from the Second Assembly of the World Council of Churches, Evanston, U.S.A. (August (1954).

Church of Scotland, *Justice and the Community*

The freedom and integrity of human personality is best preserved in a just society. There would be little dispute about certain of the characteristics of a just society. It would be generally held to be a society in which there is equality before the law, and in which freedom of speech and of peaceable assembly are guaranteed. It would also be generally agreed that a just society is one in which there is a high degree of what is called social justice.

The Christian therefore is concerned with social justice. But there is a great need for him to put to himself the Socratic question as to what he means by this social justice. When people speak of some programme or state of affairs as being more just than some other, they normally make their decision in terms of one or more of a set of four criteria:

(*a*) They may be thinking in terms of equality—that each individual should count for one. So, for example, some would argue that a society in which there was approximate equality of incomes is a more just society than one in which there is a considerable inequality of income.

(*b*) They may be thinking in terms of inequality according to some pattern or rule. So, for example, in the Middle Ages people would have said that a just society was one where wealth was distributed roughly in accordance with status in society, the baron receiving the income appropriate to a baron and the peasant the income appropriate to a peasant, or in modern society people argue that it is just that a skilled worker should receive a larger remuneration than an unskilled worker.

(*c*) They may be thinking in terms of freedom for the individual to do what he likes with his own. According to this view the most just society is one in which this freedom is at its maximum and state interference with the economic activities of private enterprise at its minimum. This conception clearly dominated much of the social thinking of the nineteenth century in Britain.

(*d*) They may be thinking in terms of an opposition between what is thought to be the good of the individual and what is thought to be the good of society as a whole, or some particular unit of it as a nation, state or a social class. Justice according to this point of view is what promotes the good of the latter rather than the good of the former. Modern totalitarianism is an extreme expression of this view.

It is necessary to see clearly the complexity and difficulty of the practical task of deciding in any particular case what course of action will in fact lead to a higher level of social justice. There is no formula in terms of which it can be simply decided along which road social justice lies. Each of the maxims outlined (*a*)–(*d*) above has its validity. Each of them taken by itself is unsatisfactory as a definition of social justice. They must be combined in some way.

Each historical period tends to a characteristic balance of the maxims outlined (*a*)–(*d*) above, in which one predominates. At the same time the one-sidedness of this balance leads to unexpected results. For instance, the medieval outlook was on the whole controlled by the interpretation of justice in terms of social status. The result was a society which was too rigid to contain the forces which gave rise to the Renaissance and Reformation. The early nineteenth century in Britain was on the whole dominated by the idea that justice meant the freedom for the individual to do what he liked with his possessions within a fairly narrowly limited system of legal controls. In reaction to this *laissez-faire* attitude there has grown up an emphasis on social justice as meaning equality as between individuals. But as this equality can be secured in modern conditions only by greatly increased state intervention, emphasis on the idea of justice as meaning the good of the whole as against the good of the individuals, grows apace with the emphasis on justice as meaning equality.

Indulging in the luxury of being wise after the event it is easy to see that Christian insight in the past ought to have been more critical. It should have seen through the exaggerated emphases which could only produce an extreme reaction. In particular, it is now very easy to see that in the nineteenth century the Church should have witnessed against the then predominating *laissez-faire* philosophy to a far greater extent than in fact it did. But the important thing is to contrive to be wise in one's own time. And that is very much more difficult.

On this issue the Commission and the Church are divided. To some the main enemy is still *laissez-faire*. It is the one-sided emphasis of the nineteenth century which remains to be further corrected. To others the main enemy is the tendency towards totalitarianism implicit in an excessive emphasis on social equality and the concomitant growth in the powers and functions of the state. As Plato and Aristotle saw many centuries ago, an unqualified democracy has an inherent tendency to degenerate into dictatorship. The preservation of constitutional government and the rule of law demands the maintenance of a powerful middle and professional class.

That this is no remote academic problem can be seen by considering its relation to very practical questions about the remuneration of work. What are the implications of 'The labourer is worthy of his hire'? Provided minimum needs are adequately covered, are we justified in accepting the market value of labour which gives a higher income to the skilled worker than to the unskilled, and a higher income still to the professional man, provided his bargaining power is adequate? How far are differentials of this sort essential for the efficient working of the economy, and how far are they barriers to fellowship? To carry the argument still further, are we justified in saying with St Paul, 'If any will not work, neither let him eat'? Or has every man a right to a minimum subsistence as his share of the common heritage or productive capacity?

What are the economic and moral bases of the right to enjoy an income out of the proceeds of past savings? How far is profit-making essential as an incentive to enterprise, and as a criterion that resources are being used economically?

Whatever views upon these difficult questions people come to, it is essential that they should be manifestly based upon honest and rational argument. It is an indispensable condition of the maintenance of a free society that it should face its problems and not shirk them.

From *The Church Faces The Challenge* (1955), The Report of the Church of Scotland Commission on Communism.

BOOKS FOR FURTHER READING

PART I

Max Beloff (editor): *The Debate on the American Revolution, 1761–1783.* (Series: The British Political Tradition.) 1950.
Alfred Cobban (editor): *The Debate on the French Revolution, 1789–1880.* (Series: The British Political Tradition.) 1950.
C. A. R. Crosland: *The Future of Socialism.* 1956.
G. C. Field: *Political Theory.* 1956.
Alexander Gray: *The Socialist Tradition, Moses to Lenin.* 1946.
James Joll: *Britain and Europe: Pitt to Churchill, 1793–1940.* 1950.
J. D. Mabbott: *The State and the Citizen.* 1948.
John Plamenatz: *Mill's Utilitarianism reprinted with a Study of the English Utilitarians.* 1949.
G. de Ruggiero: *European Liberalism* (translated by R. G. Collingwood). 1927.
G. Sabine: *History of Political Theory.* 1937.
John Strachey: *Contemporary Capitalism.* 1956.
A. J. P. Taylor: *The Trouble Makers: Dissent over Foreign Policy, 1792–1939.* (Ford Lectures delivered in the University of Oxford in Hilary Term, 1956.) 1956.

PART II

John Plamenatz: *German Marxism and Russian Communism.* 1954.
Edmund Wilson: *To the Finland Station.* 1941.
R. Carew-Hunt: *The Theory and Practice of Communism.* Revised and enlarged edition, 1957.
Isaiah Berlin: *Karl Marx, his Life and Environment.* 1939.
Isaac Deutscher: *Stalin, a Political Biography.* 1949.
E. H. Carr: *The Bolshevik Revolution, 1917–23,* vols. I, II and III. 1950–3.

PART III

Martin D'Arcy, S.J.: *Communism and Christianity.* 1956.
John F. Cronin: *Catholic Social Teaching.* 1950.
A. P. d'Entreves: *The Law of Nature.* 1951.
Michael P. Fogarty: *Christian Democracy in Western Europe.* 1957.
Philip Hughes: *The Pope's New Order.* 1943.
J. Lecler, S.J.: *The Two Sovereignties (Church and State).* 1952.
H. A. Rommen: *The State in Catholic Thought.* 1945.
F. J. Sheed: *Communism and Man.* 1938.

Various collections of Papal Encyclicals from *Rerum Novarum* onwards can be obtained in translation separately, in U.K. from the Catholic Truth Society, London.

PART IV

Adolf Hitler: *Mein Kampf*, vol. I, 1925; vol. II, 1927.
Benito Mussolini: *My Autobiography*. 1928.
Rohan d'Olier Butler: *Roots of National Socialism, 1783–1933*. 1941.

In England the best source of contemporary literature on Romantic Authoritarianism and Racialism as they appear in Europe is the Wiener Library, at present housed at 18 Adam Street, Strand, London, W.C.2. The Library's province is Central European History with particular reference to the rise and fall of the Third Reich, but it contains much of special value, some of it in English, relating to present-day manifestations of the trends discussed in this section.

PART V

The best single contemporary source of books dealing with the relationship between Protestant theology and social and political questions is the World Council of Churches, a list of whose publications can be had from 17 Route de Malagnou, Geneva.

INDEX

For EU product safety concerns, contact us at Calle de José Abascal, 56–1°, 28003 Madrid, Spain or eugpsr@cambridge.org.

www.ingramcontent.com/pod-product-compliance
Ingram Content Group UK Ltd.
Pitfield, Milton Keynes, MK11 3LW, UK
UKHW010346140625
459647UK00010B/857